AMERICAN HOUSING
AND ITS USE

A VOLUME IN THE CENSUS MONOGRAPH SERIES

AMERICAN HOUSING

AND ITS USE

The Demand
for Shelter Space

by

LOUIS WINNICK

Research Associate
Institute for Urban Land Use and Housing Studies
Columbia University

with the assistance of

NED SHILLING

Staff, Institute for Urban Land Use and Housing Studies
Columbia University

for the
SOCIAL SCIENCE RESEARCH COUNCIL
in cooperation with the
U. S. DEPARTMENT OF COMMERCE
BUREAU OF THE CENSUS

JOHN WILEY & SONS, INC., NEW YORK
CHAPMAN & HALL, LIMITED, LONDON

This monograph is dedicated to

Ernest M. Fisher

Professor of Urban Land Economics
Graduate School of Business
Columbia University

FOREWORD

The statistical results compiled by the Bureau of the Census constitute a tremendous mass of detailed information about the population of the United States and its characteristics and economic activities. To meet the requirements of government agencies, business concerns, and investigators of social problems and to satisfy the needs of individual citizens, facts must be gathered and published, showing the distribution of the population in each large and small political unit with respect to age, sex, color, marital status, occupation, income, education, national origin, and other characteristics. This information provides the basis for apportionment of representatives in Congress, for answering many questions by direct reference, and for formulating many plans, at least in preliminary form.

It is the first business of the Bureau of the Census to put into print the census results that directly answer as many such questions as possible. Along with these results, similar data from one or two previous censuses are usually included. Limitations of time, space, and money prevent any extensive statement of the relations between particular results, the long-term trends of significant totals and subtotals, the shifting proportions of the people belonging to different categories, various interesting and important relations such as those between income, occupation, and age. It is not that the Bureau of the Census fails in any sense to appreciate the value and need for such analyses, but rather that it must concentrate on its basic concern with the summary statistics that constitute its unique contribution to knowledge.

When plans for the 1950 Census were made, the need for more extensive analysis was recognized and a series of census monographs similar to those issued after the 1920 Census was proposed. Because of the pressures caused by the depression in the early 1930's and by defense and war in the early 1940's, plans for monographs based on those censuses could not be carried out. Late in the 1940's interested persons from business, research, and government agencies expressed the need for a series that would provide analyses of the most significant results of the 1950 Census. The Social Science Research Council, with the assistance of Russell Sage Foundation, took the lead in stimulating the formulation of suitable plans and in June 1950 appointed a Committee on Census Monographs to cooperate with the Bureau in organizing this project. The members of the Committee are:

Ralph G. Hurlin, Russell Sage Foundation (Chairman)

Robert W. Burgess, formerly Western Electric Company, since February 1953 Director of the Bureau of the Census

John D. Durand, United Nations

Ernest M. Fisher, Columbia University

F. F. Hill, Cornell University

Frederick F. Stephan, Princeton University

Conrad Taeuber, Bureau of the Census

Ralph J. Watkins, Dun & Bradstreet, Inc.

Paul Webbink, Social Science Research Council

J. Frederic Dewhurst, Twentieth Century Fund, and William F. Ogburn, University of Chicago, were members of the Committee during the first year and a half.

It is essential in any sound census monograph program to obtain the co-operation of authors with a broad understanding not only of the statistical information provided by the regular tabulations of the current census but also of the results of earlier censuses and other relevant knowledge and points of view from other sources and even from other countries. The preparation of a monograph should include broad exploration of new questions suggested by the new information, as well as narrowing the elements of doubt and controversy on old questions. The Social Science Research Council Committee early undertook, in consultation with leading figures in various professional fields, to develop a suggested list of monograph titles and authors and persuaded experts in the subject areas selected to undertake the preparation of memoranda outlining and discussing the topics proposed. Then, in 1951, arrangements were made for continuing cooperation between the Committee and the Bureau concerning the selection of topics, proposals of authors and consultants, and editorial supervision.

Throughout the conduct of the project there has been close collaboration with a number of interested Federal agencies and with universities and research organizations, which provided staff and facilities to help bring the project to completion. They and the Council, which also obtained necessary funds from the Rockefeller and Russell Sage Foundations, provided assistance without which the monographs could not have been prepared.

The task of preparing monographs is an essential part of the broad function of making the information secured by censuses fully available to satisfy the needs and interests of the community and to constitute a broad base for further studies in the social sciences. As Director of the Census and President of the Social Science Research Council, respectively, we wish to record our full approval of the monograph project. It is not implied, of course, that the views expressed in these reports are necessarily those of the Bureau of the Census, the Department of Commerce, or the

Social Science Research Council.   The views are those of the individual authors, each of whom has been given the freedom to interpret available materials in the light of his technical knowledge and competence.   This freedom of the individual authors is an essential element in making the most useful analyses and interpretations generally available to the community.

ROBERT W. BURGESS, DIRECTOR
BUREAU OF THE CENSUS

PENDLETON HERRING, PRESIDENT
SOCIAL SCIENCE RESEARCH COUNCIL

ACKNOWLEDGMENTS

This monograph owes much in content and organization to Dr. Leo Grebler, who, as Associate Director of the Institute for Urban Land Use and Housing Studies (Columbia University), spent long hours with me in its preparation. Thanks are also due to my former associates, Dr. David M. Blank and Dr. Chester Rapkin, for numerous ideas received in the give and take of many discussions. My wife, Dr. Wilma A. Winnick, likewise deserves mention for helpful editorial suggestions.

The staff of the Bureau of the Census gave generously of their time, meeting all requests for data and checking the final drafts. I wish to thank, in particular, Dr. Conrad Taeuber, Assistant Director of the Bureau, Howard G. Brunsman, Chief of the Population Division, Dr. Paul C. Glick, Chief, Social Statistics Branch, and Wayne F. Daugherty, Chief of the Housing Division. Their review of the manuscript saved me from several outright errors and resulted in many improvements in style. Needless to say, none of the above named is in any way responsible for whatever mistakes of fact or interpretation remain.

My personal and intellectual debts to Dr. Ernest M. Fisher, Director of the Institute for Urban Land Use and Housing Studies, are so great and go back so far, that I should like him to accept the dedication of the monograph as a small token of appreciation.

LOUIS WINNICK

Office of the Mayor
Division of Administration
City of New York

CONTENTS

CHAPTER 1

INTRODUCTION

By nearly every reasonable test, America is wealthier in housing resources than any other great nation on earth and, quite possibly, than any nation in history. There is certainly little question that Americans have more housing per person than other people. In 1950, in spite of what was felt to be a severe housing shortage, 177,313,000 rooms (nonfarm) were occupied by only 121,900,000 persons or roughly three rooms for every two persons. More precisely, to use a measure to be encountered throughout this study, the national persons-per-room ratio (PPR ratio) is 0.69.[1]

It is, of course, difficult to see so abstract a measure in proper perspective except by comparison with the density standards of other people. If the Soviet Union is accepted as the poorest of the major industrial powers, the contrast is vivid. Even before World War II, during which an appreciable amount of the Soviet housing inventory was destroyed, the intensity of occupancy of the Soviet housing stock was incredible by American standards. It has been estimated that, in 1940, urban dwellers were accommodated at the rate of 4.1 square meters of living space per person.[2] If in America a room were to average 12 square meters (approximately 125 square feet) and the data adjusted to Soviet definitions,[3] each person here would dispose of 14.9 square meters, or 3.6 times the Soviet average; in more familiar terms, occupancy in the U.S.S.R. would average nearly 3 persons per room (of 12 square meters), equivalent to the overcrowding found in the one percent of American households that is worst off. Clearly, the concepts of housing shortage and overcrowding are quite relative.

The occupancy limits, that is, the maximum number of persons who could be accommodated within a given housing inventory, are too elastic for us to develop a meaningful measure of capacity. But if the utilization of the inventory in Soviet Russia is taken to be close to the outside limit at

---

[1] The derivation of total and average (mean) number of rooms, used extensively in this monograph, is given in Appendix A.

[2] Timothy Sosnovy, *The Housing Problem in the Soviet Union*, Research Program on the U.S.S.R., New York, 1954, p. 106.

[3] The Soviet space inventory ordinarily excludes kitchens but includes all vacant space, if any. For purposes of this comparison, some 35 million kitchens were excluded from the American data and the estimated number of rooms (other than kitchens) in vacant units included.

which people in cities and towns may be housed without significant (apparently) loss in economic productivity, our 1950 nonfarm inventory was capable of absorbing over 450 million persons.   In other words, at the Soviet standard our 1950 housing stock could easily accommodate all population growth for the next century or more, after allowance for a likely rate of demolition, without building a single new unit.   Put into still other terms, if some national catastrophe were to wipe out two-thirds of our housing stock without loss of population, the surviving housing units would still be sufficient, in the Spartan regimen of forced quartering that would follow, to shelter everyone at a viable density.[4]   The very contemplation of such close companionship, however, is likely to produce a shudder in even the most gregarious American.

International comparisons of shelter resources are at least as hazardous as comparisons of income, wage rates, or consumer budgets.   Not only are there national differences with respect to living habits, acceptable space standards, the degree of rent control, and the extent of war destruction but differences in census enumeration techniques and in definitions as well.   Problems of comparison aside, as far as other European countries are concerned, our position in density levels is always favorable (table 1).   The

TABLE 1.—PERCENT DISTRIBUTION OF DWELLING UNITS BY PERSONS PER ROOM, FOR SELECTED COUNTRIES: SPECIFIED DATES

[The distributions do not always add to 100 percent]

Country and year	0.50 or less	0.51 to 1.00	1.01 to 1.50	1.51 to 2.00	2.01 to 2.50	2.51 or more
United States (nonfarm, 1950)	35.7	49.8	8.9	3.7	...	1.8
Canada (urban, 1951)[1]	31.1	52.4	11.5	3.8	0.6	0.6
Belgium (total, 1947)	5.8	36.0	19.7	20.3	4.8	11.6
Czechoslovakia (urban, 1946)[2]	2.1	15.6	...	48.3	28.6	
France (urban, 1946)	15.2	46.1	15.5	13.8	2.1	7.3
West Germany (urban, 1950)	91.2				8.8	
Sweden (urban, 1945)	15.6	48.9	19.5	11.3	1.8	2.3
Switzerland (urban, 1941)[3]	15.9	56.6	18.3	6.7	1.2	
United Kingdom (urban, 1951)	8.1		12.0	5.0	2.0	

[1] Data are for households.   [2] Places of 5,000 or more.   [3] Kitchens not counted.

Source: United States: Appendix table A–2; other countries: United Nations, Department of Economic Affairs, *Statistical Yearbook, 1953*, table 174, pp. 510–511.

[4] The Soviet death rate (crude) is reported to be about the same as our own, between 9 and 10 per 1,000.   Nor is there any evidence that incidence rates of major illnesses are significantly higher than our own.   If so, the Soviet case illustrates that a major improvement in public health services (as it has occurred in the U.S.S.R.) is a more efficient and cheaper method of reducing morbidity than raising housing standards.

density group having a PPR ratio of one or less includes 85 percent of our households compared with 81 percent for the United Kingdom, 64 percent for Sweden, 61 percent for France, and 18 percent for Czechoslovakia. At the PPR level of 0.50 or less our advantage is even more impressive.

A cursory glance at table 1 shows that the distribution of space bears at least a rough correspondence to national income levels, Canada and the United Kingdom being close to our pattern, Sweden and Switzerland somewhat lower, followed by France, Belgium, and West Germany, with Czechoslovakia at the bottom. Since real income is assumed to be an important factor in determining the per capita amount of space, the most striking feature that emerges from this quick survey of international differences is not that we are better off than everybody else, but rather that we are not as much better off as might be expected from observed differences in income and general living standards.

Of course, housing space is by no means the only criterion of housing standards, nor would housing space standards be expected to rise proportionately with real income (about which more will be said in Chapter 3). In fact, recent findings on long-run trends in American housing strongly suggest that over the past 60 years our investment in housing capital has been disappointingly small in view of the tripling of real per capita income during this period. The response has been substantially less than is suggested by any cross-sectional data on the relationship between family income and housing investment.[5] There is *prima facie* evidence of a decided shift away from shelter toward other and newer consumer durables—a shift much greater than in the case of other necessities, such as food and clothing. Disraeli's dictum that while we can have enough to eat and too much to drink we can never have enough housing may express a biological fact but not an economic truth.

The utilization of housing space: An economic interpretation

The economic analysis of housing has for some time included three related but not always integrated subjects—aggregate housing expenditures, consumer budget studies, and housing market behavior. It cannot, however, be truthfully said that the way in which people use housing space has until recently[6] formed a substantive part of any of these subjects.

The importance of aggregate expenditures on housing to the national economy is great because housing happens to be the most costly of the consumer durables. The stock of housing has become the largest single asset in America's balance sheet, comprising about one-fourth of reproducible national wealth and accounting for an even more impressive propor-

---

[5] Leo Grebler, David M. Blank, Louis Winnick, *Capital Formation in Residential Real Estate: Trends and Prospects*, Princeton University Press, Princeton, 1956.

[6] Ernest M. Fisher, and Robert Moore Fisher, *Urban Real Estate*, Henry Holt and Co., New York, 1954.

tion of our private debt. The annual fixed cash outlay on housing paid by households approaches the federal personal income tax in size and is of strategic importance in determining the level of disposable income remaining for the purchase of other goods and services. The amount (relatively small) by which the housing stock grows each year is anxiously watched as an indicator of the general state of the economy.

Outlays for housing both in terms of expenditures for the use of existing houses and expenditures on new construction are determined to a large extent by the quantity of space demanded as well as by the quality of the exterior envelope which encloses interior space and the partitions that subdivide it. Other things equal, larger houses nearly always cost more. It is not generally realized that if each existing household decided to acquire one more room, the increased demand for housing thus generated would exceed the annual level of new construction expenditures several times. It is only in recent years, during which we have witnessed a continued high level of construction expenditures in the face of declining household formation, that we have become aware of the increased housing demand rising from the requirements of an increased number of maturing children.

Budget analysis of family expenditure on housing has produced the rent-income ratio. In spite of its long history, which goes back at least as far as Schwabe and Engel, this ratio recognizes the relationship between housing space and the number and composition of occupants only insofar as some correspondence exists between the amount of rent and the quantity of space. The major budget studies of the 1930's, which provided raw material for more penetrating analysis, have hardly been exploited. In this nation of home owners, where rental units are increasingly becoming the abodes of childless couples, single individuals, and nonfamily groups, the rent-income ratio has been supplemented by the price-income ratio and the ratio of mortgage payments to income. Budget analysis has thus been increased in coverage but not in its depth of penetration into the demand for space.

Housing market analysis recognizes the fact that shelter space is distributed in America, with still minor exceptions, by market processes, which means that the amount and quality of shelter a family acquires is determined (broadly speaking) by its tastes and income in relation to the price of housing. Because housing space is very expensive, the market rationing process is quite severe, a fact known to every buyer of a new home who forgoes an extra room and to the buyer of an older but larger house who acquires more space at the expense of obsolescence. It is likely that most families would find additional space convenient if it were to cost them nothing. Our current density pattern is largely a market phenomenon that results from the economic scarcity of housing resources. The acute crowding in the Soviet Union, discussed earlier, is of course enforced by strict administrative decrees. Practically every Russian family would like, and very many would be prepared to pay for, more housing if the market were uncontrolled. But one could safely venture the prediction that, if housing markets in the Soviet Union were to be set completely free and rents (now heavily subsidized) allowed to take any course whatsoever, the average density of Russian households would remain at or close to its present high level, although it might be distributed somewhat differently. The high density would be enforced, for many years to come, by high rents in place of ukase. 勒令(化的言辞语气).

In housing market analysis the subject of space utilization usually appears in only one of its aspects: vacancies. The widespread use of vacancy series as a housing market indicator reveals an obvious though infrequently expressed awareness of a space demand function; i.e., fluctuations in demand occasioned by changes in income, population, or house prices produce fluctuations in the amount of "unutilized" space. But vacancies even in the worst of times constitute a relatively small and, in periods such as the present, an almost negligible proportion of the housing inventory. While variations in the vacancy rate are probably correlated with and reflect changes in consumers' space requirements, the level of vacancies at any moment is nothing but the "top of the iceberg" of space utilization patterns that have a much broader base.

The importance of vacancy data lies in the fact that they provide a guide to expectations of the future level of construction and to changes in the prices and rents of existing housing; as in every industry, idle capacity affects both the price structure and the volume of investment. In the fundamental equation (really, identity) underlying all housing market analysis, new construction equals household formation minus conversions plus demolitions plus the change in vacancies. Since we know little about conversions and demolitions, these being, furthermore, partially offsetting terms, changing vacancies are taken to measure the excess of new construction over household formation. It is assumed that sooner or later new construction will be brought into equilibrium with household formation; that is, new construction will be cut back if vacancies rise and will increase when vacancies decline (the movement in vacancies to be measured with reference to some previously defined normal).

All historical data confirm the fact that household formation is the principal determinant of new construction. But the relationship between the two appears to hold true only over long periods of time. We really have no way of knowing whether a deficiency in household formation this year, accompanied by a rise in vacancies, will in fact affect next year's home building. This is so because newly formed households do not, by and large, appear as customers for new houses. In every study made of the characteristics of new home purchasers, the evidence is clear that the great majority of them are established families, already provided with dwelling units. Moreover, the fact that household formation is rising or falling in his community is quite irrelevant to the would-be purchaser and has no immediate effect on current house-buying plans. The trend in household formation, therefore, is not an adequate indicator of the demand for new construction in the short-run.

A knowledge of space preferences would result in an important addition to our ability to forecast housing demand in the near-term future. This is because the motivation for buying is not primarily the lack of a separate dwelling unit, but its inadequacy. This fact emerges whenever people who plan to acquire a new home are asked to explain their motives. While many different reasons are given, the "shortage" of space in present housing arrangements stands high on the list.

Notions of an "excess" or "shortage" of space are not, of course, formed in an economic vacuum. With unchanged income a given quantity of space may become too small or too large as household size changes. But even in the absence of any change in the character of the household, dissatisfaction with one's housing space will vary with income and with the price of housing. Often, after a rise in its income, a family finds that using a living room as a bedroom, hitherto an unpleasant expedient, becomes suddenly and plainly intolerable. Requiring two children to share a bedroom is likewise considered a realistic adjustment to a fall in income or to the discovery that an extra bedroom would add $20 a month to the rent bill or $1,000 to the price of a home. Thus, changes in economic conditions affect housing demand to an important extent by altering the consumer's judgment with respect to the adequacy of his housing space.

No better example of the market impact of these changing judgments can be offered than the events which took place from 1930 to 1950. For many reasons, large amounts of "excess" space were suddenly discovered in occupied dwelling units, resulting in an enormous wave of conversions. The millions of dwelling units created out of "underutilized" housing space exceeded the number of "unutilized," or vacant, units. In the 1950's. after a long, continuous rise in income, many households found they were "over-crowded" so that even in those cities where new construction ran far ahead of population growth few or no vacancies were available.

It would be committing a logical error to conclude that, because the individual would-be home buyer pays no conscious heed to household formation, the latter is without final significance to aggregate housing demand. Even allowing for growing preferences for a single-family house in the suburbs, a sustained divergence between new construction and household formation with an attendant rise in vacancies must eventually affect house-buying decisions. Should the rise in vacancies produce a decline in the rents and prices of existing housing, many of the families who ordinarily are first-class prospects would be tempted away from the new house market by the bargains available among existing dwelling units. Also, many of the potential customers for new houses count first on selling their present homes at a reasonable price. Declining prices on existing homes would cause such families to postpone or abandon house buying plans. It is only because these market processes may take years to unfold that the usefulness of the household formation-new construction-vacancy relation as a short-run forecasting device is brought into question.

If household formation is the strategic factor in explaining long-run trends in construction, then a better understanding of the space-using propensities of consumers has value for long-run, as well as short-run, forecasting. Household formation takes place very often because a number of adults are dissatisfied with the lack of privacy in the homes they now occupy. Shifts in preferences for privacy affect not only the proportion of newly married couples who double up with parents, but also a growing number of unmarried adult individuals of all ages whose housing space requirements (in the sense of a quantity of floor area) can be met alternatively by sharing the dwelling unit of another or by an independent establishment. What makes them decide one way or the other is governed by the strength of their desire for privacy as well as by their incomes and the relative cost of alternative housing arrangements.

Research into housing space utilization must draw upon the skills of many sciences in addition to economics. But economists will have to do better than they have in the past. Apart from vacancies, the only other aspect of utilization which has interested economists has been the possible distorting effects of rent control (Chapter 5). In the main, however, the subject of space utilization has been abandoned to the sociologist and to the public health official, the economist remaining content to cast his physical measures of housing demand in terms of dwelling units: unquantified units of shelter.

The sociologist has been far more sensitive to the problem of housing space utilization because it has become a major index of social welfare. But he, as well as the public health specialist, has until recently concentrated upon the pathology of space utilization: overcrowding. Overcrowding has been assigned a major role in the etiology of a large number of social disorders ranging from the creation of slums to capital crimes. It is believed to be a factor in the incidence of many physical illnesses, such as tuberculosis; in more recent years, family conflicts and even the malformation of personality which leads to emotional and mental disturbance have been traced to the absence of sufficient privacy in the home.

Thus, an economic analysis of the utilization of American housing breaks new ground in which this monograph can be considered merely a first effort. By necessity, the rate of utilization is analyzed almost entirely in terms of the PPR ratio.[7] Despite the many shortcomings of this measure no better index is currently available. Furthermore, the analysis is re-

---

[7] The national PPR ratio (or persons-per-room ratio) is the total number of people in occupied dwelling units divided by the total number of rooms contained in such dwelling units. Likewise, the PPR ratio of any household is the number of persons in the household divided by the number of rooms in the dwelling unit they occupy. Unless otherwise noted, the data used in this study exclude farm housing.

stricted to the occupied portion of the inventory since vacant units tell us nothing about actual utilization patterns. Because changes in the quantity of housing space desired by consumers directly affect the number and composition of vacant dwelling units, the omission of the latter is clear warning that this study falls short of offering a complete account of the rate of utilization. When more is known about what determines the amount of space people actually occupy, it is hoped that this deficiency can be remedied.

Summary of findings

The findings of this study are nevertheless numerous, many going beyond the 1950 Census data which serve as the basis for the bulk of the monograph. In broadest terms and without regard for either chapter sequence or qualifying detail, some of these findings are:

1. The improvement in housing space standards of the past half century has apparently been modest. It is doubtful whether the nonfarm PPR ratio has been reduced by more than 15 or 20 percent since 1900. Furthermore, much of this gain must be attributed to the decline in household size. The very large increases in real income that have accrued to American families contributed little to the improvement in space standards, partly because the influence of income appears weaker than is commonly assumed and partly because of the very sharp long-term increase in the real cost of housing which led to smaller dwelling units. There is also reason to believe that the reduction in the amount of "house" people buy is not entirely due to its high relative cost but is the result of changing consumer tastes. The competition of other expensive consumer durables, the high cost of domestic service, and the shift of many family activities away from the home are among the factors which caused pinching on housing space. In more recent years the interest of the consumer in housing seems to have been rekindled as a result of more children and suburbanization so that the future may witness more gains than has the past (Chapter 7).

2. The distribution of housing space in 1950 was remarkably even, far more so than the distribution of income and probably more equal than is the case of any other major economic asset. As a result, severe overcrowding, i.e., more than 2 persons per room, is exceedingly rare and affects less than 2 percent of nonfarm households (less than 4 percent of the nonfarm population). The lowest income groups tend to enjoy surprisingly favorable PPR ratios; overcrowding is most frequent in the groups that lie between the bottom and the middle of the income structure (Chapter 3).

3. Judging from cross-sectional data, the most important determinant of a household's density standard is its size. By comparison, the effect of household income or the cost of shelter is relatively small. Large households with fairly high incomes are often more crowded than small house-

holds with modest means (Chapters 4 and 5). The importance of rent and income, however, is increased and the role of household size diminished, in explaining the change in utilization over the 1940–1950 decade.

4. Overcrowding among Negroes is far more severe than among whites, and the improvement since 1940 has been less noticeable. The cause for Negro overcrowding seems to lie more in low income than in racial discrimination in the housing market. Negro households apparently occupy as much space as white households of the same income, but racial barriers limit this space to low quality structures in older neighborhoods (Chapter 6).

5. The average dwelling unit has been shrinking in size for many decades. At the same time, there has been a leveling in the size of dwelling units, at least since 1940, with relatively fewer very small or very large ones and relatively more of average size. From the early 1950's on, some movement back toward larger dwelling units has appeared. But larger dwelling units no longer mean the mansions and castles of the 1890's.

6. The most densely populated regions in the country do not suffer the most from overcrowding. The reverse tends to be true. The West has more overcrowding than the Northeast, rural areas more than urban areas, and small cities more than large ones (Chapter 6).

7. The demand for larger dwelling units is in part due to the maturation of children. As children pass from infancy to school age, considerable pressure is exerted for more rooms (Chapter 8).

8. The most important reason for the long-run decline in average household size has not been the "spreading out" of adults but, rather, the changing age structure of the population, which is the result of declining birth and death rates. An older population gives rise to more married couples who have a strong propensity toward establishing separate households. But, paradoxically, a larger proportion of married people in the middle age groups leads to fewer rather than more households. On net balance, therefore, the effect of an increased proportion of married people on the number of households a given population will form (average household size) is greatly weakened (Chapter 8).

9. No evidence can be found that older people form independent households much more frequently than in the past. The rise in what is called here the "headship rate" of people over 60 has been quite small over the past 50 years and almost negligible between 1940 and 1950. Because their numbers have greatly increased, older people, of course, occupy a larger proportion of the housing inventory. But this is not at all the same thing as an increased tendency toward separate living arrangements. These findings are contrary to widespread belief and should be reviewed with care. It is indeed surprising that Social Security, more pensions, and general economic improvement have had, thus far, so little effect on the housing arrangements of the aged (Chapter 8).

10. The PPR ratio will ordinarily vary with the business cycle, but to a

much lesser extent. Fluctuations in income from prosperity to depression would tend to be largely offset by corresponding fluctuations in the cost of housing. These findings may help to explain why cyclical fluctuations in the doubling-up rate (and therefore the vacancy rate) have been so (relatively) small. People are reluctant to give up separate living space even in a depression, and this reluctance is increased by the many housing bargains which become available. The depression-induced rise in the national PPR ratio is more the result of shifts of established households into smaller dwelling units than of increases in doubling. Because of such shifts vacancies become concentrated in larger dwelling units and a wave of conversions ensues, causing the number of vacancies to increase by more than can be accounted for by the increase in doubling up (Chapter 5).

11. Rent control, which created many housing bargains, apparently, resulted in some misallocation of housing space. But the amount of extra space pre-empted by favored renters does not appear to have been very great, not enough to destroy the usefulness of rent regulation under emergency conditions. Part of the reason why the amount of "excess" space held by renters was so limited is that rent control also reduces the number of large dwelling units by stimulating conversions and transfers of single-family houses from the rental to the ownership market. Also, some renter households which might have enjoyed extra space were forced to share it with married children whose doubling rate appears to be related to the stringency of rent control.

The plan of this study is simple. After a discussion in Chapter 2 of alternative measures of housing space, substantive analysis begins in Chapter 3 with an account of the utilization patterns of various income groups. Chapter 4 concentrates upon an analysis of the PPR ratios of households of different size. The influence of the cost of housing (rent and value) on utilization is given attention in Chapter 5. This chapter falls into two parts: (a) an account of utilization patterns associated with housing carrying different price tags and (b) an attempt to quantify, via multiple correlation, the relative effects of changes in income, household size, and rent on changes in utilization.

Chapter 6 is concerned with locational and racial differences in housing utilization, while Chapter 7 offers details on the shrinkage in the average size of dwelling units. Chapter 8 attempts to probe more deeply into the causes of the decline in household size, a phenomenon of considerable importance to an understanding of long-term changes in housing space standards. This chapter also discusses the influence of household composition on housing space requirements and traces the aggregate changes in household composition that occurred between 1940 and 1950.

The technical reader will, undoubtedly, also be interested in much of the appendix material. But even the nontechnician who wishes to use any of the PPR ratio estimates contained in this study would profit from a glance at Appendix E which contains a statement on errors in the census reports on number of rooms. It goes without saying that the precision of many of the results of the monograph is affected by any and all errors in the published census volumes for which no corrections are possible.

CHAPTER 2

MEASURING THE UTILIZATION OF HOUSING

The dwelling unit is our primary physical measure of the housing inventory. Census data since 1940 permit quantification in terms of number of rooms, but, as far as is known, no room inventory figures have hitherto been presented. Neither the dwelling unit nor the room, of course, is an adequate yardstick because of the wide variability in the amount of space contained in such units. Dwelling units range in size from 1 to 50 or more rooms, while a 6 by 9 study and a baronial hall are counted equally as rooms. It is probable (though it cannot be demonstrated) that the variation in sizes of rooms is smaller than variation in size of dwelling units and that the room is therefore more useful as a spatial indicator. But it is only because it is safe to assume some rough correspondence between the total number of dwelling units, the total number of rooms, and aggregate floor area, that we can be sure that the inventory of housing space even moves in the same direction as the stock of dwelling units and rooms. What is clear is that in the past two decades, because of the importance of conversions and the reduction in the average size of new homes, our housing stock has grown more rapidly in terms of dwelling units than in terms of rooms (cf. Chapter 7) and, quite possibly, more rapidly in number of rooms than in floor area.

Measures of housing space

We do not always recognize that the dwelling unit serves as a unit of account rather than as a *standard* of measurement. That is, we have adopted the dwelling unit by convention to be the unit by which we maintain our housing accounting system. The distinction can best be made by borrowing an example from monetary economics. The dollar is both a unit-of-value account and a standard-of-value measurement. In the former role it is an unchanging unit insofar as we have kept all our financial books in terms of dollars for over 150 years. In its function as a standard of measure, however, the dollar is deficient since its value in terms of real resources varies with the price level.

The adoption of the dwelling unit for housing accounting is, however, far from arbitrary. Its convenience is great in a country which maintains a close correspondence between families and dwelling units, and it is by no means due to chance that the room or the structure (in spite of the easier identification and countability of the latter and its inclusion in every

12

census report between 1890 and 1940) has not been given more serious consideration. The dwelling unit also corresponds to the package of space traded on the market, except in special cases, such as the renting of rooms or the trading of subunits, which comprise a well-developed if not always legal market in the Negro and Puerto Rican sections of New York. After all, the typical family does not seek to buy or rent an abstract quantity of space. The space that it acquires must have certain attributes: the envelope must be distinct and separate from others, all internal space must be interconnected, it must be equipped to take care of the nutritional needs of the family. In short, the adoption of such a unit of account takes cognizance of most (but by no means all) of the realities of the housing market.

The selection of the dwelling unit as the quantum of housing accounting is unspoken testimony to our great material wealth. With the exception of room leases, we do not even consider space to be unoccupied unless such space appears in the form of a dwelling unit. Such a unit of account is obviously not equally useful to all countries. Much depends upon the types of social units and the adequacy of housing resources. In the modern world, the family has universally become the most important social group, and everywhere a separate dwelling unit for each family is at least a goal of national policy. The degree to which attainment falls short of this goal becomes a rough index of "the housing shortage." If the failure is very great, however, the dwelling unit as a unit of housing account is robbed of its content and other units must be used. While the game of drawing contrasts with Russian experience can be overplayed, it is difficult to resist the temptation to cite housing classification systems established in St. Petersburg in 1908. Only 7 percent of the married workers occupied a completely private apartment, and only 50 percent occupied space that could conceivably meet an American census definition of a dwelling unit. The latter is hardly an appropriate unit of account where room sharing is so extensive and the only concession to the proprieties of marriage is a private bunk. In the Soviet Union today the unit of account has become a square meter of living space; that is, like Irving Fisher's parity dollar, the unit of account and the standard of measurement have become identical.

TABLE 2.—PERCENT DISTRIBUTION OF ST. PETERSBURG WORKERS BY TYPE OF
ACCOMMODATION, BY MARITAL STATUS: 1908

Type of accommodation	Single workers	Married workers	Type of accommodation	Single workers	Married workers
One-half bunk	4.6	...	One room	14.8	21.4
Bunk	21.3	7.1	Apartment with roomers	...	21.4
Corner	44.4	35.7	Individual apartments	...	7.1
One-half room	11.1	7.1	Unknown	3.8	0.2

Source: S. N. Prokopovich, "Real Wages of the Industrial Worker in Soviet Russia." Unpublished manuscript, Russian Research Center, Harvard University, 1947; cited by Timothy Sosnovy in *The Housing Problem in the Soviet Union*, Research Program on the U.S.S.R., New York, 1954, p. 9.

It seems strange that a country like the United States, otherwise rich in housing data, has never applied a *standard* of measurement to determine the size of its housing inventory, although such standards have occasionally been used for other purposes. Occupancy codes are usually based upon physical measures of space. Builders estimate costs of construction on the basis of square or cubic feet. But it is a curious fact that once the new housing space enters the inventory, all value expressions (prices and rents) are nearly always without reference to the quantity of space.

Obviously, quantitative space data are necessary for a full interpretation of housing utilization patterns. It is equally obvious that such data would be difficult to develop. Apart from the unenviable task the Bureau of the Census would face in obtaining reports on physical measures, there are a great many questions on just what to measure and how. Shall we adopt a square or a cubic standard? The latter is the more complete measure, and the former can serve as a substitute only on the assumption that variation in ceiling heights is without much importance. This assumption has validity for our times, since a great deal of standardization in ceiling heights has resulted from builders' practices and building codes. The ceiling height in most of our existing housing is probably between 8 and 10 feet, the lower limit restricted by building codes and the upper by costs of construction. The use of cubic measurements goes back to earlier times of lower housing standards when emphasis was placed upon the minimum volume of air per capita as a health measure.

At the present time there is more concern over the maintenance of adequate privacy in terms of rooms and proper distances between occupants, with adequate ceiling heights taken for granted. In New York the only density requirement contained in the 1901 tenement code was a specification that no room should contain "less than 400 cubic feet of air to each adult and 200 cubic feet of air to each child under 12 years of age occupying each room."[1] The amendments to the New York City building code proposed in 1954[2] set much more elaborate density standards without any reference at all to cubic volume. All minimal requirements are stated in terms of aggregate floor area and persons per room. Likewise, the "functional analysis" of minimum space requirements made by the American Public Health Association and discussed below is framed only in terms of floor area.

The acceptance of an areal standard of measurement would involve little controversy. Questions would, however, be raised on how inclusive a floor space measure ought to be. A gross (outside wall boundary) measure is perhaps the simplest and, for many purposes of economic analysis, has much to recommend it. To obtain a better understanding of the utilization of hous-

---

[1] R. W. DeForest and L. Veiller, *The Tenement House Problem*, The Macmillan Co., New York, 1903, Vol. II, p. 192.

[2] *New York Times*, November 17, 1954.

ing, however, some concept of effective net space would be required. Effective space is difficult to define since its size is dependent upon actual living patterns. It is at present the custom in many European countries to exclude the kitchen from the space inventory, and at one time Germany, Switzerland, and Sweden (and perhaps other northern lands) excluded unheated rooms.[3] In this country no such exclusions are made, and as far as is known, have never been seriously contemplated. There is more complete, though not universal, agreement, on excluding corridors, stairways, closets, and rooms below some minimum size.

Should a living space concept be broadened to include outside space in the case of single-family houses? Depending on climate and season, the distinction between exterior and interior space is not clear-cut and is becoming increasingly blurred in contemporary architectural philosophy. Apart from the esthetic unity of interior and exterior space, there are obvious functional links. A garage equipped as a workshop is as much a recreation area as a hobby room, a backyard stocked with furniture may become a living room, and an outside play area for children is perhaps as important as one indoors. The availability of such exterior facilities reduces the need for indoor space so that a 5-room single-family house on a sizable lot may be the spatial equivalent of an 8-room apartment in a crowded city area. The extension of the living space concept to exterior areas is not entirely illogical even if a national space inventory cast in these terms would be much less useful for resource analysis.

Functional space requirements

At any rate, a living space definition (other than a measure of gross floor area minus specified if arbitrary exclusions) must await much more knowledge of how households utilize available space. The amount of work that has been done on this subject has not, thus far, been very great and is descriptive of a rather limited range of types of households without regard to income and rent levels.[4] These studies are based on the actual functioning of households of various sizes pursuing ordinary activities in the home and have as their major purpose the setting of space norms for various households. Among the more carefully drawn of these is the schedule of minimum space requirements prepared by the American Public Health Association. These norms take account of both health requirements (minimal distance between beds) and living requirements (area required for furniture and equipment based on average dimensions of selected items). While it would not be difficult to find points of disagreement with the bases upon which the norms rest, the same is likely to be true for practically any other

---

[3] Edith Wood, "The Statistics of Room Congestion," *Journal of the American Statistical Association,* September 1928.

[4] Pioneering research has been performed by the John Pierce Foundation, a number of public agencies, particularly the Public Housing Authority, and the American Public Health Association. Among individuals, the names of Svend Riemer, Nicholas Demerath, and Glenn H. Beyer stand out.

set of norms. The APHA standards are, at the very least, inferences made by a group of reasonably informed specialists using all available data and therefore merit attention.

The space requirements set up by the APHA (table 3) are concerned more with function than with privacy,[5] and are therefore independent of any subdivisions into rooms, which are given later. In effect, these needs could be satisfied by a single large room. It should also be noted that household composition is not considered. Clearly, a different schedule could be drawn for each household size depending on age, sex, and relationship of household members.

TABLE 3.—PERCENT DISTRIBUTION OF MINIMUM FLOOR SPACE REQUIRED FOR BASIC HOUSEHOLD ACTIVITIES, BY NUMBER OF PERSONS IN HOUSEHOLD

[Amount of floor space in square feet. The space requirements for each activity are adjusted for overlapping uses]

Household activity	1 person		2 persons		3 persons	
	Amount	Per-cent	Amount	Per-cent	Amount	Per-cent
Total..........................	380	100.0	765	100.0	989	100.0
Sleeping and dressing................	74	19.5	148	19.3	222	22.4
Personal cleanliness and sanitation.......	35	9.2	35	4.6	35	3.5
Food preparation and preservation.......	8	2.1	76	9.9	97	9.8
Food service and dining..............	53	13.9	70	9.1	91	9.2
Recreation and self-improvement........	125	32.9	164	21.4	221	22.3
Extra-familial association.............	17	4.5	17	2.2	34	3.4
Housekeeping.....................	48	12.6	91	11.9	110	11.1
Care of the infant or ill..............	...	...	124	16.2	124	12.5
Circulation between areas.............	20	5.3	20	2.6	35	3.5
Operation of utilities.................	...	...	20	2.6	20	2.0

Household activity	4 persons		5 persons		6 persons	
	Amount	Per-cent	Amount	Per-cent	Amount	Per-cent
Total..........................	1,159	100.0	1,420	100.0	1,550	100.0
Sleeping and dressing................	296	25.5	370	26.1	444	28.6
Personal cleanliness and sanitation.......	35	3.0	70	4.9	70	4.5
Food preparation and preservation.......	97	8.4	118	8.3	118	7.6
Food service and dining..............	105	9.1	119	8.4	146	9.4
Recreation and self-improvement........	286	24.7	357	25.1	383	24.7
Extra-familial association.............	34	2.9	51	3.6	51	3.3
Housekeeping.....................	127	11.0	146	10.3	149	9.6
Care of the infant or ill..............	124	10.7	124	8.7	124	8.0
Circulation between areas.............	35	3.0	45	3.2	45	2.9
Operation of utilities.................	20	1.7	20	1.4	20	1.3

Source: American Public Health Association, *Planning the Home for Occupancy*, Public Administration Service, Chicago, 1950, p. 15.

---

[5] This separation can never be rigidly maintained. The constant floor space increments to the activity of "sleeping and dressing" in table 3 imply a considerable degree of privacy. In Chaucer's time even the privileges of rank did not always include a private bed on a journey, three occupants being a common arrangement.

Total space requirements increase consistently with the increase in household size but at a slower rate. Thus, the percentage increases in square feet of space as household size rises from one to six persons are as follows: 101.3, 29.3, 17.2, 22.5, and 9.21. The per capita quantities of space in square feet are: 380, 383, 330, 290, 284, 256.[6] Even on the basis of norms, an increased rate of utilization (PPR ratio) is implied for larger households. Census data for 1950 in terms of persons per room confirm the broad outlines of this schedule. The average for 1-person households is 0.38 persons per room for renters and 0.22 for owners, while the average for 6-person households is 1.08 and 0.86, respectively (Chapter 4). Both the functional analysis and actual living arrangements reveal clearly how average household size affects the average rate of utilization. Abstracting from other historical changes (such as those in income, housing costs and tastes), the long-term decline in household size therefore carries with it some implication that intensity of occupancy, or the rate of utilization of housing, should have tended to decrease.

The tendency for the rate of utilization to increase with household size is due in part to the large amount of "overhead" space that is either invariant to any increase in the size of the household or that increases more slowly. Waiving the jump from one to two persons, as household size increases from two to six, the space needs for activities, such as "care of the infant or ill" and "operation of utilities," remain constant, and most of the remainder, except "sleeping and dressing" and to some extent "recreation and self-improvement," have low response elasticities. Thus, while the proportion of total space requirements for "sleeping and dressing" increases from 19.3 to 28.1 percent, the food preparation—"food service"—group declines from 19.0 to 17.0 percent and "housekeeping" from 11.9 to 9.6 percent. The only other important items that show a substantial increase are the social activities (recreation and extra-familial association), which rise from 23.6 to 28.0 percent. Thus, as the household gains in size, the greatest demand for extra space is exerted for bedrooms and social activity, while the hard core of the dwelling unit meets the extra demand through more efficient utilization as well as by a relatively small expansion. This gain in efficiency is fortunate, since large families, other things equal, must economize on rent (Chapter 5).

The translation of minimum space requirements into room counts is quite difficult and open to a considerable range of possibilities, depending upon the composition of the household or the size of the rooms. The room schedule for households of various sizes derived from the APHA is shown in table 4.

---

[6] That the space utilization schedules do not decline smoothly is due to the lumpy character of the space requirements for certain activities. Thus, as household size increases from one to two persons, the family is presumed to take up housekeeping and large areas are given over to "food preparation" and "housekeeping."

TABLE 4.—MINIMUM SIZE OF DWELLING UNIT BY NUMBER OF ROOMS AND SIZE OF HOUSEHOLD

Number in household	Number of rooms	Number in household	Number of rooms
1 person............................	1–2	4 persons............................	4–6
2 persons...........................	2–4	5 persons............................	5–7
3 persons...........................	3–5	6 persons............................	5–8

Source: APHA, *op. cit.*, p. 39.

This schedule obviously permits the estimation of minimal persons-per-room ranges and, as far as it goes, offers a standard against which actual performance can be measured.   The table illustrates, however, the difficulty in interpreting persons-per-room ratios unless the structure of the household population is known.   Thus, after allowance for kitchen and living room, a 6 person household can be served by as few as three bedrooms if it consists of two parents, two girls reasonably close in age, and two boys reasonably close in age.   But six bedrooms would be necessary, according to APHA standards, if the household had the following composition: father, grandmother, two boys aged 21 and 9, two girls aged 12 and 4.   In other words, the acceptable limits on the persons-per-room ratio range from 0.75 to 1.20.   The 1950 Census reports disclose that the actual average PPR ratio for 6-person households falls nearly in the middle of this range.   The averages for other household size classes were either as good as or better than APHA norms (Chapter 4).

The persons-per-room ratio

The persons-per-room ratio is the principal measure of the utilization of housing space that can be derived from census data.   It is clear that, in the absence of areal measurements, this ratio remains an imperfect tool for quantitative analysis though an infinite advance over a persons-per-dwelling-unit ratio, which is a mere statement of household size.   The PPR ratio, of course, tells us nothing of the arrangements within a dwelling unit that affect its utilization and, like any simple measure, is incapable of expressing the complexity of the phenomenon it is intended to describe.   The PPR ratio of a given dwelling unit represents an egalitarian allocation of a given number of cubicles within a house among its occupants.   Apart from the assumption that all persons are alike in their space requirements and that all rooms are alike in size and capacity to render satisfaction, there is a further assumption that all enumerated rooms are actually used.   Many large houses, particularly in rural areas, contain rooms that pass census definition but are hardly habitable from the standpoint of access or heating.[7]   A living room may, like the Swedish *finrum* or the Victorian parlor, be kept in hallowed isolation even at the cost of congestion elsewhere in the house.

---

[7] J. M. Mackintosh, *Housing and Family Life*, Cassell and Co., Ltd., London, 1952, p. 10.

Moreover, the intensity with which we use housing space varies over the course of a day, with the days of the week, and with the season of the year;[8] these variations are not subject to measurement by census PPR ratios. In the daily rhythm of family activity not all rooms are simultaneously occupied, even in the case of households with PPR ratios higher than one. Intensity of use traces out a pattern over a typical day with idle capacity probably greatest during the daytime and least in the early evening when kitchen, living room, and even some bedrooms are used for recreation and study. During the night, idle capacity is represented by the living room and kitchen. Recreation space obtains its greatest use over the weekend, and during the summer the intensity of use is lower in most climates than it is in the winter.

The PPR is probably most open to criticism because of its inability to differentiate households of various size and composition. We have no way of demonstrating that a PPR ratio of 0.50 achieved by one person in 2 rooms is more or less satisfactory than the same PPR ratio for five persons in 10 rooms. An additional infant may be readily accommodated in a dwelling unit of average size, while a mother-in-law or lodger may crowd even the largest. Already in some countries PPR ratios are partially standardized for household composition by assigning infants 25 percent, and children below a certain age, 50 percent of the weight of an adult. No effort, however justified, has been made thus far to assign weights higher than one to any adult or to take account of occupants other than persons. It is not so long ago (and is characteristic of other countries even today) that household composition reached lower down into the animal kingdom to include a cow, a pig, or a goat.[9] Even to speak of a *persons*-per-room ratio is to record the march of progress and civilization. Whatever his other failures, man is at least rapidly obtaining the exclusive use of residential real estate. Nevertheless, the use of "adult equivalents" would be a welcome improvement offering more realism than simple per capita measures because it is a device for standardizing compositional variations.

The PPR ratio, however, is well adapted to describe the *potential* privacy of internal arrangements. It is entirely probable that our requirements for privacy are increasing, and that more and more demand for housing space will reflect such desires regardless of changes in household size. The demand for more privacy expresses itself in greater separation of children by age and sex and in study, den, play, and hobby rooms. It is even conceivable that future standards may require separate bedrooms for

[8] Svend Riemer and N. J. Demerath, "Family Life and Housing," mimeographed paper contributed to the research conference on *The Role of Social Research in Housing Design*, sponsored by the Social Science Research Council, Ann Arbor, 1951.

[9] The New York City Tenement Code of 1901 went so far as to include the prohibition, "no horse, cow, calf, swine, sheep, or goat shall be kept in a tenement house. . . ." DeForest and Veiller, *op. cit.*, p. 192.

husband and wife, allegedly an arrangement now found among the wealthier classes. A requirement for separate bedrooms on the part of married couples in 1950 would have led to a gross demand for nearly 30 million additional rooms and a net demand, i.e., after allowing for those who already have spare bedrooms, of perhaps 20 million rooms or the equivalent of 4 to 5 million dwelling units. Desires for greater privacy involving more study-recreational space could have equally large leverage.

Alterations in tastes, though manifested less clearly than changes in income and prices, have far-reaching effects on the long-run level of construction, more so in terms of aggregate dollar expenditures than in numbers of dwelling units built. The increase in real expenditures per new dwelling unit since 1950, an increase largely accounted for by larger houses and one that is in contrast to a long trend in the opposite direction, may have been brought about by sustained prosperity, a rise in the birth rates of second and third children, and a refocusing of interest on the home that has accompanied suburbanization. It is too early to tell whether this phenomenon reflects a basic change and will prove to be a lasting reversal of a long-term trend or a mere episode.

CHAPTER 3

THE PERSONS-PER-ROOM RATIO: INCOME

The tasks of this chapter are (*a*) to describe the 1950 distribution of housing space among the nonfarm household population, and (*b*) to begin an exploration of the determinants of the rate of utilization (PPR). At every step handicaps arising from lack of special tabulations, which resources for this study did not allow, will be embarrassingly plain. Moreover, it will be necessary to discuss separately the effect of each of a number of variables. Such an approach is, of course, unsatisfactory since any given PPR ratio is the combined result of both independent and interdependent causes. Nevertheless, except for a multiple correlation analysis based on local area data (Chapter 5), no other treatment is possible. In spite of these limitations, the available sources (published census tables supplemented by a limited amount of non-census data) are sufficiently rich to afford a number of observations, some strongly supported and others merely suggestive, concerning the factors governing the space-using propensities of the American people.

In 1950 the national PPR ratio (nonfarm) averaged 0.69 for occupied dwelling units. No over-all deficiency of housing space can be said to have existed with respect to the commonly accepted maximum density standards of 1.51 or even 1.01 persons per room. The overwhelming majority of American households are adequately provided with housing space; five-sixths of the households have at least one room for every person, and one-third have at least two rooms per person. At the extremes of the density range, however, one finds 2,000 households of 10 or more persons jammed into single rooms, and 26,000 one-person households occupying units of 10 or more rooms (table 5).[1]

Extreme overcrowding (2.01 or more) is quite uncommon and is found in only 18 households out of every 1,000. The percentage of overcrowded households is higher for renters than for owners, and the proportion of home-owner households drops sharply as the density range is traversed from low to high density groups.

The utilization pattern takes a somewhat different form when space is

---

[1] The derivation of the eight density groups shown in table 5 is explained in Appendix A. At other points in this chapter the broader density groupings published by the Bureau of the Census are used.

TABLE **5.**—PERCENT DISTRIBUTION OF NONFARM HOUSEHOLDS BY PERSONS PER ROOM, BY TENURE: 1950

Persons-per-room ratio	Percent of reporting households and population						Owner households as proportion of total households
	Total		Owner		Renter		
	Popu-lation	House-holds	Popu-lation	House-holds	Popu-lation	House-holds	
0.17 or less...............	0.6	1.6	0.9	2.5	0.2	0.5	80.6
0.18 to 0.33...............	6.3	12.0	8.1	15.2	3.5	8.1	68.4
0.34 to 0.50...............	15.5	22.1	18.8	25.7	11.2	18.3	61.1
0.51 to 0.75...............	24.4	25.1	26.1	25.2	22.5	25.1	53.0
0.76 to 1.00...............	29.2	24.7	28.0	21.3	30.7	28.7	45.5
1.01 to 1.50...............	14.1	8.9	11.6	6.8	17.3	11.3	40.2
1.51 to 2.00...............	6.0	3.7	4.0	2.2	8.5	5.4	31.4
2.01 or more..............	3.9	1.8	2.5	1.2	5.6	2.6	33.3

Source: Appendix table A–2.

distributed in terms of population rather than households.[2]   The extent of overcrowding greatly increases and there is a corresponding reduction in the relative importance of the low-density groups.   The relative importance of the overcrowded groups (1.51 or more) is almost doubled, rising from 5.5 to 9.9 percent, while the very low density group (0.33 or less) drops from 13.6 to 6.9 percent.   There has not always been sufficient recognition of the striking differences in utilization measures between household and population proportions, even on the part of those who are most concerned with the problems of overcrowding.

The inequality in the distribution of housing space can best be described by a Lorenz curve, a graphic device most commonly used for the demonstration of inequality in the distribution of income.   The degree of inequality is related to the size of the area between the Lorenz curve and a diagonal representing a line of equal distribution.   It can be seen in figure 1 that this area is of considerable size though not as large as will be found for income.

In interpreting figure 1, note should be taken that the Lorenz curve is drawn in terms of proportions of population rather than households and that the data are arranged in order of the most crowded to the least crowded, i.e., persons living in housing with a PPR ratio of 1.51 or more comprised 10 percent of all persons but held only 3.2 percent of all occupied rooms; persons enjoying a PPR ratio of 0.33 or less accounted for 6.6 percent of the household population and about 17 percent of total space (table 6).

---

[2] In presenting data on the PPR ratio a choice is presented between two units, the person and the household.   While all census tabulations are given in terms of households, a reading of Appendix A will make clear that the latter, because of the variation in household size, is an inappropriate unit for certain kinds of quantitative analysis, particularly in deriving weighted averages and their changes over time.   Much of the data will nevertheless be given in household units where (a) it is not possible to convert to population units, (b) a point can be made equally well even if less accurately with the use of household data, and (c) the household is the unit being analyzed.

FIGURE 1.—LORENZ CURVE SHOWING DISTRIBUTION OF HOUSING SPACE (MEASURED BY ROOMS), FOR NONFARM OCCUPIED DWELLING UNITS: 1950

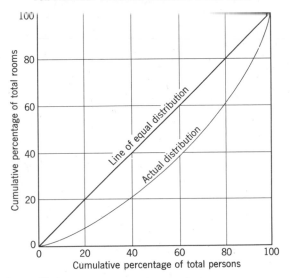

Note: Based on data in table 6.

Differences in the rate of utilization can be attributed to many inter-related factors: income, the cost of housing space, the type of space units available, household size, household composition, tenure, location, race, age of head, plus a host of other factors many of which can be subsumed under "tastes," i.e., sheer individual differences in preferences for housing relative to other ways of spending income. Not all of these factors are of equal importance, nor are the data sufficient to permit anything like a full analysis of each. This chapter is primarily concerned with the influence of income.

TABLE 6.—CUMULATIVE PERCENT DISTRIBUTION OF PERSONS AND ROOMS, BY PERSONS PER ROOM, FOR NONFARM OCCUPIED DWELLING UNITS: 1950

Persons-per-room ratio	Percent of persons	Percent of rooms	Persons-per-room ratio	Percent of persons	Percent of rooms
More than—			More than—		
0	100.00	100.00	1.25	17.38	6.93
0.17	99.44	97.22	1.33	14.09	5.21
0.33	93.36	82.62	1.50	9.84	3.21
0.40	88.64	74.28	1.75	7.00	2.03
0.50	77.68	58.66	2.00	3.86	0.92
0.60	70.25	49.87	2.50	2.31	0.47
0.75	53.18	32.79	3.00	0.98	0.15
0.80	47.33	27.69	5.00	0.21	0.02
1.00	23.99	10.73	12.00	...	...

Source: Appendix table A–2.

Relationship between income and density

Analysis of the effect of income on density levels is complicated by a number of interrelationships. First, space requirements are linked to household size which, up to a certain point, varies with income. Second, additional space is certainly not the only manifestation of higher housing standards; as income levels continue to rise, more and more (relatively) is put into housing quality rather than quantity, that is, the average value or rent *per room* rises as the value or rent of a dwelling unit increases (Chapter 5). Third, as income increases both quantitative and qualitative improvements in housing become less pronounced because the consumer finds more preferred ways of disposing of his added income. The third factor explains the negative slope of the typical Engel curve.

The fact that income helps to determine the rate of utilization, while long a matter of common observation, was not given a statistical basis until the middle thirties when the National Health Survey was made. This survey, which naturally concentrated on the problem of overcrowding, yielded the results given in table 7 which indicate that high-income families tend to crowd less frequently than poor ones.

TABLE 7.—URBAN HOUSEHOLDS BY PERSONS PER ROOM AND INCOME: 1935 AND 1936

[Data for nonrelief households]

Family income	Percent of households with PPR ratio of—		
	1.01 or more	1.51 or more	2.00 or more
All families	16.1	5.9	3.8
Under $1,000	17.0	7.1	5.0
$1,000 to $2,000	11.8	2.9	1.5
$2,000 and over	7.7	1.4	0.7

Source: U. S. Public Health Service, "The National Health Survey: 1935–1936," Preliminary Reports, Bulletin No. 5, p. 8.

The adoption of very broad income classes in the National Health Survey, however, tended both to obscure and oversimplify the income-density relationship. Furthermore, the data were presented only for one end of the density spectrum. The 1950 Census data permit not only a much closer look at the same type of distribution, but also the derivation of average PPR ratios by income (based on the population in, and rooms held by, a given income class). Nevertheless, the data in table 7 anticipate one finding that has never been sufficiently emphasized, namely, that the proportion of overcrowding (1.01 or more) in the lowest income class, 17.0 percent, is not significantly higher than the proportion of overcrowding found for all households, 16.1 percent. In nearly all the 1950 data this rather startling finding receives full corroboration: the people with the lowest incomes have surprisingly good density standards, and the relation between density and income is not as strong or as straightforward as is often believed

Of all households reported in the Census of 1950, 60.6 percent were in the density group of 0.75 persons per room or less; but this density class contained no less than 68 percent of the households with income of $1,000 or less (table 8). Likewise, while 14.5 percent of all households were crowded (1.01 or more), the proportion of crowded households in the lowest income class was only 13.4 percent. Not only did the poorest (in terms of income) fare better than the general population, but no income class except the $10,000 or more has so high a proportion in the lowest density group.[3] Quite clearly, at the lowest income levels, income is not representative of consumer expenditures or living standards.

TABLE **8.**—PERCENT DISTRIBUTION OF NONFARM HOUSEHOLDS BY INCOME, BY PERSONS PER ROOM AND TENURE: 1950

Persons-per-room ratio and tenure	Total report-ing	Income								
		Under $1,000	$1,000 to $1,999	$2,000 to $2,999	$3,000 to $3,999	$4,000 to $4,999	$5,000 to $5,999	$6,000 to $6,999	$7,000 to $9,999	$10,000 and over
TOTAL										
Total.........	100.0	100.0	100.0	100.0	100.0	100.0	100.0	100.0	100.0	100.0
0.75 or less........	60.6	68.1	57.5	55.1	56.2	59.8	63.7	65.6	65.6	77.1
0.76 to 1.00........	24.9	18.6	22.1	26.1	28.8	28.3	26.6	25.7	25.6	17.7
1.01 or more.......	14.5	13.4	20.4	18.8	15.0	11.9	9.7	8.7	8.9	5.2
OWNER										
Total.........	100.0	100.0	100.0	100.0	100.0	100.0	100.0	100.0	100.0	100.0
0.75 or less........	68.4	79.7	70.3	64.2	62.3	64.1	67.6	67.8	68.4	80.0
0.76 to 1.00........	21.4	12.1	16.0	21.9	26.3	26.5	24.7	24.2	24.3	15.8
1.01 or more.......	10.2	8.2	13.8	13.9	11.3	9.4	7.7	7.0	7.3	4.1
RENTER										
Total.........	100.0	100.0	100.0	100.0	100.0	100.0	100.0	100.0	100.0	100.0
0.75 or less........	51.0	56.6	47.1	47.3	49.4	54.0	57.9	60.2	59.8	68.2
0.76 to 1.00........	28.7	25.0	27.0	29.8	31.6	30.8	29.3	28.3	28.1	23.4
1.01 or more.......	19.3	18.5	25.9	22.9	19.0	15.3	12.7	11.5	12.0	8.4

Source: *1950 Census of Housing*, Vol. II, *Nonfarm Housing Characteristics*, Part 1, Chapter 1, United States, table A–7.

Separate data for owners and renters in each of the three density groups show the same pattern, with particularly striking results in the case of owner households. While home owners enjoy better density standards than renters, whatever tabulation or time period is selected (a fact which appears over and over again in this study), it is astounding to find four-fifths of the owner households with the lowest incomes enjoying a PPR of

---

[3] Higher income groups may, of course, have larger rooms than the lower income group. If so, differences in density patterns are understated.

0.75 or less, roughly the same as the highest income class. Overcrowding is proportionately lower at the very bottom of the income scale than it is in the next four $1,000 intervals up the income ladder.

Renters not only have a higher over-all average density, 0.82 as compared to 0.63 for owners, but also characteristically show a more normal response to differences in income. Owners are, of course, financially better off than renters, as is evidenced by median incomes of $3,363 and $2,926, respectively, in 1949. In fact, higher income is one determinant of home ownership since the home ownership ratio rises with income (table 9). Differences in income, however, cannot fully explain why owners show a lower rate of utilization of housing space, since the latter is true even when income is held constant; i.e., the density levels of owners are lower than those of renters within each income class. As one searches for another explanation of the lower rate of utilization for home owners, the simple fact comes to mind that the single-family house typically contains more rooms than do dwelling units in other structure types. But the rate of utilization remains lower for owners even when type of structure is held constant.[4] The truth of the matter is, although it cannot be adequately demonstrated, that owners are probably less inclined to reduce the amount of space in accordance with changes in personal circumstances and probably more inclined to anticipate future space requirements. A greater amount of inertia and lower mobility is necessarily imposed by home ownership, and these factors may be reinforced by differences in the social characteristics of home owners. Not only is it ordinarily easier for a renting household to change residence as family income changes, but renters usually have fewer ties to a neighborhood and therefore less reason for not moving.

The fact remains that, while 68 percent of owner households in 1950 enjoyed the lowest of the three major density levels, the same was true for only slightly more than half the renters. Twice as many renters (relatively) were overcrowded as were home owners. Like owners, the lowest income renters were better off than some of the superior income classes but to a considerably lesser extent. The proportion of the lowest income renter households at a density of 0.75 or less (51 percent) is not exceeded by that of any group with incomes under $5,000, and the proportion at a density of 1.01 or more (18.5 percent) is less than that of any income group under $4,000. In the case of owners the comparable incomes are $10,000 and $5,000. Thus, the sensitivity of response to income seems to vary with tenure.

The income-density relationship for all income classes is most quickly and most accurately seen by shifting to average PPR ratios based on total

[4] The proportion of overcrowded households in rented 1-family houses in 1935–1936 was more than twice as great as in owner-occupied 1-family houses. U. S. Public Health Service, *Urban Housing and Crowding*, Public Health Bulletin #261, Washington, D.C., 1941, p. 19.

persons (rather than households) and total rooms in each income class.[5] All the data relevant to this measure are summarized in table 9, which also serves as a source for relationships other than the income-density: income-household size, income-space, and income-tenure.

TABLE 9.—PERSONS-PER-ROOM RATIO, HOUSEHOLD SIZE, NUMBER OF ROOMS, AND HOME-OWNERSHIP RATIO, BY INCOME, FOR NONFARM HOUSEHOLDS: 1950

Tenure	Under $1,000	$1,000 to $1,999	$2,000 to $2,999	$3,000 to $3,999	$4,000 to $4,999	$5,000 to $5,999	$6,000 to $6,999	$7,000 to $9,999	$10,000 and over
AVERAGE HOUSEHOLD SIZE									
Total	2.55	3.09	3.34	3.47	3.49	3.49	3.56	3.75	3.65
Owner	2.59	3.10	3.46	3.61	3.65	3.67	3.74	3.92	3.81
Renter	2.52	3.08	3.24	3.31	3.27	3.23	3.27	3.40	3.19
AVERAGE NUMBER OF ROOMS									
Total	4.09	4.18	4.43	4.65	4.88	5.08	5.30	5.67	6.81
Owner	5.01	5.02	5.18	5.32	5.51	5.72	5.93	6.20	7.61
Renter	3.32	3.50	3.79	4.03	4.18	4.27	4.41	4.62	4.93
PERSON-PER-ROOM RATIO[1]									
Total	0.62	0.74	0.76	0.74	0.71	0.69	0.67	0.66	0.53
Owner	0.53	0.63	0.67	0.68	0.67	0.65	0.64	0.63	0.51
Renter	0.77	0.89	0.86	0.83	0.79	0.76	0.75	0.75	0.66
HOME-OWNERSHIP RATIO									
Percent of households	50	45	46	53	57	60	63	67	75

[1] Derived from unrounded data.

Source: *1950 Census of Housing*, Vol. II, *Nonfarm Housing Characteristics*, Part 1 Chapter 1, United States, tables A–5 and A–7.

The income-density patterns for all households and for owners and renters separately are traced in figure 2. The nature of these patterns has been partly anticipated in the discussion of household distribution. The income-density curves do not show a continuous decline with income but rather an initial sharp rise followed by a gradual descent. For all households peak density is found at the $2,000–$3,000 income level, and the lowest income class is below the average density of every income class except the $10,000 or more. The difference between owners and renters also shows up markedly. The curve for renters clearly displays a more sensitive reaction to income. The peak occurs well down in the income scale at $1,000 to $2,000 and falls off quite sharply before leveling off at the $6,000 level. The peak for owners is not reached until $3,000 to $4,000, and the subsequent decline is quite gradual.

In the curves for both owners and renters there is considerable flatness

---

[5] For a description of the method used to arrive at these totals, see Appendix A.

FIGURE 2.—PERSONS PER ROOM BY INCOME AND TENURE, FOR NONFARM HOUSEHOLDS: 1950

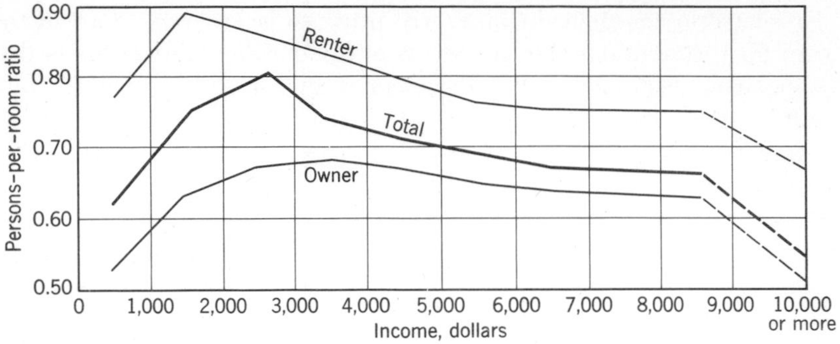

Note: Based on data in table 9.

along the middle income ranges, indicating that the improvements in housing standards are becoming qualitative rather than quantitative. The curve for renters lies well above that for owners throughout its length, that is, renters in any given income class have a higher PPR ratio than do owners in the same class. But the gap between them tends to narrow as income increases.

The fact that improvements in density are quite modest as income rises supports the proposition that housing space is more evenly distributed than income. But when to this is added the observation that the lowest income households enjoy unusually favorable (i.e., better than average) density levels, the difference in the degree of inequality between income and the use of housing space can be expected to be appreciable.

This difference is clearly seen in table 10 in which households are distributed by income and, within income classes, by proportion of total income and total space. When the proportions of households in each income class are matched with the proportions of total income they received and with their holdings of space (percentage of rooms), the inequality of income is found to be much greater than the inequality of space use. No account is taken in any of the data of the fact that some families own or rent a summer home and consequently have more housing space at their disposal than is shown in published census data. Since this is likely to be truer of the rich the degree of inequality of space distribution is somewhat understated. In any event, the lowest income class, which represented 16 percent of all households, received only 2.1 percent of household income but held 14.2 percent of total space. At the other extreme, households with an income of $10,000 or more, comprising 3.3 percent of total households, accounted for 17.3 percent of total income and only 4.7 percent of total space. At no income level is there as much as a 2-percentage point spread between household and space proportions, whereas the income and household proportions differ by as much as 14 percentage points. It is doubtful that many economic goods can be found whose distribution, when related to consumer income, will prove to be so even. Part of the reason for the favorable density levels of low income households is that they include a disproportionately large number of small households. But, as will be shown later, the density levels of low-income households remain favorable even when household size is held constant. Consequently, other reasons for this phenomenon will be sought subsequently.

For both owners and renters income inequality was roughly the same; that is, the relative differences between household and income shares were of about the same order.

TABLE 10.—PERCENT DISTRIBUTION OF INCOME AND OF HOUSING SPACE, BY INCOME CLASS AND TENURE, FOR NONFARM HOUSEHOLDS: 1950

Subject	Total report-ing	Income								
		Under $1,000	$1,000 to $1,999	$2,000 to $2,999	$3,000 to $3,999	$4,000 to $4,999	$5,000 to $5,999	$6,000 to $6,999	$7,000 to $9,999	$10,000 and over
TOTAL										
Percent of—										
Households.......	100.0	16.1	13.4	18.9	19.4	12.2	7.8	4.3	4.7	3.3
Persons..........	100.0	12.5	12.7	19.2	20.6	12.9	8.3	4.7	5.5	3.6
Income..........	100.0	2.1	5.4	12.6	18.2	14.6	11.4	7.5	10.9	17.3
Rooms..........	100.0	14.2	11.9	17.7	19.5	12.8	8.5	4.9	5.8	4.7
OWNER										
Percent of—										
Households.......	100.0	15.1	11.4	16.4	19.3	13.2	8.8	5.1	6.1	4.6
Persons..........	100.0	11.5	10.4	16.6	20.4	14.1	9.4	5.6	7.0	5.1
Income..........	100.0	1.8	4.1	9.9	16.2	14.2	11.6	8.0	12.3	21.9
Rooms..........	100.0	13.8	10.5	15.6	18.8	13.3	9.2	5.5	7.0	6.3
RENTER										
Percent of—										
Households.......	100.0	17.1	15.7	21.5	19.6	11.0	6.6	3.4	3.3	1.7
Persons..........	100.0	13.8	15.5	22.3	20.8	11.6	6.9	3.6	3.7	1.8
Income..........	100.0	2.6	7.3	16.5	21.1	15.2	11.2	6.8	8.7	10.6
Rooms..........	100.0	14.6	14.3	21.1	20.6	11.9	7.4	3.9	4.0	2.2

Source: See table 9.

CHAPTER 4

THE PERSONS-PER-ROOM RATIO:
HOUSEHOLD SIZE

In practically every analysis based upon available census data, household size emerges as a strategic determinant of the rate of utilization at any particular time, and changes in household size seem to be a key to understanding historical changes in the rate of utilization. The household size-density relation is quite simple: large households live under more crowded conditions. Further, the density ratios increase by a constant amount as household size increases; that is, the relationship is virtually linear (figure 3). The slope of the household size-density schedule is considerable, average density rising from 0.29 for the 1-person household to 1.58 for the 9-person household, or an almost uniform gain in density of 0.16 with each addition to household size. In other words, although total space increases consistently with household size, the rise is less rapid than the increase in household size. Attention was called in Chapter 2 to this phenomenon which has as its basis (a) the more efficient utilization of the "overhead" rooms, i.e., kitchen and living rooms, and (b) the need on the part of larger households to devote more of their budgets to food and

FIGURE 3.—PERSONS PER ROOM BY HOUSEHOLD SIZE AND TENURE, FOR NONFARM HOUSEHOLDS: 1950

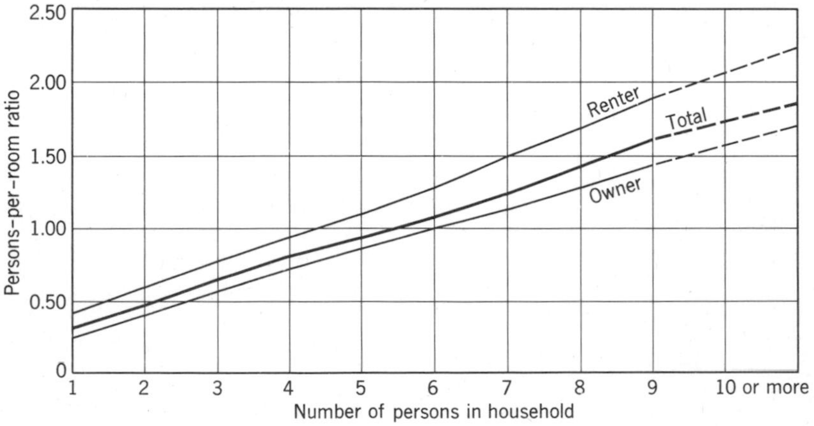

Note: Based on data in table 11.

clothing.[1] The compromises that large families make are reflected not only in economizing on space but, judging from rent and value data in the next chapter, by compromising with housing quality as well.

As always, the rate of utilization of owners is lower than that of renters for any given household size class. Just as renters' space use showed a more sensitive response to income (compared to owners), renters also appear to adjust their housing space more readily to changes in household size; the amount of space added per additional person is somewhat greater than for owners (0.22 rooms compared to 0.17). The higher mobility of renters apparently permits them more opportunities for adjusting their use of space as personal circumstances change.

In considering either the income-density relation or the household size-density relation, the connection between household size and income emerges as a complicating factor. To a certain extent higher income is accompanied by higher average household size.

TABLE 11.—AVERAGE NUMBER OF ROOMS AND PERSONS-PER-ROOM RATIO, FOR NONFARM HOUSEHOLDS, BY SIZE: 1950

Household size	Total		Owner		Renter	
	Average number of rooms	Persons-per-room ratio	Average number of rooms	Persons-per-room ratio	Average number of rooms	Persons-per-room ratio
1 person	3.41	0.29	4.61	0.22	2.63	0.38
2 persons	4.39	0.46	5.22	0.38	3.52	0.57
3 persons	4.75	0.63	5.43	0.55	3.99	0.75
4 persons	5.07	0.79	5.61	0.71	4.35	0.92
5 persons	5.40	0.93	5.91	0.85	4.63	1.08
6 persons	5.60	1.07	6.14	0.98	4.77	1.26
7 persons	5.67	1.23	6.28	1.12	4.79	1.46
8 persons	5.67	1.41	6.31	1.28	4.80	1.67
9 persons	5.70	1.58	6.60	1.42	4.83	1.86
10 persons or more [1]	5.92	2.03	6.49	1.82	5.02	2.39

[1] Estimated average = 12 persons.

Source: 1950 Census of Housing, Vol. II, Nonfarm Housing Characteristics, Part 1, Chapter 1, United States, table A–5.

Some of the gain in purchasing power is, therefore, more apparent than real. An adjustment of the income-density relation to a per-capita income basis [2] does not, however, disturb its essential characteristics (figure 4). The main effect is to give the curves a little more "normal" appearance; i.e., the improvement in utilization is seen to be somewhat more responsive to the rise in income.

---

[1] Eric Schiff, "Family Size and Residential Construction," American Economic Review, March 1946, pp. 97–112.

[2] No allowance is made for the fact that unrelated individuals are included in the population totals but not in the income figures.

FIGURE 4.—PERSONS PER ROOM BY PER-CAPITA INCOME AND TENURE,
FOR NONFARM HOUSEHOLDS: 1950

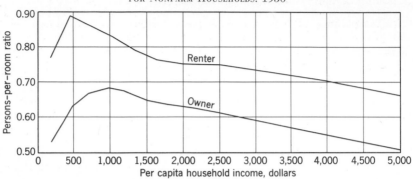

Note: Based on data in tables 8 and 11.

Because of the interrelation between income and household size, it is difficult to measure, from these data, the precise influence of household size on the use of housing space.   One would expect density to vary with household size independently of income, that is, the density of households with the same income should rise with increase in household size.   Published census material does not permit a test of this hypothesis, but partial confirmation can be obtained from the 1935–1936 family budget studies (table 12). Reading across the rows of this table, one finds a strong rise in the PPR ratio with increased family size,[3] income held constant.   More important, reading up and down the columns of the table, one finds but a small decline in the PPR ratio with increased family income, household size held more or less constant.   The income-density function is well defined but seems to be much weaker than the household size-density function.   In Chicago, for example, the PPR ratio for type III families slopes down the income range rather mildly from 0.91 to 0.64 and for type VII from 1.32 to 1.14.   For given income classes, however, the slope from the small to the large household is such as to more than double all PPR ratios.   The finding of a relatively weak income effect and a relatively strong effect of household size on PPR ratios is thus confirmed by family budget data more stratified than the census figures but limited to a few cities.

Table 12 confirms another finding derived from the 1950 Census data.   Even when household size is held constant, the peak PPR ratio does not always occur in the lowest income class; some of the nine income-density curves one could draw from this table would bear at least a family resemblance to the curve shown in figure 2.   The family budget data suggest that the favorable density levels of the lowest income households cannot be due merely to small size of households in this group.   Though

---

[3] See note to table 12 for definition of family types.

the low income classes include a disproportionate share of 1- and 2-person households, other factors must be considered.

TABLE **12.**—PERSONS-PER-ROOM RATIO BY INCOME FOR SPECIFIED FAMILY TYPES, FOR
SELECTED AREAS: 1935 AND 1936

Income	Type I family			Type III family			Type VII family		
	Chi-cago	Colum-bus	East Central[1]	Chi-cago	Colum-bus	East Central[1]	Chi-cago	Colum-bus	East Central[1]
$ 500 to $ 749	0.45	0.43	0.50	0.91	1.11	1.02	1.32	(2)	1.97
$ 750 to $ 999	0.58	0.46	0.51	0.88	0.82	0.91	1.56	1.40	1.50
$1,000 to $1,249	0.51	0.40	0.41	0.95	0.79	0.82	1.35	1.34	1.47
$1,250 to $1,499	0.56	0.43	0.42	0.89	0.73	0.84	1.26	1.22	1.23
$1,500 to $1,749	0.54	0.45	0.45	0.86	0.72	0.79	1.31	1.16	1.28
$1,750 to $1,999	0.53	0.42	0.48	0.85	0.74	0.70	1.27	1.17	1.16
$2,000 to $2,249	0.50	0.40	0.36	0.90	0.70	0.75	1.23	1.19	1.09
$2,250 to $2,499	0.48	0.41	0.39	0.82	0.73	0.70	1.26	1.07	1.02
$2,500 to $2,999	0.53	0.39	0.43	0.80	0.69	0.72	1.15	1.07	1.15
$3,000 to $3,499	0.49	0.37	0.34	0.75	0.72	0.65	1.15	1.06	1.03
$3,500 to $3,999	0.48	0.32	0.36	0.75	0.71	0.67	1.17	1.19	(2)
$4,000 to $4,999	0.50	0.35	0.33	0.74	0.66	0.62	1.17	0.95	(2)
$5,000 to $7,499	0.44	0.34	...	0.82	0.66	1.10	0.91	...	
$7,500 to $9,999	0.58	} 0.32	{ 0.34	0.71	(2)	0.68	1.14	(2)	} 0.98
$10,000 or more	0.46		...	0.64	(2)	...	(2)	(2)	

Note: Nonwhite and foreign-born excluded from the tabulations. Type I family consists of a couple without children; type III is a couple with 2 children under 16 years; type VII comprises a married couple with 1 child, plus 5 or 6 other members of any age or sex. The PPR ratios of each family type are based on all persons in the household, including servants.

[1] Three middle-sized cities.

[2] Not available.

Source: U. S. Bureau of Labor Statistics, *Family Expenditures in Selected Cities, 1935–1936,* Vol. I, Housing Bulletin No. 648, 1941, pp. 132–163.

For one, the lowest income class in any given year will include some families and individuals who are recent and perhaps temporary members: a businessman having a poor season, a worker suffering layoffs. Such people will not adjust their housing or space standards unless the setback proves to be more permanent or their assets are exhausted. In fact, there is probably a longer lag in adjusting housing expenditures to a suddenly lowered income than is the case for other consumer outlays. Second, the lowest income classes contain a large proportion of the aged. Older people may continue to occupy more space than they "need" for a variety of reasons. Their purchasing power may exceed their income because they are net dis-savers living off accumulated assets. If they are home owners, the mortgage may have been paid off[4] so that their cash outlays for housing are relatively low; the rent for smaller accommodations may be as much as current ownership expenses. While the opportunity existed in the postwar market for a profitable sale, many older people

[4] A special census tabulation shows that home owners over 65 years of age comprised about 15 percent of all home owners but accounted for only 5 percent of all mortgaged homes.

doubtlessly preferred to hold on to excess space in order to keep their homes available for family visits and celebrations. If renters, the aged are often to be found in the rent-controlled portion of the inventory, in which case smaller units may be available only at rents higher than those currently paid.

The composition of each density class by income and household size

Enough has been said concerning the income-density and the household size-density relations to suggest that households living at low densities (0.75 or less) are made up of both the poor and the rich and contain a disproportionate number of small households. The group of crowded households is comprised of the moderately poor and the large households. To make these findings more explicit, the households in each class may be distributed first by income and then by household size. The structure of each density class with reference to income is shown in table 13 in the form of indexes. If all income classes contributed proportionately to each density group, all indexes would read 100.0. An index above 100.0 means that a given income class plays a disproportionately large role in a density group; the contrary is true for an index less than 100.0. Rich households, $10,000 or more, for example, account for a small share of overcrowded households, but at the same time they constitute an even smaller share of all households; hence, the index for this group is only 37.5 in the density group of 1.01 or more. It is only by comparison of these two shares (expressed in the form of an index) that density structure can be properly analyzed.

TABLE **13.**—INDEX OF SHARES OF EACH INCOME CLASS RELATIVE TO SHARE OF EACH DENSITY CLASS, FOR NONFARM HOUSEHOLDS, BY TENURE: 1950

Persons-per-room ratio and tenure	Under $1,000	$1,000 to $1,999	$2,000 to $2,999	$3,000 to $3,999	$4,000 to $4,999	$5,000 to $5,999	$6,000 to $6,999	$7,000 to $9,999	$10,000 and over
TOTAL									
0.75 or less..............	112.5	95.5	91.0	92.8	98.4	105.1	109.3	108.3	128.1
0.76 to 1.00..............	74.4	88.8	105.3	115.9	113.1	106.4	102.3	102.1	71.9
1.01 or more..............	91.9	141.0	129.3	103.6	82.0	66.7	60.5	60.4	37.5
OWNER									
0.75 or less..............	115.9	102.6	93.9	90.7	93.9	98.9	100.0	100.0	115.2
0.76 to 1.00..............	55.6	74.6	102.4	122.7	122.7	115.9	113.7	113.1	73.9
1.01 or more..............	80.1	135.1	136.8	111.3	92.4	75.0	68.6	72.1	39.1
RENTER									
0.75 or less..............	109.8	91.1	91.2	94.9	104.5	112.1	114.7	115.2	135.3
0.76 to 1.00..............	87.1	84.3	103.7	109.6	107.3	103.0	97.1	100.0	82.4
1.01 or more..............	95.3	133.8	118.6	98.0	79.1	66.7	58.8	63.6	41.2

Note: An index number of 100.0 results when the proportion of households in the specified income class is the same as the proportion in the specified density class.

Source: *1950 Census of Housing*, Vol. II, *Nonfarm Housing Characteristics*, Part 1, Chapter 1, United States, table A-7.

The paradoxical finding of low density among the very poor is again shown in the high indexes of households with less than $1,000 income in the lowest density class. But the relatively largest contribution to the group of households enjoying low density comes from the middle to upper income classes. Families in this income range who are or remain renters (cf. the tenure ratio by income, table 9) do so in part because of the absence of density pressure. From the middle to the top of the income scale, renter households are found relatively more frequently in the low density group and less frequently in the high density group than home owners. In these income groups, there are wider differences in average household size between renters and owners than at the bottom of the income scale.

The moderate density group (0.76 to 1.00) contains less than a proportionate share of low income households. As one might expect, this is the density class of the middle income family. The highest indexes are found among households with $3,000 to $5,000 income, both owners and renters. Up to these peaks the share of households in the moderate density group increases with rise in income, and the increase is accompanied by declining indexes for the same income classes in the crowded density group. Conversely, as one goes beyond the $3,000 to $5,000 income range he finds the share of middle income households in the moderate density group declining, and this decline is accompanied by increasing indexes for the same income classes in the low density group. The moderate density group seems to serve as a "way station" as housing standards improve with income.

The crowded group draws primarily from the moderately poor, particularly from households with $1,000 to $3,000 in income. Middle and upper income households contribute relatively lightly to this group. Households with incomes of $10,000 or more, which comprise 3.2 percent of all households, are only 1.2 percent of the highest density class (an index of 37.5). It is perhaps surprising to find the highest income class represented at all among the overcrowded. Apart from lags in making adjustments in housing space, such a result is probably due to the well-to-do households which prefer small but expensive urban apartments, but which may have an additional dwelling unit at their disposal (a farm or a weekend house in the country, or a house in Hollywood in addition to an apartment near Manhattan's theater district). More generally, the presence of high-income households among the overcrowded can perhaps be attributed to the fact, long known, that housing stands quite low in the preference scale of some families throughout the income scale.

The structure of each density class with respect to household size is shown in table 14. In analyzing the shares of given household size classes in the various density groups, we have an opportunity for observing much finer detail, i.e., eight instead of three density groups. The use of index numbers, found convenient in the analysis of density classes by income,

TABLE 14.—PERCENT DISTRIBUTION OF NONFARM HOUSEHOLDS BY SIZE, BY TENURE AND PERSONS PER ROOM: 1950

Persons-per-room ratio and tenure	Total reporting	Household size									
		1 person	2 persons	3 persons	4 persons	5 persons	6 persons	7 persons	8 persons	9 persons	10 persons or more
Total	100.0	9.7	29.3	23.2	18.6	10.0	4.7	2.2	1.1	0.6	0.6
0.17 or less	100.0	82.1	17.9	....	....	....	....	....	....	....	....
0.18 to 0.33	100.0	39.4	53.1	4.1	2.0	1.4	....	....	....	....	....
0.34 to 0.50	100.0	9.7	57.6	27.4	4.3	0.1	0.6	0.3	....	....	....
0.51 to 0.75	100.0	....	24.3	45.2	21.5	7.0	1.8	....	0.2	....	....
0.76 to 1.00	100.0	6.2	12.0	14.9	37.3	19.6	7.1	2.1	0.5	0.1	0.1
1.01 to 1.50	100.0	....	....	14.6	22.3	23.0	21.4	11.0	4.3	2.6	0.9
1.51 to 2.00	100.0	....	21.5	....	17.2	21.5	9.7	10.8	11.3	3.0	5.1
2.01 or more	100.0	....	....	14.1	7.1	19.0	9.2	15.8	8.7	10.9	15.8
Owner, total	100.0	7.2	28.1	23.0	20.0	11.4	5.4	2.5	1.2	0.6	0.6
0.17 or less	100.0	81.3	18.7	....	....	....	....	....	....	....	....
0.18 to 0.33	100.0	27.0	65.1	5.3	2.6	....	....	....	....	....	....
0.34 to 0.50	100.0	2.5	55.0	34.6	5.8	1.2	1.8	....	....	....	....
0.51 to 0.75	100.0	....	9.8	45.1	30.9	10.6	2.7	0.5	0.3	0.2	....
0.76 to 1.00	100.0	2.0	3.8	6.2	42.8	28.7	11.5	3.7	0.9	0.2	0.3
1.01 to 1.50	100.0	....	....	6.1	12.3	24.3	26.8	16.9	7.4	4.6	1.8
1.51 to 2.00	100.0	....	14.0	....	12.6	18.5	8.6	14.4	16.7	5.0	10.3
2.01 or more	100.0	....	....	12.1	7.8	15.5	8.6	13.8	8.6	12.9	20.7
Renter, total	100.0	12.5	30.6	23.4	17.1	8.5	4.0	1.9	1.0	0.6	0.5
0.17 or less	100.0	86.8	13.2	....	....	....	....	....	....	....	....
0.18 to 0.33	100.0	67.5	29.8	1.7	1.0	....	....	....	....	....	....
0.34 to 0.50	100.0	20.9	61.0	15.6	1.9	0.3	0.2	....	....	....	....
0.51 to 0.75	100.0	....	40.6	45.0	10.8	2.8	0.7	0.1	....	....	....
0.76 to 1.00	100.0	9.7	18.8	22.3	32.8	12.1	3.3	0.7	0.2	0.1	....
1.01 to 1.50	100.0	....	....	20.4	29.0	22.0	17.7	7.1	2.1	1.3	0.3
1.51 to 2.00	100.0	....	25.1	....	19.4	23.1	10.1	9.0	8.7	2.0	2.6
2.01 or more	100.0	....	....	15.3	6.9	20.7	9.6	15.7	8.4	10.0	13.4

Source: *1950 Census of Housing*, Vol. II, *Nonfarm Housing Characteristics*, Part 1, Chapter 1, United States, table A–5.

proves too awkward for household size, and straight percentage shares are given instead in table 14.

Each of the density groups contains households of varying size,[5] but as density increases the larger households become increasingly dominant. Thus, 1-person households which account for 9.7 percent of all households make up five-sixths of the lowest density group (PPR ratio of 0.17 or less). Nearly 1 out of 5 households consists of 4 persons, but they account for 3 out of 8 households living at the moderate density level of 0.76–1.00 and 1 out of 50 households in the 0.18–0.33 group.

Overcrowding, on the other hand, is most often found among the large households. Households of 10 or more persons (average of 12 persons), though relatively quite rare (0.6 percent of all households), comprise nearly 16 percent of the extremely overcrowded groups (2.01 plus); over 50 percent of the latter are made up of households with 7 persons or more. Above the more generally accepted level of crowding (1.51 or more) are found almost 2 million households, nearly half of whom consist of 6 or more persons.

The tenure distribution of the various density groups (given in table 5) clearly indicates that the overcrowded households tend to be renters, while the lower density classes are mostly home owners. While one-half of all households were owners in 1950, renters outnumbered owners more than 2 to 1 in the crowded groups of 1.51 or more. In the lowest density class, 0.17 or less, there were 4 owners for every renter, and in the next higher group, 3 owners for every renter.

Effect of declining household size on the PPR ratio

The relationship between household size and the rate of utilization is so significant that the question arises as to whether the historic decline in average household size has operated to reduce the average PPR ratio. Between 1940 and 1950 both average household size and the average PPR ratio fell (table 15), the former by 7 and the latter by 5.5 percent. The drop in the PPR ratio was accompanied by a lower proportion of households in the high density group and a higher proportion with favorable densities signifying, among other things, a greater equality in the distribution of space.

Obviously, not all of the decline in the national PPR ratio is due to an altered household size distribution. Over the decade other factors, such as increased income and home ownership, were also conducive to improve-

---

[5] The density groups were tabulated from the cross-tabulation of persons in households and rooms in occupied dwelling units. Since these variables are discrete some household size classes cannot possibly be included in certain of the density groups (Appendix A). For example, the one-person household cannot fall into a density group higher than 1.00 nor into the 0.51–0.75 group, the 2–person household cannot enter into the 1.01–1.50 or 2.01 plus group. The dashes in the table indicate that a restriction of this type exists.

TABLE **15.**—PERCENT DISTRIBUTION OF NONFARM HOUSEHOLDS BY PERSONS PER ROOM,
BY TENURE: 1950 AND 1940

Year and tenure	Persons-per-room ratio					Average persons-per-room ratio	Average house-hold size
	0.50 or less	0.51 to 1.00	1.01 to 1.50	1.51 to 2.00	2.01 or more		
TOTAL							
1950...................	35.6	50.0	8.9	3.7	1.8	0.69	3.29
1940...................	32.0	50.4	10.5	4.8	2.3	0.72	3.53
OWNER							
1950...................	43.5	46.4	6.8	2.2	1.2	0.62	3.43
1940...................	43.6	44.6	7.4	2.8	1.6	0.62	3.60
RENTER							
1950...................	26.9	53.8	11.3	5.4	2.6	0.80	3.12
1940...................	23.9	54.4	12.6	6.2	2.9	0.83	3.48

Source: *1950 Census of Housing*, Vol. II, *Nonfarm Housing Characteristics*, Part 1, Chapter 1, United States, table A–5; *1940 Census of Housing*, Vol. II, *General Characteristics*, Part 1, U. S. Summary, table 10, p. 38.

ment in space standards. Waiving for the moment other variables, such as prices and rents, geographical shifts, and changes in household composition having mixed effects on utilization, one may pose these questions. Accepting the 1950 household size-density relation for all households, owner households, and renter households as a basis for analysis, how much of a decline in the nonfarm PPR ratio should have resulted from the shift in the structure of household size? From increased home ownership?[6] And how does the actual decline in this ratio of 4.1 percent compare to these expected values? Using standardization techniques, the answers are as follows: Changes in household size alone should have caused about a 6-percent decline in the over-all PPR ratio, the shift to home-ownership a 3-percent decline, the two in combination a 10-percent decline.[7]

The actual drop of about 4 percent in the PPR ratio was remarkably small compared to that which might have been anticipated from shifts in household size and tenure. Obviously, during this decade important offsetting influences were at work acting on consumer behavior in such a way that some or all given household size classes reduced the amount of housing space used. There is no way of directly testing such an hypothesis from nationwide totals because of the lack of requisite data. However, for one city, Philadelphia, the 1934 Real Property tabulation of household

[6] The census definition of income changed between 1940 and 1950 from a wage and salary base to income from all sources preventing any direct quantification of the income effect. In the next chapter an indirect measure of the influence of income is obtained via correlation analysis which confirms the finding that its effect is relatively weak.

[7] Stated differently, the average number of rooms per dwelling unit declined, between 1940 and 1950, by 3.6 percent. The shift to smaller households and the increase in home ownership, however, should have led to a 2.3 percent *increase* in the average number of rooms, if the 1950 relation of number of rooms by number of persons and tenure had remained unchanged. Obviously, it did not.

size and number of rooms is published in sufficient detail to permit the derivation of a household size-density schedule that can be directly measured against a comparable 1950 schedule (table 16).

The evidence presented in table 16 is clear. For nearly all given household size classes the PPR ratio rose between 1934 and 1950, i.e., the household size-density curve shifted upward. Even the significant movement towards more home ownership, a powerful depressor of the rate of utilization, merely retarded, but did not overcome, the tendency for households of given size to reduce their holdings of space. Households in Philadelphia (and quite likely in the Nation as a whole) in 1950 occupied fewer rooms than did their counterparts in 1934. The over-all rate of utilization declined from 0.66 to 0.64 only because of the large increase in the proportion of small households which use relatively greater amounts of space.[8]

TABLE 16.—PERSONS-PER-ROOM RATIO BY HOUSEHOLD SIZE, BY TENURE, FOR
PHILADELPHIA: 1950 AND 1934

Household size	1950			1934			Percent change, 1934 to 1950[1]		
	Total	Owner	Renter	Total	Owner	Renter	Total	Owner	Renter
1 person	0.29	0.18	0.39	0.25	0.15	0.34	+19.2	+15.0	+13.9
2 persons	0.43	0.34	0.59	0.39	0.29	0.50	+10.1	+11.9	+17.3
3 persons	0.56	0.48	0.72	0.50	0.43	0.60	+10.9	+11.9	+21.1
4 persons	0.68	0.62	0.86	0.63	0.56	0.71	+ 9.4	+11.1	+21.1
5 persons	0.80	0.74	0.98	0.75	0.69	0.83	+ 6.7	+ 7.8	+17.7
6 persons	0.92	0.85	1.10	0.88	0.81	0.96	+ 5.3	+ 5.8	+15.3
7 persons	1.04	0.95	1.24	0.99	0.92	1.08	+ 4.2	+ 3.7	+14.5
8 persons	1.13	1.03	1.35	1.10	1.02	1.19	+ 2.7	+ 1.4	+13.4
9 persons	1.22	1.09	1.47	1.22	1.14	1.30	...	− 4.1	+12.6
10 persons or more	1.55	1.15	1.82	1.51	1.47	1.55	+ 2.5	−21.9	+17.3

[1] Computed from unrounded data.

Source: *1950 Census of Housing*, Vol. II, *Nonfarm Housing Characteristics*, Part 4, Chapter 107, Philadelphia, table A–5; and Federal Works Progress Administration, *Report of Philadelphia Real Property Survey*, 1934.

The finding, inferred from the census aggregate data and clearly demonstrated by the Philadelphia data, that the rate of utilization tended to rise for given household size classes from depression to prosperity is of considerable significance and stands in opposition to widespread beliefs. Although the income effect on density was seen to be relatively weak, it was far from negligible, especially when adjusted for household size[9] (cf. the family budget data in table 12). Nevertheless, a typical household of,

[8] As in the case of the 1940–1950 change in the aggregate nonfarm PPR ratio, the effect of shifting household size was more important than the increase in home ownership in producing this decline, the relative weights of the two factors being in the ratio of over 2 to 1.

[9] It is true that the shift in household size distribution, which creates a larger number of households from a given population, and the rise in home ownership are, in part, the result of the increase in incomes so that some of the impact of general increases in income on density is made indirectly by way of a complex path.

say, 3 or 4 persons, having in 1950 probably twice the real income of its 1934 counterpart, was found to be occupying less, rather than more, space.

Some important modifications were, of course, simultaneously taking place on the supply side of the market. One important trend was the shift toward smaller dwelling units (Chapter 7) as a result of conversions and the declining size of new houses and apartments. Normally in most markets, particularly one as competitive as the housing market, i.e., where supply cannot be controlled because it is in the hands of a very large number of sellers, it is supply that adapts to demand rather than the reverse. A large part of the reason for smaller dwelling units was, therefore, smaller households. Another was the rising cost of housing space. Moreover, this period was far from normal. Restrictions on building and rent control during much of the decade imposed formidable limitations on the free exercise of consumer sovereignty; consequently, no analysis of the 1940–1950 changes in the housing market can be completely economic.

Nevertheless, one must still look to the consumer in attempting to understand why households of given size were using less space. Consumer behavior might be explained (a) by the sharp absolute and relative rise in prices and rents (at least for uncontrolled housing). As the data in Chapter 5 show, the increased cost of housing space had a measurably deterrent effect on utilization; (b) by shifts in household composition; and (c) by a change in tastes, which caused housing to take a lower place in the consumer scale of preferences as a result of the competition of high priced durables—television, automobiles, washers, air conditioning, and so forth, for which a great postwar hunger existed.

CHAPTER 5

THE PERSONS-PER-ROOM RATIO:
VALUE AND RENT

The relationship between housing space utilization and the value or rent of housing will be discussed along two lines. First, utilization patterns associated with housing bearing different price tags will be described on the basis of cross-sectional data. Second, changes in utilization that take place in reaction to a change in rent or value will be analyzed through the use of time series. The second is obviously the more interesting and important task. Because the cost of housing is a major item in family budgets it is reasonable to expect that the quantity of housing space used by consumers is subject to normal market reactions, namely, other things equal, a higher price will lead to retrenchment on space and a lower price to more liberal use of space.

That the cost of housing space restricts its use hardly needs demonstration. It is a fact observed in the sales office of any new housing project and one that is largely responsible for the shrinkage in the size of new dwelling units as construction costs vaulted after World War II. The real question is: *how much* curtailment of space, measured in terms of the PPR ratio, will result from given price increases, or, more technically, what is the magnitude of the price "elasticity" with respect to per capita use of space?

The extent of price-induced changes in space utilization has never been ascertained. Certainly critics of rent control who hold that legislated housing bargains lead to excessive use of housing space must implicitly assume a rather sizable reaction. An empirically derived measure of the influence of changes in rent on the PPR ratio is therefore quite relevant not only to a general understanding of housing market behavior but is also useful for weighing the implications of rent control policy. But an analysis of the response in space utilization to price changes is an extremely difficult task. While it is believed that the results derived from multiple correlation analysis will shed some light on both general market behavior and the effects of rent control, much more work remains to be done. This occasion is also used to explore, to the limit that census data permit, a number of other hypotheses concerning the influence of rent control on the housing market. To avoid disappointment, it is best to state at once that the answers to questions of rent control do not always emerge with incontestable finality.   An attack on the problem via census data can be made only with the aid of bold assumptions and catch-as-catch-can technique.

The rent/value-utilization relation: cross-sectional data

Turning to descriptive materials derived from the Census of 1950, a number of useful relationships can be traced between the PPR ratio and value and rent.   The most obvious finding is that people who occupy more expensive dwelling units ordinarily have lower PPR ratios, chiefly because they have more space (table 17 and figure 5).   Clearly, people who pay higher rent also have, on the average, a higher income, so that it comes as no surprise that the rent-PPR curve bears a resemblance to the income-PPR curve.   The patterns are far from identical, however, as a reference to figure 2 in Chapter 3 will show.   It might almost be said that the rent-utilization curve looks about what one might have expected the income-utilization pattern to be, namely, that there is a consistent improvement in utilization as economic status improves.   The rent-PPR curve drops continuously (but at a changing rate) from the lowest to the highest rent and contains none of the "abnormality" the income-PPR curve displayed for the low-income people.

FIGURE 5.—PERSONS PER ROOM BY VALUE AND CONTRACT MONTHLY RENT OF NONFARM OCCUPIED DWELLING UNITS, BY TENURE: 1950

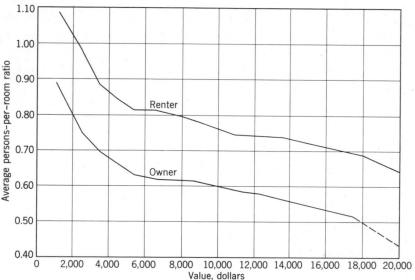

Note: Based on data in table 17.

TABLE 17.—HOUSEHOLD SIZE, NUMBER OF ROOMS, AND PERSONS PER ROOM, BY VALUE
AND CONTRACT MONTHLY RENT OF NONFARM OCCUPIED DWELLING UNITS: 1950

Value and rent	Average number of persons	Average number of rooms	Average persons per room [1]	Value and rent	Average number of persons	Average number of rooms	Average persons per room[1]
VALUE [2]				CONTRACT MONTHLY RENT			
Less than $2,000....	3.48	3.91	0.89	Less than $10.....	3.27	2.96	1.11
$2,000 to $2,999....	3.49	4.64	0.75	$10 to $14.......	3.31	3.38	0.98
$3,000 to $3,999....	3.48	4.98	0.70	$15 to $19.......	3.29	3.72	0.88
$4,000 to $4,999....	3.48	5.23	0.66	$20 to $24.......	3.22	3.82	0.84
$5,000 to $5,999....	3.44	5.44	0.63	$25 to $29.......	3.21	3.96	0.81
$6,000 to $7,499....	3.47	5.59	0.62	$30 to $34.......	3.12	3.83	0.82
$7,500 to $9,999....	3.49	5.68	0.61	$35 to $39.......	3.10	3.86	0.80
$10,000 to $14,999..	3.50	6.05	0.58	$40 to $49.......	2.96	3.78	0.78
$15,000 to $19,999..	3.50	6.77	0.52	$50 to $59.......	2.92	3.93	0.74
$20,000 or more....	3.57	8.31	0.43	$60 to $74.......	2.93	3.98	0.74
				$75 to $99.......	2.98	4.27	0.70
				$100 or more.....	3.54	4.80	0.64

[1] Computed from unrounded data.

[2] Restricted to single-family units on 1-unit properties.

Source: *1950 Census of Housing*, Vol. II, *Nonfarm Housing Characteristics*, Part 1, Chapter 1, United
States, tables A–1, A–2, and A–5.

Reasons for the dissimilarities are not difficult to find. For one, the
relation between rent and income is far from perfect. Although this
relation has been generalized from scores of studies and given a characteristic shape, the simple correlation between rent and income is not very
high.[1] Families in any given income class differ greatly in the amount of
rent they pay, while families in any rent class report a wide range of income. At the low end of both the rent and income scales the following is
true: there is a greater likelihood that a family paying a low rent will be
"poor" (low income) than that a "poor" family will pay a low rent. A
family's income for any single year may sometimes be a deceptive indicator of its average economic position in the community over a longer
period of time. This is why many students regard consumption expenditures rather than income to be a more reliable index of economic status,
even though consumption (particularly rent) may adjust slowly to changing circumstances. The inclusion of households which were only temporary
"residents" of the low-income class and therefore had favorable PPR
ratios was one of the reasons, it will be remembered, for the "abnormal"
appearance of the income-density curve.

The most important reason why the rent/value-density relation is more
consistent than the income-density relation lies in the fact that value and

[1] The correlation between rent and income was +0.41. Thus, only about one-sixth of the variation
in rent could be attributed to variation in income.

rent bear a closer relationship to size of dwelling unit than does income. More spacious homes cost more on the average. At the same time, the average PPR ratio for the smaller dwelling units is higher than for the more spacious ones. As a matter of fact, the PPR ratio drops consistently with increasing size of dwelling units (table 18). When these two findings, a direct relationship between space and price and an inverse relation between space and the average PPR ratio, are combined, the nature of the price-density relation of figure 5 becomes quite understandable. Low-price units tend to be both small and crowded (table 17).

TABLE **18.**—PERSONS PER ROOM AND VALUE AND CONTRACT MONTHLY RENT, FOR NONFARM OCCUPIED DWELLING UNITS, BY SIZE: 1950

Number of rooms	Owner-occupied dwelling units		Renter-occupied dwelling units	
	Value	PPR ratio	Contract monthly rent	PPR ratio
1 room	$3,898	2.32	$32.17	1.73
2 rooms	2,828	1.32	35.27	1.15
3 rooms	3,885	0.94	38.99	0.92
4 rooms	6,431	0.80	39.69	0.83
5 rooms	8,764	0.66	43.16	0.72
6 rooms	11,460	0.61	44.60	0.65
7 rooms	14,795	0.55	48.75	0.60
8 rooms	17,757	0.49	50.03	0.53
9 rooms	23,205	0.45	56.69	0.49
10 rooms or more	32,789	0.27	66.63	0.36

Source: See table 17.

This comparison between income and density and rent/value and density suggests that the second of these two relationships is superior (for most purposes) in analyzing the connection between the economic power of a household and its demand for space. A rent/value-density relationship gets closer to the heart of the matter because it is less affected by (*a*) the temporary "residents" in the lower income groups and (*b*) the very small but very poor households whose low PPR ratios, while real enough, are subject to some ambiguity as indexes of welfare.

Rent/value-income ratios

Since the value or rent of housing bears a relation to the income of the household, the utilization of housing can also be examined directly in terms of the value- or rent-income ratio. These well-known ratios have the following properties: (*a*) on the average, the more income people have the more expensive is the housing they utilize; and (*b*) the increase in housing expenditures does not keep pace with the improvement in income, hence the ratio tends to fall as income rises. In general, groups with a high value- or rent-income ratio contain the poorer segments of the population, while the richer segments are found in low value- or rent-income groups (table 19). One might then expect the most favorable utilization patterns to be found among the low price-income ratio classes (rich) and unfavorable patterns, or high PPR ratios, at the other end of the scale.

This expectation is not borne out (table 19). Actually, the most overcrowding is found in the lowest rent/value-income ratio class and the least relative amount of overcrowding in the highest rent/value-income ratio class. The explanation for this curious result is the weak relation between income and utilization and the poor correlation that exists between rent and income. As a consequence, the price-income ratio is an even poorer guide to space utilization than is income alone. In the case of income only a distortion but not a complete reversal of the "normal" or expected pattern was found.

TABLE **19.**—PERSONS PER ROOM BY GROSS RENT/VALUE-INCOME RATIOS, FOR NONFARM OCCUPIED DWELLING UNITS: 1950

Persons-per-room ratio	Ratio of gross rent to income					Ratio of value to income [1]				
	Less than 0.10	0.10 to 0.14	0.15 to 0.19	0.20 to 0.29	0.30 or more	Less than 1.00	1.01 to 1.49	1.50 to 1.99	2.00 to 2.99	3.00 or more
Total.....................	100.0	100.0	100.0	100.0	100.0	100.0	100.0	100.0	100.0	100.0
0.75 or less...................	42.4	49.1	50.6	52.9	58.4	45.7	60.6	66.2	70.3	81.2
0.76 to 1.00..................	31.9	30.6	30.6	29.6	25.4	27.2	26.4	25.1	23.4	14.5
1.01 or more..................	25.7	30.3	18.8	17.5	16.2	27.1	13.0	8.8	6.4	4.3
Median income...........dollars..	4,607	3,884	3,256	2,564	1,138	3,796	4,286	4,190	3,656	1,989

[1] One-family structures only.

Source: *1950 Census of Housing*, Vol. II, *Nonfarm Housing Characteristics*, Part 1, Chapter 1, United States, table A–9.

The low correlation between rent and income produces a result that so far has escaped the attention of many analysts: while the rent-income ratio declines with increasing income (the familiar Engel curve), it *rises* with increasing rent. That is, households who pay higher rent tend to have, on the average, higher incomes, but the increase in income is (relatively) less than the increase in rent. Thus, in 1950, households with a rent expenditure of $10 to $15 had an average income of $1,909, and households paying $50 to $59 rent had an income of $4,012, or a rent-income ratio 100 percent higher. This is so because the low rent-income ratio class contains large numbers of relatively well-to-do households who spend comparatively little on rent. The quantity of housing they obtain is determined by what they actually spend on rent and not by what they could "afford" to spend.

One of the reasons for the poor correlation between rent and income is variation in household size. Many of the lowest income households which typically have high rent/value-income ratios tend to be very small and not subject to overcrowding. Second, many of the higher income families with low rent/value-income ratios are large and subject to high PPR ratios. While their higher income does allow them to purchase more space, they do not buy all they "need" because of other pressures on their budgets. It is a well-known fact that with given incomes large families spend less on rent even though they frequently obtain larger quantities of space. The relation between the price-income ratio and household size is clearly inverse for home owners and nearly so for renters: the larger the household the lower the ratio.

TABLE **20.**—GROSS RENT-INCOME AND VALUE-INCOME RATIOS, FOR NONFARM OCCUPIED DWELLING UNITS, BY HOUSEHOLD SIZE: 1950

Household size	Rent-income ratio	Value-income ratio
1 person...	0.26	[1]3+
2 persons...	0.18	2.4
3 persons...	0.18	2.1
4 persons...	0.17	2.0
5 persons...	0.17	1.9
6 persons...	0.17	1.7
7 persons or more...	0.18	1.5

[1] Open-end class; exact value indeterminate.

Source: See table 19.

FIGURE **6.**—MEDIAN MONTHLY RENT OF NONFARM OCCUPIED DWELLING UNITS, BY FAMILY SIZE AND INCOME: 1940

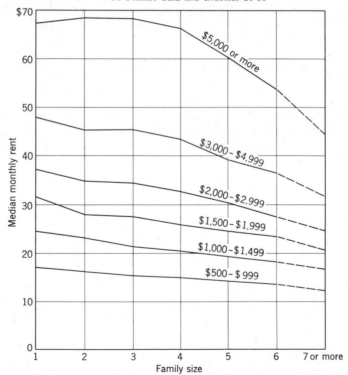

Source: 1940 Census, *Families—Income and Rent*, table 1a.

The drop in rent expenditures with increasing household size when income is held constant is shown in figure 6.   Each line, which represents
a given income class, slopes down to lower rent as household size increases.
When household size (but not income) is held constant it can be demonstrated that, for renters, low rent is associated with higher PPR ratios
(figure 7, based on 1934 Real Property Inventory data for Philadelphia).
The 10 household size classes form a ladder of curves that ascends with
household size, each curve sloping downward as rent increases.   Reading
the curves vertically, it can be seen that at any given rent larger households

FIGURE 7.—PERSONS PER ROOM BY RENT OF OCCUPIED DWELLING UNITS, BY HOUSEHOLD SIZE,
FOR PHILADELPHIA: 1934

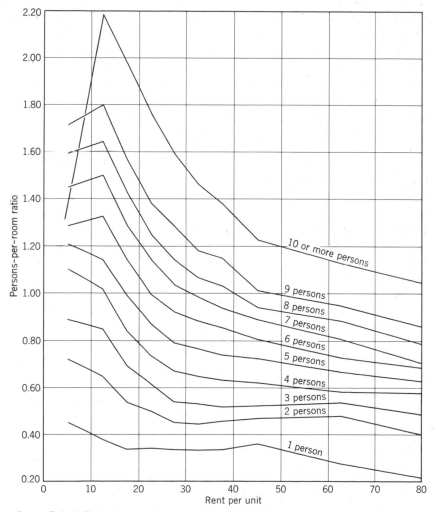

Source: Federal Works Progress Administration for Pennsylvania, *Report of Philadelphia Real Property
Survey, 1934*, Project No. 4744.

have higher densities.   Reading horizontally, one finds that a given favorable
density standard is achieved by larger households only by paying substantially higher rent.   Thus, at a $40 rental the PPR ratio is about 0.34 for
the 1-person household and 0.84 for the 6-person household.   At the same
time, a 3-person household obtained a PPR ratio of 0.60 by paying only $23
a month, while the 4-person household had to pay over $50 a month to be
as well off in terms of density.   Regardless of how high the rent paid (at
least within the range of these data) the average 7-or-more-person household is always more crowded than the 2-person household.

The interplay of all four variables—income, rent, household size, and
housing space—cannot be observed in published census data, but it is well
illustrated by another source, the BLS budget study of 1935–1936.   Table
21 shows that at given income levels larger families spend less on rent and
obtain more rooms, but the increase in space is less than the increase in
family size, resulting in higher densities.   Large households (types VI and
VII, with at least 5 persons) having an income of $1,500 to $1,749
obtained an average of 5.4 rooms at an average rent of $29.35, whereas a
type I family (2 persons) having the same income occupied an average of
only 3.9 rooms at the higher average rent of $34.30 per month.

If large households buy more space but pay less for it, it is entirely
reasonable to suppose that the quality of their housing suffers.   While
detailed quality indexes cannot be applied to census data, the housing
occupied by large households was clearly of lower quality judging by dilapidation rates.   In 1950 about 1 out of 8 units occupied by owner households containing 7 or more persons was classified as dilapidated, as compared to 1 out of 20 for all owners.   In the case of renters the story is
even worse: nearly 1 out of every 3 large renter households (i.e., containing 7 or more persons) lived in dilapidated units, compared to 1 out of 9
for all renters.

TABLE 21.—AVERAGE RENT AND NUMBER OF ROOMS, BY INCOME AND FAMILY TYPE,
FOR CHICAGO: 1935 AND 1936

[For definition of family types I and VII, see table 12 in Chapter 4; a type VI family consists of at least 5
people: married couple plus at least 3 children under 16 years old]

Income	Type I family		Types VI and VII families	
	Average rent (dollars)	Number of rooms	Average rent (dollars)[1]	Number of rooms[2]
$750 to $999	27.50	4.0	24.60	4.6
$1,500 to $1,749	34.30	3.9	29.35	5.4
$2,500 to $2,999	42.80	4.1	38.95	6.2

[1]Average of contract rent for renters and estimated rent of owners.

[2]Average for type VI and type VII families given separately in the original source.

Source: U. S. Bureau of Labor Statistics, *Family Expenditures in Selected Cities, 1935–36*, Vol. I, Housing, pp. 137 and 360.

Summarizing the results thus far, higher priced housing units are associated with better density levels owing to the fact that such dwelling units are nearly always larger. The influence of household size is so overriding, however, that the more useful findings are obtained by holding household size constant. Large households, other things equal, find it more difficult to attain favorable density standards than do smaller households. They tend to devote a smaller proportion of their income to housing because of the claims made by food and clothing on their budgets and therefore cannot obtain as much per capita space as the smaller households in the same income group. Large households, therefore, remain crowded in spite of the fact that their dwelling units are larger than average. Furthermore, these larger dwelling units often are poor in quality.

Adjustments of the PPR ratio to change in value and rent

The question whether (and by how much) a change in the price of housing affects utilization cannot be answered from cross-sectional data, although it is occasionally possible to do so for commodities or services more homogeneous than housing. Nor can a mere comparison of 1940 and 1950 aggregate census data reveal the nature of price effects on utilization. The PPR ratio decreased over the decade in spite of very large increases in the cost of housing space; only from the fact that this decrease was so modest in view of the rise in income and fall in household size could an inference be drawn that consumers were reacting to rising prices.

The one practical method of learning something about the effects of price change from census data is to observe trends in utilization and prices for a large number of cities [2] for which both 1940 and 1950 Census reports are available. A survey of the decade changes in the principal cities shows many differences in the movements of both PPR ratios and values and rents. While the rate of utilization declined in most cities, it remained unchanged in some and actually rose in others. Single-family house values nearly tripled in Fort Worth but rose by little more than 50 percent in Jersey City. Does some systematic relation exist between the variations in the rise in house values and the modifications made by consumers in the use of space? Was, as one should expect, the decline in utilization least (algebraically) where the cost of housing space increased the most?

The analysis required for an answer to these questions is best carried out by correlation. A separate correlation must be made for owners and renters since no adequate method exists for combining house values and rents into a single value index. In figure 8, a simple scatter diagram is

[2] Such political entities, which are smaller than local housing market areas, are not the optimal geographical units to single out for analysis. However, the abandonment of the 1940 metropolitan district in favor of the standard metropolitan area removes the possibility of measuring decade changes in housing for market areas larger than cities. The errors involved in using correlations of geographic areas to derive conclusions about behavior of individuals are discussed by W. S. Robinson, "Ecological Correlations and the Behavior of Individuals." *American Sociological Review*, June 1950.

FIGURE **8.**—PERCENT CHANGE IN MEDIAN VALUE OF SINGLE-FAMILY OWNER-OCCUPIED DWELLING UNITS, BY PERCENT CHANGE IN PERSONS-PER-ROOM RATIO, FOR NONFARM HOUSEHOLDS: 1940 to 1950

[Based on 94 cities with 100,000 inhabitants or more in 1950]

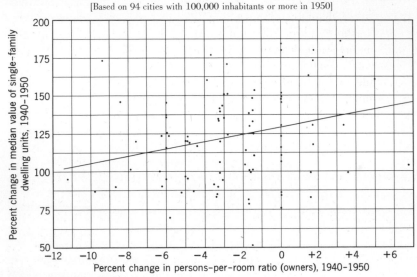

Source: Appendix table D–1.

presented covering home owners in some 90 large cities to illustrate both the existence of correlation and the large amount of dispersion about the least-squares regression line. Apparently home owners in these cities were not indifferent to the higher cost of housing in deciding how much space to hold.

The reaction to higher price is, however, weak,[3] perhaps understandably so. Home owners, because of inertia or ignorance, do not always perform the close economic calculation of businessmen. The knowledge that their homes had risen so greatly in value did not always lead to an awareness that holding more space than was justified by family requirements was an expensive luxury. As long as actual monthly cash outlays reflected the lower price levels at which they had purchased, the real cost of housing space remained hidden. Even when there was awareness, disposing of one house and buying another is a task not lightly undertaken. Also, the capital gains tax penalized those who would sell a large house in order to buy or rent a smaller one.[4]

Much of the dispersion shown in figure 8 is also created by leaving out of account changes in other variables such as income, household size, and composition. A higher degree of confidence in the results and a better understanding of price reactions could be obtained from a multiple cor-

---

[3] The correlation coefficient was low, 0.23, but clearly significant at the .05 confidence level.

[4] Furthermore, the correlation involves the changing value of single-family houses only. Many owners reduced their holding of housing space by creating one or more additional units via conversion. Such cases, however, are excluded (since the houses are no longer 1-family), tending to understate the actual effect of price rise on the utilization of owners.

relation. In order to conserve resources but still provide some information on the effects of rent control, the application of multiple correlation analysis was restricted to the rental sector. The equation of multiple correlation was further restricted by including only the three variables whose relation to space utilization has been studied—income, household size, and rent. Expressed in words, the equation of multiple correlation for the rental sector, $X_1 = K_1 + k_2X_2 + k_3X_3 + k_4X_4$, asks the question, how was the percentage change in the PPR ratio of renter households (X_1) influenced by the percentage change in rent (X_2), the percentage change in household size (X_3), and the percentage change in income (X_4)? The first term K_1 is merely a constant about which more will be said later. The solution of the equation, therefore, yields information not only about the relative importance of rent changes but also permits quantification of the roles of household size and income hitherto referred to in the vaguer terms as having "strong" or "weak" effects on utilization.

Before presenting the results a word is necessary about the data, given in Appendix D, on which the correlation is based. The change in rent is taken for each city to be the percent increase in average contract rent as reported by the Bureau of the Census, adjusted for change in the number of rooms, i.e., the percentage increase in contract rent per room. An adjustment for shrinkage in the size of dwelling units comes closer to measuring the effective increase in the cost of housing space. The increase in average contract rent is, of course, influenced by changes in the composition of the rental inventory (new construction, demolitions, conversions, etc.) and by changes in the number and kinds of utilities included in contract rent, as well as by "true" rent increases. Since some of the increase in contract rents reflects an improvement in housing quality, equipment, and services, the "true" amount of rent rise is undoubtedly overstated. No unique measure of "true" rent increase, however, is available.[5]

---

[5] To cite an example, suppose that two grades of butter are available on the market at 40 and 80 cents a pound, respectively, sold in equal quantities, so that the average price is 60 cents. If, for some reason, the cheaper grade disappears, the average price of available butter rises to 80 cents, an increase of 33 percent. While some reduction in purchases is likely to result, the shrinkage in consumption would probably be smaller than if both grades had risen by 33 percent but had remained on the market. The former users of the cheaper grade have a little less reluctance to buy the more expensive butter because they are getting something for the extra money, i.e., a better grade of butter. The steady purchasers of the higher grade would not reduce their purchase at all since the price to them is unchanged. Economic theory is still in dispute on how best to interpret the rise in the average price of butter. Is it a "true" price rise or a mere change in the composition of commodities leading to an increase in the cost of living? The reduction in consumption is real enough, but the student finds difficulty in selecting an appropriate price index to account for the shrinkage.

Similarly, if a landlord splits up a large rent-controlled unit, having a ceiling rent of $50 a month, into two smaller units which are rented on the free market at $40 each, the price of housing space has increased by 60 percent with dubious gains in quality (certainly not as clear cut as in the case of butter). For the consumer this increase in rent represents a pure price rise and the PPR ratio of his household is adjusted accordingly. It is unlikely that the old BLS rent index adequately reflected such increases since the objective of the index is to sample rents of identical dwelling units; similar large units under control may still rent at $50. It should also be noted that the average rent per dwelling unit would fall unless converted to a per room basis.

In lieu of the changes in contract rent as reported by the Bureau of the Census, it would have been possible to use the BLS rent index (old series) which is designed to arrive at a measure of "true" rent changes. But the BLS index cannot always accomplish this task. Furthermore, its coverage extended to but 30 cities for which utilization data are available and to only a certain portion of the renter population. Judging from analysis of rent changes by year built, the BLS index probably understates the "true" rent increase. The reader is referred to Appendix C for a comparison of different measures of rent increase. The question asked here is how utilization in a given city adjusted to the increased cost of housing regardless of the causes of such increase. Data for cities covered by the BLS index are used later in this chapter to answer other questions.

The decade change in the median income of the experienced labor force, the only group for which comparable 1940 and 1950 income data can be obtained, is assumed to represent the change in income of renters. Although the average income of experienced workers probably differed from that of renter households it is hoped that the *percentage changes* of both groups were reasonably close; i.e., that the gains achieved by people in the experienced labor force can be taken as an index of the gains made by renters as a group.

The percentage change in household size of renters is measured from average household size in 1940 for a given city compared to its 1950 average, both of which figures are published. The percentage change in the PPR ratio is based upon the estimates made, during the course of this study, for each city of the total number of renter-occupied rooms and the total number of renter occupants (Appendix D).

Results of multiple correlation analysis

The results of the multiple correlation are as follows: X_1 (percentage change in PPR ratio) $= 4.79 + 0.07X_2$ (percentage change in average contract rent) $+ 0.40X_3$ (percentage change in renter households size) $- 0.05X_4$ (percentage change in income). The above coefficients are net of intercorrelation; for example, the fact that income may also affect household size has been taken account of.

The coefficient of multiple correlation is highly significant (Appendix D), and all the variables are seen to act on space utilization in the direction inferred from all the preceding discussion; that is, utilization varies directly with rent and household size and inversely with income. A rise in income causes the PPR ratio to fall, while a rise in rent or household size causes the PPR ratio to rise. The relative size of the regression coefficients also confirms the previous findings of a weak income-density but a very strong household size-density relation. The regression coefficient for household size (0.40) is 8 times as large as the income coefficient (0.05). The new finding pertains to the relative size of the rent coefficient (0.07), which appears higher than that for income but much lower than that for household size. The fact that rent is potentially more important than income in determining density may also help to explain why, earlier in this chapter, the rent utilization function was found to be more consistent than the income-utilization function.[6]

The equation can be interpreted in the following manner: If, over the decade, none of the selected variables—rent, household size and income— had changed, the rate of utilization would have nevertheless increased by 4.79 percent (the value of K) as a result of the net effect of all variables (including changes in consumer tastes) not included in the equation.[7] If each of the variables—rent, household size, and income—had increased by, say, 10 percent, the PPR ratio would have risen by 4.3 percent (on the average) with practically all of the rise in utilization accounted for by the change in household size, since rising rent and rising income would tend to offset each other.

As it stands, the equation of multiple correlation is merely an estimating device. If the actual changes in utilization which occurred over the decade are to be understood, empirical values need to be substituted for X_2, X_3, and X_4. While a given percentage change in household size has potentially 8 times the impact of a like change in income and 6 times the impact of a like change in rent, actual changes in household size between 1940 and 1950 were small compared to the sharp rise in rents and income. In the tested cities, average household size declined less than 13 percent, but average rent rose 78 percent and average income doubled. When account is taken of these facts, the equation becomes X_1 (the change in the PPR ratio) $= 4.79\%$ $(K_1) + 5.67\%$ (rent) $- 5.05\%$ (household size) $- 9.04\%$ (income). The rise in income over the decade was so great that despite the ordinarily weak income-density relation, it is seen to be the most important of the three factors used to explain the actual decline in utilization which occurred.[8] Likewise, the rise in rent appears to have

---

[6] The partial correlations given in Appendix D yielded the following additional findings which are consistent with observations derived from other data and presented elsewhere in this monograph: (a) a positive relation between the increase in a city's income and the increase in its rent; (b) a positive relation between an increase in income and an increase in household size; (c) a negative relation between increase in household size and increase in rent. All of the partial relationships were statistically significant. The fact that practically every one of the observations gleaned from the multiple correlation of city data proved to be consistent with other known relationships increases the confidence which may be placed in the results of the multiple correlation equation. It also suggests that the city data from the 1940 and 1950 Housing Censuses may be used to explore a fuller range of housing market hypotheses by formal correlation techniques.

[7] Strictly speaking, this inference would be correct only if the 89 cities upon which the correlation is based had contained numerous examples of zero changes in all three variables. This is not the case, hence the inference is only presumptive having no more or less validity than any other mechanical extrapolation.

[8] It was noted in Chapter 4 (table 16) that in Philadelphia over the period 1934 to 1950, while the over-all persons-per-room ratio decreased, the PPR for each household size class increased. Thus, the effect of all factors other than changes in the household size distribution was to increase the PPR; the downward pressure exerted on utilization by rising income was not sufficient to overcome the effect of these factors.

been great enough to offset the ordinarily powerful effects of a drop in household size. Together, the rise in income and the decline in household size would have caused a 14.1 percent drop in utilization. The rise in rent reduced this possibility by nearly 6 percentage points, while the operation of all other factors lowered it further by 4.8 percentage points. On net balance, the PPR ratio for the observed cities therefore declined by less than 4 percent.

Implications for theory of housing market behavior

The results of the multiple correlation and a scrutiny of the partial correlations presented in Appendix D suggest a number of observations on housing market behavior which, for lack of better data taken from a more normal period, must be considered a form of intellectual musing rather than a piece of scientific analysis. First, it appears that the changes in income necessary to produce significant changes in the national PPR ratio must be sizable. A 10-percent rise or fall in national income, other things equal, would hardly leave a mark. Major depressions are another story, but major depressions or declines in income are also accompanied by significant declines in rent. Since the responses of the PPR ratio to movements in income and rent are in opposite directions and of similar magnitudes, large-scale economic fluctuations will be accompanied by dampened swings in the PPR ratio—ignoring the influence of cyclical swings in household size about which nothing is known. The PPR ratio does not remain entirely free from cycle swings since income both decreases and increases more than rent over a business cycle; i.e., the rent-income ratio rises in depression and falls during recoveries. The PPR ratio for Philadelphia, for example, declined between 1934 and 1940. Nevertheless, cyclical fluctuations in the PPR ratio are likely to be much less severe than cyclical fluctuations in income.

Second, the same facts, i.e., offsetting influences of rent and income, can be offered in explanation of why cyclical swings in the rate of doubling up appear to have such an astonishingly small amplitude. If the Real Property Inventory data are to be trusted, the doubling rate in 1934 at the trough of a major depression averaged about 6 percent,[9] roughly the same as in 1940 and 1950, a little more than two percentage points higher than in the very prosperous year 1955, and barely higher than the 1910 rate of 5 percent estimated by the Bureau of the Census. Only in 1947, a truly exceptional year in which the upsurge in the demand for housing could not in any way be adequately accommodated by additions to the supply, did the doubling rate break through an apparent long-run narrow range of 4 to 6 percent. Given strong preferences for private living arrangements, a

---

[9] The comparison cannot be exact. In the Real Property Inventory, parent-children and sub- and secondary families were included in the doubling-up total, and some cases of married sons excluded. On the basis of comparable definitions, the 1940 doubling rate was probably a little higher than in 1934.

family's reluctance to double up as its income is reduced is further increased by the many housing bargains which become available.

Third, if the doubling rate is truly subject to fairly narrow swings [10] it is no wonder that vacancy rates even in depressions remain relatively low. Since the standing stock of housing is at the mercy of fluctuations in demand, there is no *a priori* reason why the national vacancy rate should not rise to 25 or 30 percent. Instead, during our worst depression the Real Property Inventory of 1934 reported a vacancy rate of 8 percent including many dilapidated units. In 1940, marketable vacancies composed less than 6 percent of the inventory and roughly 2 percent in 1950 and 1955. The relatively small amplitude in the vacancy rate appears to be largely the result of an even smaller range of movement in doubling up.

Nevertheless, the vacancy rate appears to have a wider swing than the doubling rate, suggesting that during a depression the increase in vacancies is not solely the result of increases in doubling. Why should this be so? Again, our findings offer a few suggestions. Both the aggregate data and the partial correlations disclose that a drop in income would produce a more pronounced decline in the number of rooms occupied than in the PPR ratio. The implication here is that the primary path by which the national PPR ratio rises during a depression is the shifting of established households into smaller dwelling units rather than through an increase in the doubling rate.[11] Retrenchments in budgets cause families indeed to economize on housing expenses, but this is accomplished by reductions in space standards rather than through the total abandonment of privacy implied in doubling up.

If this is so, vacancies in depression years should become concentrated among the larger dwelling units.[12] The sudden undesirability of large dwelling units in turn causes many landlords, if they are to maintain gross income, to repackage housing space into smaller and lower priced units, and a large-scale conversion movement gets under way. During the 1930's conversions totaled more than a million units, almost supplanting new construction as the primary source of growth in the supply of dwelling units. It is the appearance of these converted units during a time when household

---

[10] The phenomenon of doubling up has hardly received the empirical attention corresponding to its prominence in theoretical discussions. It will be seen in Chapter 8 that a decline in the doubling rate between 1940 and 1950 for many age groups can be obscured by sharp increases in the marriage rate. The opposite may happen during a depression as marriages fall off. If true, an additional explanation is offered for the apparently narrow cyclical swings in the over-all doubling rate, i.e., the number of newly married couples increases as the tendency to double up decreases and vice versa.

[11] There may be a somewhat greater effect on single-person household formation, particularly of the young. It is inferred, however, from the analysis in Chapter 8 that older individuals may react more to changes in rents than to changes in income.

[12] This hypothesis could be tested by comparative analysis of all the cities for which both Real Property Inventory and 1950 Census data are available. Because of limited resources, such a comparison was made only for New York City where in 1934 vacant units with 6 or more rooms were nearly 18 percent of all vacancies compared to 8 percent in 1950, while the corresponding percentages for 1- and 2-room units were 6 and 12.

formation is low which may explain why the over-all vacancy rate rises by more than the rate of doubling up.[13]

What about periods of rising income? The first guess is that the processes mentioned above should reverse themselves. That is, the fall in the rate of utilization accompanying a return to more prosperous times should manifest itself by some decline in the doubling rate, resulting in the filling of vacancies, and by a movement of established households into larger dwelling units. Some undoubling surely takes place and vacancies certainly begin to fill up. As for shifts to larger units, however, it was noted in Chapter 4, on the basis of both national data for 1940 to 1950 and more complete information for Philadelphia for 1934 and 1950, that households of given size had shifted to smaller, not to larger, dwelling units. One important reason offered for this significant phenomenon was the very sharp movement in house prices, construction costs, and uncontrolled rents. Another reason, it was said, may have been some change in consumers' tastes that caused them to shift away from housing to other consumer durables and luxury services. A third may have been the interferences with the normal operations of the housing market caused by war and postwar restrictions.

It is difficult to believe, however, that the impulse to acquire more space as economic status improves has been entirely or permanently repressed. One may still hazard the guess that, if the experience of the 1952–1955 period, which marked slow but steady increases in income and reasonable stability in house prices, rents, and construction costs, continues, consumer desire to improve space standards will eventually express itself. If so, an important sustaining force for housing demand will be provided. Some evidence for such a change in consumer desire has indeed emerged since 1950 or so. The demand for more space per person in response to higher real income will not of itself be spectacularly strong. But when coupled with the demand for more space arising from the needs of a large population of maturing children (Chapter 8), the trend toward larger units may prove to be substantial. Such demand will have its major impact on new construction since the standing stock of housing is more readily adapted to the splitting of large units than the reassembly of small units into larger ones. Expenditures for additions and alterations will also tend to rise as many home owners add rooms to existing dwelling units.

A demand for larger units may create vacancies among the smaller units, but the demographic structure of our population is such (Chapter 8) that the bulk of these units are likely to be occupied by old couples and 1-person households as soon as their rents or prices become favorable.[14]

---

[13] Many vacancies in the earlier phases of the depression also result from the completion of new structures started before the downturn.

[14] Many other small dwelling units are likely to be abandoned. Quantification is not possible, but many students of the housing market have observed the disappearance since 1954 of large numbers of small units that had been created during the housing shortage. If the view advanced here that vacan-

Implications for rent control policy

The implications of these findings for analyzing the effects of rent control on the housing market are also clear.   In the face of a sharp rise in
the level of income, rent fixing will undoubtedly lead to overuse of space.
However, since the relative effect of rent on the PPR ratio is small, the
amount of such "excess" space will be of moderate proportions.   Just how
large this quantity was in 1950 is impossible to measure with any desir-
able degree of precision.   Only complete data on utilization tabulated
separately for controlled and uncontrolled rental units could provide an
accurate answer.   But if speculation, which has already gone a little beyond the limits of cautious scholarship, may be further extended, a rough
estimate can be made from the correlation equation.   If during the decade
all changes occurred as they had but rents had remained free, rising to,
say, double the actual 1950 level, renters might have given up about 1
million rooms or the equivalent of a little over 250,000 dwelling units.

Misallocation of housing space, while not impressive in dimension, undoubtedly is one of the reasons why the PPR ratio for renters declined
more than for owners between 1940 and 1950, 3 percent compared to less
than 1 percent.[15]   The greater gain in space used by renters has already
been noted by Grebler[16] (who attempted to place this effect of rent control
in proper quantitative perspective).   Other analysts, not having available
to them the results of the 1950 Census, often exaggerated the quantitative
importance of space misallocation, indeed, elevating this factor to one of
the most important causes of the postwar housing shortage.[17]   On the
whole, it would seem that misallocation of space was probably far from
negligible,[18] but hardly serious enough to destroy the usefulness of rent
restrictions under emergency conditions from the standpoint of national
economic policy.   A number of factors will be found in the discussion

---

cies affect large dwelling units in depression and small dwelling units during sustained prosperity with-
stands fuller investigation it follows that cyclical swings in vacancies might be much wider if the vacancy rate were defined in terms of rooms rather than dwelling units.

[15] The drop in the PPR ratio for renters in the rent-controlled sector of the inventory (which by
1950 was probably not more than two-thirds of all rented units in the tested cities) was undoubtedly
greater than the 3 percent shown for all renters.   The larger decline (4 percent) in the PPR ratio for
owners and renters combined, given in Chapter 4, is a peculiarity of weighting.   There was a shift
throughout the decade towards home ownership giving the sector of the market which normally has
more favorable density a higher weight.

[16] Leo Grebler, "Implications of Rent Control," *International Labour Review*, April 1952.

[17] Milton Friedman and George J. Stigler, *Roofs or Ceilings?*, The Foundation for Economic Education, Inc., New York, 1946.

[18] If the excessive use of space attributed to rent control was pronounced one might expect that increases in the proportion of rented dwelling units occupied at densities of 0.50 or less would bear
some relation to the change in rent.   No correlation could be found.   However, a weak relationship
was derived in a correlation of changes in the proportion of renter households living at the more moderate density of 0.75 or less.   The "excess" space was of course entirely enjoyed by the occupants of
rent-controlled units at the expense of other renter households who paid full market rents and presumably economized on space.

below to explain why the opportunity to enjoy excess space is reduced by counteracting forces that rent control itself sets into motion.

The probable amount of excess space used by renters is insufficient in itself to account for the differential changes in utilization between renters and owners. A more important explanation seems to be the sharper increase in the growth of very small households among renters, particularly 1-person households, which caused average household size of renters to decline by 10 percent compared to a decline of 5 percent for owners. The proportion of 1-person households rose from 9.0 to 12.8 percent for renters while remaining virtually unchanged for owners. Of the total increase in the number of renter households over the decade, over 75 percent is accounted for by growth in 1-person households. These differential changes in the number and proportion of small households having very low PPR ratios, of course, lower the PPR ratio for renters as a whole.

Did rent control, however, play a part in explaining these differences in the redistribution of household size? Did artificially low rents lead to an increased number of secretaries occupying their own dwelling unit or of "solitary old ladies rattling around in spacious apartments"? Again no final answer can be given, but a correlation of changes in the BLS rent index and changes in the proportion of 1-person renter households for the BLS sample cities shows no relation. Nor does the analysis in Chapter 8 of changes in the proportion, age class by age class, of "unmarried" older people who head their own households reveal any significant rise over the decade. It is probable that rent control caused some acceleration in the growth of small renter households but hardly enough to show up in these simple tests.

Does rent control have distorting effects other than overuse of space? To answer this question, variations in the BLS rent index for the same 30 sample cities were related to variations in new construction, tenure shifts, and doubling-up rates in these cities. No evidence could be found of a positive relation between the proportion of new rental housing (adjusted for population growth) and the size of rent changes. Cities with the lowest change in rents (presumably with the most rent control) showed, relatively, about as much new rental construction as did cities in which rents rose sharply. However, another procedure yielded different results[19] so that the question remains far from settled. It has long been argued that rent control stifles new construction, but such arguments frequently fail to take account of the fact that rents on new construction were, by and large, free. Indeed, to the extent that misallocation of space forces the unfortunate

---

[19] Without adjustments for population growth and using change in average contract rent for 94 cities rather than the BLS index, a weak but significant *negative* correlation was found. Less reliance is placed on this second test since new construction is a factor in causing higher average contract rent. Also, it is theoretically incorrect not to adjust for population growth since little new construction is expected in static cities regardless of rent policy.

"have nots" into the market for new housing, demand for the latter is stimulated. Rent control may, of course, inhibit investment in rental housing even with freedom to set economic rent levels because prospective investors fear (a) future rollbacks and (b) the development of a low rent "psychology" on the part of consumers. There is undoubtedly much truth in this. There was indeed little rental construction after World War II except under the Section 608 program of the National Housing Act, which made the operation both highly profitable and virtually riskless to the builder. Nevertheless, perhaps because of the removal of investment risk in Section 608 operations, there was no apparent discrimination against rental construction in the more rigidly rent-controlled cities when account is taken of population growth.

It is fair to say that correlation tests may be too simple for so complex a question. In cities such as New York and Washington, where rent control was tight, strong preferences existed for rental units. Renters flocked to new apartment developments having rent levels that compared unfavorably with the monthly costs of home ownership. In cities where the preference for home ownership is overwhelming, builders may have been loath to provide new rental units even when rents on existing units showed large percentage increases.

No significant correlation could be established between the changes in the home ownership ratio and variations in the BLS index. The hypothesis tested here is that a combination of rent restriction and free price movements in the home ownership market caused owners of rented single-family houses to sell them to owner-occupants. Because it is primarily the single-family house that is subject to such tenure shifts, the test was repeated by substituting data on tenure shifts exclusively for single-family houses for the larger sample of 105 cities for which Bureau of the Census reports on average contract rents in 1940 and 1950 are available. The latter test,[20] which is more clearly relevant, reveals the existence of some tendency for homes to move more readily into the ownership market where the rise in rents was smallest. If this is so, then rent control may be said to cause many of the larger housing units to become unavailable to renters at favorable rents. Rent control also induced conversions which removed many larger units from the rent-controlled supply. Both the drop in the rate of utilization for renters and the amount of misallocated space might therefore have been more sizable if rent control had not brought in its wake these two counter-acting movements which reduced the number of opportunities for occupying "extra" space.

Did rent control affect the amount of doubling up? Newly married couples and returning veterans were, of course, at a disadvantage in the

---

[20] When done separately for the "home owner" and "renter" cities, i.e., the cities which in 1940 had home ownership ratios of over 70 percent and less than 50 percent, respectively.

postwar housing market since their opportunity to bid for dwelling units was limited primarily to the free market. A simple correlation, clearly significant, based on 105 cities discloses that the 1940–1950 increase in the doubling rate (married couples without own households) was indeed higher in the cities with low rent increases. Thus, rent control would appear to have visited inequity on the "have nots" in addition to forcing many of them into high-cost housing which put their family budgets under serious pressure.[21] But it is equally probable that much of the doubling up occurred in rent controlled units occupied by the relatives of the "have nots." Many occupants of rent-controlled housing were forced to share their space with newly married children unable to afford the very much higher rents in new construction. This observation offers another example of how rent control creates a self-correcting influence which reduces the amount of under-occupied housing space.

[21] Grebler, *op. cit.*

CHAPTER 6

THE PERSONS-PER-ROOM RATIO:
LOCATION AND RACE

Location can affect the rate of utilization in a number of ways. Apart from the more general regional differences in economic opportunities, income, population, and household size, the use of housing space can be influenced by climate and geographical differences in land values and construction costs. In many parts of the South and West, where the climate is mild, many family activities can be transferred outdoors during most of the year, and the need for interior housing space reduced accordingly. On the other hand, central heating systems, basements, and expensive insulation can often be eliminated, hence more resources are available for a larger house if desired.

High land values might also tend to create relatively high PPR ratios by restricting the horizontal extension of housing space, although, within the limits of zoning restrictions, the number of stories can be multiplied and land coverage varied. The urban apartment and tenement buildings in which many of our overcrowded households live are found in association with high site values. The single-family house has been pushed out of the core of the city. And it is a matter of common observation that the home buyer often finds a larger house for the same price if he ventures farther out into the suburbs. High-cost land, other things equal, competes with the shell of the house by reducing the amount of disposable capital.

Construction costs also vary among regions and in urban compared to rural areas, though probably less so today than formerly. While self-building is more common in rural areas, making larger houses less expensive, financial terms are more favorable in urban areas, builder competition is keener and building productivity higher.

Regional differences

Although the foregoing discussion might lead to the expectation that crowding is more severe in the heavily populated nonfarm areas of the East than in the "newer" regions, the facts are contrary. Table 22 discloses the most favorable utilization picture in the Northeast Region and the least favorable in the South and West. In the low density groups (0.33 or less) are found about 15 percent of Northeast and North Central households (nonfarm), only 11 percent of the Southern, and 13.5 percent of the Western households. In the overcrowded groups (1.01 or more), the respective percentages are 11.2, 12.3, 20.6, and 14.0. Overcrowding is serious in the South; in terms of population rather than households, one-third of the South fails to meet the modern density standard of no more than one person per room. Within the South, crowding is particularly widespread in the East South Central states (table 23), where nearly one out of four households lives in a dwelling unit with more than one person per room. Half of the Nation's severely overcrowded households, with densities of more than two persons per room, are found in the South.

TABLE 22.—PERCENT DISTRIBUTION OF NONFARM HOUSEHOLDS BY PERSONS PER ROOM AND TENURE, FOR REGIONS: 1950

Region and tenure	Persons-per-room ratio								Average persons-per-room ratio	Average household size	Average number of rooms
	0.17 or less	0.18 to 0.33	0.34 to 0.50	0.51 to 0.75	0.76 to 1.00	1.01 to 1.50	1.51 to 2.00	2.01 or more			
TOTAL											
Northeast	2.0	13.5	21.9	27.1	24.4	8.2	2.3	0.7	0.66	3.34	5.08
North Central	1.8	12.8	23.4	24.9	24.5	7.9	3.1	1.3	0.67	3.21	4.85
South	1.1	9.9	19.8	23.6	25.0	11.1	5.9	3.6	0.78	3.41	4.40
West	1.1	11.4	23.5	24.5	25.7	8.3	3.7	2.0	0.70	3.03	4.31
OWNER											
Northeast	3.5	18.3	25.3	26.5	19.9	5.2	1.0	0.4	0.57	3.57	6.23
North Central	2.7	15.8	26.3	24.6	21.6	6.6	1.8	0.8	0.62	3.35	5.45
South	1.9	13.5	24.1	24.4	21.8	8.5	3.7	2.2	0.68	3.47	5.11
West	1.6	13.7	26.5	24.9	22.2	6.9	2.6	1.6	0.65	3.23	4.99
RENTER											
Northeast	0.7	9.3	19.0	27.5	28.3	10.8	3.5	0.9	0.75	3.14	4.18
North Central	0.6	8.5	20.0	25.2	28.8	9.9	5.0	2.1	0.76	3.00	3.93
South	0.3	6.0	15.2	22.7	28.4	13.9	8.4	5.2	0.92	3.34	3.62
West	0.3	8.4	19.6	23.9	30.2	10.1	5.1	2.5	0.81	2.77	3.43

Source: *1950 Census of Housing*, Vol. II, *Nonfarm Housing Characteristics*, Part 1, Chapters 2 to 10.

Low incomes, large households, and a heavy concentration of nonwhite population account for the relatively poor showing made by the South. The South has the lowest per capita money income of any region among both nonfarm white and nonwhite residents.[1] About 60 percent of all Negroes (nonfarm) live in the nonfarm areas of the South and comprise one-fifth of the region's nonfarm population. The concentration of Negro population in the South is a factor in both the region's low income level and its high average household size, for Negroes have relatively large families. Average household size in the South, 3.41 persons in 1950, was larger than in any other region. At the same time, Southern dwelling units tend to be small, containing an average of 4.40 rooms compared to the national average of 4.78. The result is an average PPR ratio of 0.78 as against the national average of 0.69.

[1] Herman P. Miller, *Income of the American People*, John Wiley & Sons, Inc., New York, 1955, p. 70.

TABLE **23.**—PERCENT DISTRIBUTION OF NONFARM HOUSEHOLDS BY PERSONS PER ROOM AND TENURE, FOR DIVISIONS: 1950

Division and tenure	0.17 or less	0.18 to 0.33	0.34 to 0.50	0.51 to 0.75	0.76 to 1.00	1.01 to 1.50	1.51 to 2.00	2.01 or more
TOTAL								
New England............................	2.5	14.6	23.7	26.3	23.5	7.1	1.8	0.5
Middle Atlantic.........................	1.9	13.2	21.4	27.3	24.6	8.5	2.5	0.7
E. North Central........................	1.8	12.4	23.7	25.5	24.8	7.8	2.9	1.2
W. North Central.......................	1.9	13.6	23.5	23.4	24.0	8.4	3.6	1.6
South Atlantic..........................	1.3	10.6	20.0	24.7	24.7	10.7	5.3	2.8
E. South Central........................	0.9	8.9	18.6	22.9	25.2	12.3	6.8	4.4
W. South Central.......................	1.0	9.5	20.5	22.4	25.2	10.9	6.3	4.3
Mountain...............................	0.9	9.5	19.4	22.2	26.9	11.3	5.8	4.6
Pacific.................................	1.1	11.9	24.7	25.1	25.4	7.4	3.1	1.4
OWNER								
New England............................	4.2	18.7	25.1	25.5	19.8	5.2	1.1	0.4
Middle Atlantic.........................	3.3	18.2	25.4	26.9	19.9	5.1	1.0	0.3
E. North Central........................	2.7	15.3	26.1	25.2	22.1	6.4	1.6	0.7
W. North Central.......................	2.7	16.9	26.7	23.3	20.3	6.9	2.1	1.0
South Atlantic..........................	2.3	14.7	24.4	24.9	21.5	7.9	3.0	1.4
E. South Central........................	1.6	12.6	23.3	24.8	21.8	9.5	4.0	2.4
W. South Central.......................	1.6	12.5	24.3	23.5	22.1	8.6	4.3	3.1
Mountain...............................	1.3	11.8	22.3	22.6	23.7	10.1	4.6	3.6
Pacific.................................	1.7	14.2	27.8	25.6	21.7	6.0	2.0	1.0
RENTER								
New England............................	0.9	10.6	22.3	27.2	27.0	8.9	2.4	0.6
Middle Atlantic.........................	0.7	8.9	18.0	27.6	28.7	11.3	3.8	1.0
E. North Central........................	0.6	8.5	20.5	25.8	28.5	9.6	4.7	1.9
W. North Central.......................	0.6	8.4	18.6	23.6	29.6	10.7	5.9	2.6
South Atlantic..........................	0.4	6.5	15.6	24.4	27.9	13.4	7.5	4.2
E. South Central........................	0.2	5.1	13.7	21.0	28.7	15.3	9.6	6.4
W. South Central.......................	0.3	5.8	15.7	21.0	29.0	13.7	8.7	5.8
Mountain...............................	0.3	6.6	15.4	21.8	31.1	12.8	7.5	4.6
Pacific.................................	0.3	8.9	20.8	24.5	30.0	9.3	4.4	1.9

Source: See table 22.

At the other extreme, the most favorable utilization pattern is found in the Northeast. Its average PPR ratio of 0.66 is the lowest for any region, and the same is true of its percentage of overcrowded dwelling units. The low PPR ratio found in this section of the country is not due to small households but to large dwelling units. Its average household size is nearly as high as in the South. Its dwelling units, however, with an average of over 5 rooms, are the largest in the nation.

The Northeast is, of course, the oldest settled portion of the country. Since there has been a long-run trend toward fewer rooms, part of the reason for more spacious dwellings is the fact that they are older. Another reason is the relatively high per capita income found in this region. Nevertheless, the fact that the Northeast has a lower average PPR ratio than more thinly populated areas, such as the West, indicates that no close relationship exists between population density and housing density, at least for the larger geographic units. While a more systematic testing of such a relationship would prove worthwhile, its existence cannot be demonstrated by any of the evidence uncovered in this study. New York

City, for example, one of the most densely populated cities, with perhaps the highest average unit land values, has by no means the highest PPR ratio. Even the renter households of the Northeast, which are concentrated in its large cities, had a lower proportion of overcrowding (1.01 or more) and more spacious dwelling units than renter households in other areas.

The North Central Region calls for little comment: its density distribution is close to the national pattern and only slightly less favorable than the Northeast's. More striking are the data for the West, where the average density of 0.70 is exceeded only by the South. It is somewhat surprising to find this (relatively) sparsely peopled region, whose average income approximates that of the Northeast, having 14 percent of all its households, and nearly 18 percent of its renter households, overcrowded. Furthermore, overcrowding is even more prevalent in the Mountain division than in the more populated states on the Pacific Coast (table 23). Nor is its relatively high PPR ratio due to large household size. The West, with its heavy in-migration and its retirement havens, is the region *par excellence* of the small household; its average household size of 3.03 is the lowest in the Nation.

The explanation seems to lie in the small homes found in the West. The average dwelling unit contains about 4.31 rooms and, whether occupied by owner or renter, is smaller than in any other region. While a smaller dwelling unit for a smaller household is, as we have seen, perfectly normal, a higher PPR ratio is not, especially since the income level of the West is so favorable. It is difficult to find entirely convincing reasons to explain why Western homes contain so few rooms. Certainly one reason is that its housing stock is relatively new and, therefore, has shared fully in the trend towards fewer rooms and style changes calling for an elimination of dining rooms. Also, an appreciable portion of the Western housing inventory was built under high cost conditions. Perhaps, too, in this region, where the more advanced architectural designs are found, the room is an even more inadequate measure of space than elsewhere. There may be, in the West, a preference for fewer but larger multipurpose rooms.

All four regions shared in the decline of the national PPR ratio over the decade. The improvement in the South was most noticeable, its PPR ratio decreasing 8.6 percent compared to a roughly 4 percent drop in the national average. Thus, the gap between the South and the rest of the country was narrowed. In fact, there was a general narrowing of regional variations in utilization, a trend observed for income, prices, wage rates, interest rates, and many economic indexes.

In all regions other than the South (and in the Nation as a whole) improved utilization was accompanied by both a decline in household size and in the average size of dwelling units, the former being larger than the latter. The relatively greater gain achieved by the South was the result of a substantial decrease in household size at the same time that average dwelling unit size increased slightly.

TABLE 24.—PERCENT CHANGE IN HOUSEHOLD SIZE, NUMBER OF ROOMS, AND PERSONS-PER-ROOM RATIO, FOR NONFARM HOUSEHOLDS, FOR REGIONS: 1940 TO 1950

Region	Household size	Number of rooms	Persons-per-room ratio
Northeast..	−9.0	−5.8	−3.4
North Central....................................	−7.2	−3.6	−3.2
South...	−7.6	+1.1	−8.6
West..	−2.9	−0.2	−2.6

Source: *1950 Census of Housing*, Vol. II, *Nonfarm Housing Characteristics*, Part 1, Chapters 2 to 10; and *1940 Census of Housing*, Vol. II, *General Characteristics*, Part 1, U. S. Summary, tables 8a and 9.

Other locational differences

The absence of any clear-cut relationship between population density and housing density is seen again in tabulations segregating urban and rural-nonfarm areas and population inside and outside standard metropolitan areas (table 25). In urban areas, 61.4 percent of the households enjoyed densities of 0.75 or less, compared to 58 percent of rural-nonfarm households, and the proportion of overcrowded households (1.01 plus) was nearly one-third lower. There was also more overcrowding outside of metropolitan areas than within, even for renter households. At the same time, one finds larger proportions of households outside of standard metropolitan areas with very favorable density standards (0.33 or less). Utilization patterns appear to become more heterogeneous as one leaves the major metropolitan centers, corresponding to the heterogeneity of people encountered outside these centers. On the one hand, the outside areas show the rural characteristics of large households and low income. On the other hand, many well-to-do suburbanites are located there in very spacious homes. The differences found in the density distributions for the two types of areas are, however, lost in the averages. Both inside and outside of standard metropolitan areas, the average PPR ratio, average household size, and the average number of rooms are virtually identical at 0.69, 3.27, and 4.72, respectively.

Variations in housing density by size of city are not very pronounced. According to the 1950 data,[2] density distributions for cities of 100,000 or over were nearly the same as for all urban areas, i.e., 60 percent at 0.75 or less, and 13.5 percent at 1.01 or more. A full city-size class analysis can be obtained only with difficulty from published 1950 Census data and has not been attempted. But the 1940 Census and the survey tabulations

---

[2] *1950 Census of Housing*. Vol. I, *General Characteristics*, Part 1, U. S. Summary, p. 102.

TABLE **25.**—PERCENT DISTRIBUTION OF HOUSEHOLDS BY PERSONS-PER-ROOM RATIO, BY TENURE, INSIDE AND OUTSIDE STANDARD METROPOLITAN AREAS, AND URBAN AND RURAL NONFARM: 1950

Area and tenure	0.17 or less	0.18 to 0.33	0.34 to 0.50	0.51 to 0.75	0.76 to 1.00	1.01 to 1.50	1.51 to 2.00	2.01 or more
Total:								
Inside standard metropolitan areas............	1.2	11.0	22.1	26.5	26.0	8.6	3.3	1.4
Outside standard metropolitan areas...........	2.4	13.9	22.1	22.5	22.6	9.4	4.5	2.7
Owner:								
Inside standard metropolitan areas............	1.9	14.1	25.7	27.0	22.5	6.4	1.7	0.7
Outside standard metropolitan areas...........	3.5	17.7	25.2	22.1	19.3	7.3	3.1	1.8
Renter:								
Inside standard metropolitan areas............	0.4	7.8	18.5	26.1	29.4	10.9	4.9	2.0
Outside standard metropolitan areas...........	0.8	8.6	17.8	23.0	27.1	12.2	6.5	4.0
Urban.................................	61.4				25.3	13.3		
Rural nonfarm...........................	57.9				22.6	19.5		

Source: *1950 Census of Housing,* Vol. 1, *General Characteristics,* Part 1, U. S. Summary, table 11; Vol. II, *Nonfarm Housing Characteristics,* Part 1, Chapter 1, United States, table 5.

by city-size class confirm the absence of significant differences among urban areas. If anything, crowding seems to be somewhat more severe in the smaller cities of 2,500 to 5,000 than elsewhere.[3] Apparently, big cities and crowded housing do not necessarily go together. Casual observers may mistake the crowded apartment block for the crowded dwelling unit or are perhaps struck by the crowding in the well-publicized slum sections of most metropolises while they overlook the favorable housing densities at which the majority of big city dwellers live.

Density patterns among nonwhites

The 1950 Census of Housing contains practically no cross-tabulation of housing or household characteristics by race upon which housing utilization measures can be based. There are, therefore, no comprehensive recent data from which to draw a picture of crowding in Negro housing. The few facts presented here are taken from a variety of sources. Fragmentary though they may be, they permit the unstartling disclosure that Negroes have substantially higher PPR ratios than whites. Furthermore, Negroes may not have shared fully in the general improvement in utilization which took place in recent years, in spite of unmistakable gains in employment and income, the provision of public housing, and (possibly) reductions in the intensity of discrimination.

---

[3] U. S. Bureau of the Census, *Housing—Special Reports,* Series H–44, No. 1. "Characteristics of Dwelling Units for Groups of Places Classified According to Size, Urban and Rural: 1940." The proportion of overcrowding (1.51 or more) in these places was 7.7 percent compared to 5.4 percent for places of 50,000 or more, 4.7 percent for places of 500,000 or more, and 7.4 percent for places of 250,000 to 500,000.

Overcrowding among Negro households was already partially reflected in the regional data given earlier.[4] In 1947, the most recent year for which reliable data are available,[5] nearly four times as many Negro households, proportionately, lived under conditions of severe overcrowding (1.51 or more) as white households, 15 and 4 percent, respectively. In 1940 the corresponding percentages were 18.4 and 6.1 (table 26). Thus, while the density levels of both whites and nonwhites improved, the gain of the latter was so slight that the relative distance between the two groups actually widened. In 1940, of all overcrowded households (1.51 or more) about one in four were Negroes, although the latter comprised only between 8 and 9 percent of the nonfarm household population. A fuller comparison of racial differences in utilization by tenure and area is given in table 26.

TABLE **26.**—PERCENT DISTRIBUTION OF NONFARM HOUSEHOLDS BY PERSONS PER ROOM, BY TENURE AND COLOR: 1940

Area, tenure, and color	Total reporting	Persons per room				
		0.50 or less	0.50 to 1.00	1.01 to 1.50	1.51 to 2.00	2.01 or more
Total:						
White	100.0	33.0	50.8	10.0	4.2	1.9
Nonwhite	100.0	20.8	45.3	15.4	11.4	7.0
Owner:						
White	100.0	44.2	44.7	7.2	2.6	1.4
Nonwhite	100.0	32.4	42.2	12.7	7.4	5.3
Renter:						
White	100.0	24.7	55.4	12.2	5.4	2.3
Nonwhite	100.0	17.2	46.3	16.3	12.7	7.5
Urban:						
White	100.0	32.3	53.2	9.6	3.6	1.2
Nonwhite	100.0	21.5	47.2	15.2	10.6	5.4
Rural nonfarm:						
White	100.0	35.1	43.9	11.2	6.0	3.9
Nonwhite	100.0	18.9	39.5	16.0	13.8	11.8

Source: *1940 Census of Housing,* Vol. II, *General Characteristics,* Part 1, U. S. Summary, p. 38.

As is the case for whites, overcrowding among Negroes is more severe among renters than owners and in rural nonfarm compared to urban areas. Home ownership was, of course, far less common among Negroes, 23.9 percent in 1940, compared to 42.7 percent for whites, so that the relatively good showing of Negro home owners applied to but a small minority of the Negro population. Over the decade 1940 to 1950, the gain in home ownership among Negroes was relatively greater than among whites. Nevertheless, in 1950 the home ownership ratios were still far apart, standing respectively at 35 and 55 percent.

[4] Negroes and nonwhites are used interchangeably since the quantitative difference in most census tabulations is negligible.

[5] U. S. Housing and Home Finance Agency, *Housing of the Nonwhite Population, 1940 to 1947.*

Ignoring for the moment more fundamental factors, such as low income and racial discrimination, the proximate causes of Negro overcrowding are large households and small dwelling units. Negro households averaged 3.8 persons in 1940 compared to 3.6 for whites,[6] and they averaged 3.7 persons in 1950 as against 3.3 for whites. The decline in Negro household size over the decade was slight compared to whites. In 1947, 12 percent of Negro households contained 7 or more persons as against 5 percent for whites.

Because of increased home ownership and continued migration from rural nonfarm areas (where high housing densities prevail), the small decline in density between 1940 and 1947 may have accelerated so that complete analysis of 1950 data would show further improvements even after allowance for a rise in the rate of doubling up.

The relatively high doubling rate for Negroes is, of course, one of the factors accounting for higher household size. Another is the higher birth rate and the prevalence of more children. In 1950 the doubling rate (married couples without own households) among nonfarm Negroes was over 15 percent compared to about 6 percent for whites.[7] In 1940 the comparable rates were 14.1 and 6.7 percent.[8] Thus, while doubling among whites diminished, the rate for Negroes actually increased over the decade.

Negroes not only have a higher doubling rate but also a "looser" form of household organization arising, in part, from fewer marriages and more divorces, separation, and widowhood. Detailed data on household status for urban Negroes (appendix table B–3) show, for example, that the tendency to live with nonrelatives (household lodger) was about 2½ times as great as for whites. Also, the percentage of Negroes living in households headed by a relative other than a member of the immediate family was much larger than the corresponding ratio for whites. A lower proportion of Negroes are married,[9] and women head households with twice the frequency found among the white sector.

Despite the prevalence of large households often containing extra adults, Negroes tend to occupy relatively small dwelling units averaging in 1947 about one room less than whites. More detailed 1940 data on differences in the amount of occupied space are given in table 27, showing that Negroes consistently had less space than whites regardless of tenure or

---

[6] In 1940, however, median household size (nonfarm) was actually smaller than for whites. The fact that the average was higher results from the high proportion of very large households found among Negroes.

[7] *1950 Census of Population*, Vol. II, *Characteristics of the Population*, Part 1, U. S. Summary, table 105, p. 190.

[8] *1940 Census of Population*, Vol. IV, *Characteristics by Age*, Part 1, U. S. Summary, table 11, p. 28.

[9] Leading, incidentally, to a result which assumes considerable importance in the analysis presented in Chapter 8: a lower proportion of household heads in the younger age groups and a higher proportion among the middle-age groups.

area.   In rural-nonfarm areas the exceptionally small size of rented dwelling units reflects the persistence of the one-room shack.   Negro owners
in the urban areas with a median of 4.90 rooms (a figure still below the
median for white owners) were the only group among the nonwhites who
occupied dwelling units that matched the 1940 nonfarm average of 4.86
rooms.

A large proportion of the small dwelling units of urban Negroes who
are renters are in large multifamily structures.   Although it has been
noted earlier that the apartment house areas of the nation do not have no-
toriously high PPR ratios, the Negro apartment dweller in urban areas has
fewer rooms than his white counterpart, making overcrowding an inevi-
table outcome.   Nevertheless, bad as the lot of the urban Negro may be,
his density standards are much above those of Negroes in rural-nonfarm
areas, an improvement which results more from gains in housing space
than from reductions in household size.

TABLE **27.**—MEDIAN NUMBER OF ROOMS FOR URBAN AND RURAL-NONFARM OCCUPIED
DWELLING UNITS, BY TENURE AND COLOR OF OCCUPANTS: 1940

Area and tenure	White	Non-white	Area and tenure	White	Non-white
Urban..................	4.89	3.64	Rural nonfarm..........	4.82	3.18
Owner occupied..............	5.75	4.90	Owner occupied..............	5.32	3.83
Renter occupied..............	4.23	3.35	Renter occupied..............	4.20	2.87

Source: *1940 Census of Housing,* Vol. II, *General Characteristics,* Part 1, U. S. Summary, table 8d, p. 28.

There is, Gunnar Myrdal has said, nothing more obvious about the low
level of the Negro's standard of living than his poor housing conditions.
While these can be attributed both to low income (resulting from employment barriers) and to racial discrimination in the housing market, there
is no clear answer at the moment to the question as to the relative weights
of each of the two factors.   The data which are necessary but which are
not available for an answer to this question would require the stratification
of all statistical materials on dwelling units and occupants by comparatively
narrow income classes.   Nevertheless, the weight of the present evidence
seems to be that low income is a more strategic factor in the unfavorable
density standards of nonwhites than housing discrimination *per se.*

In the first place, in view of the probable improvement in utilization
since 1940, it is not very likely that the proportion of overcrowded households among Negro renters (the majority of all Negro households) in 1950
was appreciably higher than the proportion for all renters for the income
classes within which most Negroes are included (Chapter 3).   Second, and
more directly to the point, the budget studies of 1935–1936[10] by the

---

[10] U. S. Bureau of Labor Statistics, *op. cit.,* pp. 72–73.   Likewise, the National Health Survey of the
same period revealed about equal degrees of overcrowding among Negro and white families on relief.

Bureau of Labor Statistics reveal that, income class for income class, Negro households had more rooms than whites in virtually all survey cities and that PPR ratios were either equal to, or lower than, those for whites with comparable incomes. If these observations still obtain today, then it would be fair to conclude that the high proportion of overcrowding among Negroes as a group is the result of a disproportionate concentration in low income classes.

There is reason to believe that housing discrimination is a far more important factor in explaining the low quality of Negro housing than in explaining an unfavorable density pattern. Racial discrimination shatters the mechanism by which housing supply adjusts to demand, that is, a growing Negro population cannot obtain the housing it wants even with the means to pay for it. Although the substantial growth of the nonfarm Negro population has been accompanied by an expansion of residential areas available for Negro occupancy, this expansion has taken place mainly in the older, run-down sections of the community. The result is that Negroes manage to increase their housing space inventory but only at the price of accepting housing of inferior quality. While housing densities of many Negro households are bad, a complete evaluation of racial differences in housing standards through the use, say, of the American Public Health Association (APHA) scale, would probably yield relatively lower ratings for Negroes as far as the physical characteristics of dwelling unit and neighborhood (such as dilapidation rates, ventilation, lack of plumbing, undermaintained buildings, community facilities) are concerned, than for overcrowding.

CHAPTER 7

SPACE TRENDS IN THE HOUSING INVENTORY

There is little doubt that the decline in the rate of utilization observed over the 1940–1950 decade was an extension of a longer run trend toward improvement in per capita space standards. Such a trend would be a natural outcome of smaller households and of the somewhat greater long-term rise in real family income than in the real cost of housing. One opposing tendency, however, has limited the extent of any such improvement: over the long run the consumer has been buying and leasing smaller and smaller dwelling units. All evidence points directly to the conclusion that the homes of yesteryear were larger, not only in terms of number of rooms, but also, judging from value data adjusted for price change,[1] in over-all physical dimensions.

The reduction in the number of rooms per dwelling unit, however, appears to have been at a lesser rate than the decrease in household size, a relationship which makes a *prima facie* case for a long-run decline in the PPR ratio. Between 1900 and 1950 average household size (nonfarm) is estimated [2] to have declined by about 20 percent, while the median number of rooms declined by a minimum of 10 percent and, if allowance is made for a systematic bias[3] in the data shown in table 28, by perhaps as much as 15 percent. The long-run improvement in space standards has therefore been most modest, certainly less than the advance of other living standards. Perhaps the most important reason for this phenomenon is the fact that housing space has become more and more expensive compared to other consumer goods. Over the past 60 years residential construction costs have risen twice as fast as the cost of all other goods and services included in gross national product. Another reason for the apparently slight improvement in space standards, and one that has been mentioned

---

[1] Leo Grebler, David M. Blank, and Louis Winnick, *Capital Formation in Residential Real Estate: Trends and Prospects*, Princeton University Press, Princeton, 1956. Between 1890 and 1950 the average real value per new dwelling unit built, despite addition of more plumbing, wiring, and equipment, declined by about 40 percent.

[2] *Ibid.*, Chapter VII.

[3] Cross tabulations of rooms by year built do not indicate the actual number of rooms contained in a dwelling unit as originally built. Because of their size and location, older units in the housing inventory have been prime candidates for conversion. It is, therefore, safe to say that the 1950 data understate original average size and therefore the rate of decline.

frequently in this study, may be the displacement of housing by other expenditure items in consumer budgets. The evidence seems to indicate that housing has indeed fallen victim to the newer, expensive consumer durables. The $600 average annual cost of automobile ownership (capital and operating) estimated by the Bureau of Labor Statistics in 1950 was actually higher than average contract rent in that year. If the average home owner (to whom such a choice would be unthinkable) were to subsitute more and better housing for his car, such a sum could have financed a house nearly twice as expensive as the one he was currently occupying.

It is fair to say, however, that though the consumer buys fewer rooms (and less "house" measured in terms of the real quantity of resources embodied in a dwelling unit) than his grandfather, he may not have suffered a commensurate loss in usable living space. There was an appalling amount of "dead space" in the form of stairways, corridors, and unusable corners in the typical 2½-story frame house of the past. Furthermore, the tendency toward smaller homes appears to have been reversed in recent years. It is too early to tell, however, whether this reversal which began in the early fifties represents a permanent break with an historical trend.

TABLE **28.**—MEDIAN NUMBER OF ROOMS FOR URBAN AND RURAL-NONFARM OCCUPIED DWELLING UNITS, BY YEAR BUILT: 1950

Year built	Total	Urban	Rural nonfarm
1945 or later	4.26	4.35	4.16
1940 to 1944	4.39	4.43	4.30
1930 to 1939	4.56	4.80	4.12
1920 to 1929	4.81	4.87	4.47
1919 or earlier	4.76	4.63	5.29

Source: Leo Grebler, David M. Blank, and Louis Winnick, *op. cit.*, Chapter VII. From a special tabulation of preliminary 1950 Census data.

The slow shrinkage in the number of rooms per dwelling unit can be seen in detail in a comparison of 1940 and 1950 Census inventory data (table 29). In 1950 the median number of rooms per nonfarm dwelling unit was 4.57, a reduction of over 3 percent from the 1940 average of 4.73 rooms. Some of the decline in the over-all averages is due, of course, to regional shifts. The West and Southwest, where houses are customarily smaller, accounted for an increasing share of new construction as population moved "toward the sun."

The decline in the median number of rooms would have been even greater had it not been for the swing to home ownership; former renters increased their space standards by buying a single-family home even though this house may have been small relative to the prevailing size of owner-occupied homes. This observation is evidenced by the fact that the shrinkage in rooms for each of the tenure classes was greater than that for all dwelling units.   From 1940 to 1950, the median number of rooms per rented dwelling unit fell by 8.3 percent, from 4.11 to 3.77, and that for owner-occupied units by 1.8 percent, from 5.39 to 5.32 rooms.   In urban areas (errors due to the change in definition aside) the shrinkage was even greater, being over 9 percent for rented and 5.6 percent for owner-occupied dwelling units.   It is in this sector of the housing inventory that the impact of conversions was greatest.

Because of the decline in the average number of rooms, the room inventory increased at a lower rate than the inventory of occupied dwelling units, 31.5 compared to 33.7 percent.   But the increase in the household population was only 24 percent,[4] hence the decline in the national PPR ratio.

The reduction in the number of rooms per dwelling unit was accompanied by a considerable "compression" in the size distribution of dwelling units over the decade from 1940 to 1950.   Not only did the share of the larger dwelling units (containing 6 or more rooms) decline but, unless the data are badly distorted,[5] the proportion accounted for by small units with 1 or 2 rooms also seems to have dropped.   At the same time, the share of medium-sized dwelling units containing 3 to 5 rooms increased. Despite the declining relative importance of large and small units, there was an appreciable growth in absolute numbers even in these categories. One- and two-room units increased by 7.5 and 22.2 percent, respectively, 6-room units by nearly a fourth, 7-room units by over one-fifth.   The gain in 8-room units was almost negligible; only above this size, i.e., 9 or more rooms, was there a decline in actual numbers.

The great surge towards home ownership during the decade resulted in a sensational growth of nearly 73 percent in the number of owner-occupied dwelling units.   The owner-occupied inventory gained over 8 million units, substantially more than all the dwelling units built for owner-occupancy over this period.   The additional units, of course, resulted from the change in tenure of large numbers, perhaps more than 2 million, of existing single-family houses occupied by renters in 1940.   Such a movement back to owner-occupancy is characteristic of any period of prosperity following a depression (during which an opposite movement occurs as a result of foreclosure).   But it was seen in Chapter 5 that the shift in tenure was

---

[4] The increase in household population would appear somewhat greater (25.5 percent) if allowance is made for the growth in the Armed Forces.   If all military personnel (who in 1950 were not living in dwelling units) had remained in civilian life, the 1950 PPR ratio would have been a trifle, i.e., less than one percent, higher even under the unlikely assumption that no expansion in the room inventory would have ensued.

[5] The comparative analysis of the Post-Enumeration Survey with census totals, shown in Appendix E, indicates a relatively large shortage in the 1- and 2-room dwelling unit categories.   Even allowing for these errors, some decline in the share of small dwelling units undoubtedly occurred, particularly if it is granted that unrevealed shortages also existed in 1940 when no post-census survey was made.   It is easy for enumerators to miss small dwelling units because they are often located in out-of-the-way places.

TABLE 29.—Nonfarm Occupied Dwelling Units, by Number of Rooms and Tenure: 1950 and 1940

[Minus sign (−) denotes decrease]

Year, area, and tenure	Total	Number of rooms 1	2	3	4	5	6	7	8	9 or more	Median number of rooms
Total:											
1950	38,731,181	1,185,582	3,061,085	5,990,004	8,521,226	8,390,265	6,494,582	2,668,785	1,351,712	1,067,940	4.57
1940	29,290,742	1,102,714	2,503,554	4,211,334	5,384,020	6,152,353	5,253,878	2,191,708	1,323,412	1,167,769	4.73
Percent increase, 1940 to 1950	32.2	7.5	22.2	42.2	58.3	36.4	23.6	21.8	2.1	−8.6	−3.4
Owner occupied:											
1950	19,512,658	205,395	475,485	1,262,207	3,627,357	5,136,590	4,737,385	2,092,617	1,100,503	875,119	5.32
1940	11,306,145	159,105	334,400	695,533	1,505,951	2,690,936	2,834,595	1,384,829	891,833	808,963	5.59
Percent increase, 1940 to 1950	72.6	29.1	42.2	81.5	141.6	90.9	67.1	51.1	23.4	8.2	−4.8
Renter occupied:											
1950	17,036,048	809,166	2,243,792	4,285,488	4,372,681	2,918,158	1,561,092	504,657	202,065	138,949	3.77
1940	16,123,633	823,270	1,927,305	3,168,425	3,490,732	3,149,651	2,201,535	719,317	366,314	277,084	4.11
Percent increase, 1940 to 1950	5.7	−1.7	16.4	35.3	25.3	−7.3	−29.1	−29.9	−44.8	−49.9	−8.3
Urban											
Total:											
1950	29,044,249	836,198	2,233,219	4,581,659	6,194,988	6,486,395	5,044,138	1,965,051	953,480	749,121	4.60
1940	21,339,428	760,796	1,710,499	3,104,302	3,815,290	4,648,797	4,001,856	1,559,344	916,878	821,666	4.78
Owner occupied:											
1950	14,185,434	99,752	241,586	772,119	2,447,660	3,904,773	3,708,058	1,564,608	805,234	641,644	5.40
1940	7,647,769	56,969	134,421	367,792	888,194	1,908,180	2,106,239	979,656	625,870	580,448	5.72
Renter occupied:											
1950	13,912,199	664,056	1,846,028	3,618,666	3,523,329	2,421,882	1,246,668	372,961	131,272	87,337	3.74
1940	12,717,114	640,276	1,447,012	2,543,632	2,736,664	2,574,079	1,775,720	536,704	261,272	201,755	4.13
Rural Nonfarm											
Total:											
1950	9,686,932	349,384	827,866	1,408,345	2,326,238	1,903,870	1,450,444	703,734	398,232	318,819	4.47
1940	7,951,314	341,918	793,055	1,107,032	1,568,730	1,503,556	1,252,022	632,364	406,534	346,103	4.61
Owner occupied:											
1950	5,327,224	105,643	233,899	490,088	1,179,697	1,231,817	1,029,327	528,009	295,269	233,475	5.03
1940	3,658,376	102,136	199,979	327,741	617,757	782,756	728,356	405,173	265,963	228,515	5.24
Renter occupied:											
1950	3,123,849	145,110	397,764	666,822	849,352	496,276	314,424	131,696	70,793	51,612	3.92
1940	3,406,519	182,994	480,293	624,793	754,068	575,572	425,815	182,613	105,042	75,329	4.05

PERCENT DISTRIBUTION

	Total	1 room	2 rooms	3 rooms	4 rooms	5 rooms	6 rooms	7 rooms	8 rooms	9 rooms or more
Total:										
1950	100.0	3.1	6.9	15.5	22.0	21.7	16.8	6.9	3.5	2.8
1940	100.0	3.8	8.5	14.4	18.4	21.0	18.0	7.5	4.5	4.0
Owner occupied:										
1950	100.0	1.1	2.4	6.5	18.6	26.3	24.3	10.7	5.6	4.5
1940	100.0	1.4	3.0	6.2	13.3	23.8	25.1	12.2	7.9	7.2
Renter occupied:										
1950	100.0	4.7	13.2	25.2	25.7	17.1	9.2	3.0	1.2	0.8
1940	100.0	5.1	12.0	19.7	21.6	19.5	13.7	4.5	2.3	1.7
Urban										
Total:										
1950	100.0	2.9	7.7	15.8	21.3	22.3	17.4	6.8	3.3	2.6
1940	100.0	3.6	8.0	14.5	17.9	21.8	18.8	7.3	4.3	3.8
Owner occupied:										
1950	100.0	0.7	1.7	5.4	17.3	27.5	26.1	11.0	5.7	4.5
1940	100.0	0.7	1.8	4.8	11.6	25.0	27.5	12.8	8.2	7.6
Renter occupied:										
1950	100.0	4.8	13.3	26.0	25.3	17.4	9.0	2.7	0.9	0.6
1940	100.0	5.0	11.4	20.0	21.5	20.2	14.0	4.2	2.1	1.6
Rural Nonfarm										
Total:										
1950	100.0	3.6	8.5	14.5	24.0	19.7	15.0	7.3	4.1	3.3
1940	100.0	4.3	10.0	13.9	19.7	18.9	15.7	8.0	5.1	4.3
Owner occupied:										
1950	100.0	2.0	4.4	9.2	22.1	23.1	19.3	9.9	5.5	4.4
1940	100.0	2.8	5.5	9.0	16.9	21.4	19.9	11.1	7.3	6.2
Renter occupied:										
1950	100.0	4.6	12.7	21.3	27.2	15.9	10.1	4.2	2.3	1.7
1940	100.0	5.4	14.1	18.3	22.1	16.9	12.5	5.4	3.1	2.2

Source: *1950 Census of Housing*, Vol. I, *General Characteristics*, Part 1, U. S. Summary, table 9, and *1940 Census of Housing*, Vol. II, *General Characteristics*, Part 1, U. S. Summary, table 8b.

apparently accelerated by rent control which made a sale of the fee more advantageous than a leasehold.

Because of the enormous over-all growth in the owner-occupied inventory, gains were registered in every size class, including the largest houses. None of these gains was small; even 1-room owner-occupied units rose by nearly 30 percent and the 9-or-more-room units by nearly a fourth. But the growth in the middle size ranges was truly remarkable when it is considered how sluggish adaptations in the supply of housing often may be. The number of 4-room units went up nearly 2½ times and the number of 5-room units nearly doubled. In 1950, 4- and 5-room units together comprised 45 percent of owner-occupied dwelling units compared to 37 percent in 1940.

In the meantime, the inventory of rented dwelling units experienced but little growth, less than 6 percent over the decade. In fact, so small was this gain that the shrinkage in the average size of rented dwelling units resulted in an actual *decline* in the total number of rooms occupied by renters, perhaps for the first time in history.[6] The number of rented units increased by slightly over 1 million, despite the fact that nearly 1½ million new units were built (according to census data on year of construction) and perhaps 2 million added by conversion (according to semiofficial estimates). While the number of demolitions and changes due to reclassification is unknown, much of the net difference of 2½ million units was undoubtedly attributable to tenure shifts.

The loss of single-family rented units to the ownership market and the widespread practice of splitting up large dwelling units into smaller ones caused net decreases in the number of rented dwelling units containing 5 or more rooms. These decreases ranged from 7 percent for 5-room units to 50 percent for units with 9 or more rooms. Dwelling units containing 2 to 4 rooms showed the greatest absolute and relative gains. In view of the wave of conversions, it is difficult to accept entirely the data in table 29 which show that the number of 1-room rental units actually declined over the decade. It is more likely that this category of the housing inventory was affected most by census enumeration errors. But it must also be realized that the 1-room rented unit was already present in large numbers in 1940 as a result of the depression. Moreover, though data on conversions are scarce, it does not seem that the 1940–1950 wave of conversions resulted in as many 1-room units as is commonly believed. Lipstein's [7] sample of conversions in the Baltimore and Norfolk-Portsmouth areas indicates that only 2 to 4 percent of all converted dwelling units were

---

[6] Again, omitting the possibility of a greater census undercount in 1950 than was the case in 1940. The Post-Enumeration Survey of 1950 indicates that rented dwelling units were more likely to be missed than owner-occupied units.

[7] Benjamin Lipstein, "How Important Are Conversions in the Current Housing Scene," *Housing Research*, Spring, 1952.

1-room units; the heaviest concentration (42 to 47 percent) appears in 3-room units, a finding consistent with census data giving this renter size class the highest growth rate during the decade.

The trend toward smaller houses, visible in census data, is confirmed by trends in new construction. As was already stated, new houses, if viewed as bundles of real economic resources, had been shrinking for at least half a century. Data on spatial dimensions, however, are available only for more recent periods. New single-family homes insured under Section 203 of the National Housing Act contained 6.2 rooms in 1936 and only 4.9 in 1950.[8] No similar decline can be seen in rental housing projects financed with FHA insured mortgages. Here, both prewar and postwar project dwelling units averaged about 4 rooms (median). The supply of new rental housing apparently had been adapted much earlier to the smaller household. One would have to go back to the twenties and even earlier periods to find numerous examples of large dwelling units in new multi-family structures. The proportion of new residential construction accounted for by single-family houses increased so sharply in recent decades that the average size of *all* new units, however, fell by less than the separate data on single-family houses show.

Meanwhile, evidence is mounting that since the early 1950's the size of new houses has started to rise. BLS field surveys indicate that the 1954 house is 5 percent larger than the 1951 house, which in turn was bigger than the 1947 house.[9] Data on new homes bought with FHA insured mortgage loans confirm this trend.

That some return to larger sized houses should occur is in accord with the analysis presented in Chapter 5. There, it will be recalled, the results of the multiple correlation equation suggested that a sustained period of prosperity, during which construction costs and the prices and rents of existing housing remained reasonably stable, might be accompanied by a slow but continuous reduction in the PPR ratio. It was reasoned that any desire to improve space standards as real income rises would receive further powerful reinforcement from the space needs of a larger and increasing population of children passing through the 6-to-18-year-old age groups (cf. Chapter 8), at which time separation of the sexes and a desire for personal privacy become pressing enough to make successful claims on the family budget.

Moreover, the suburbanization movement has caused a restoration of interest in the home; housing may be rising again in the consumer's hierarchy of values. New owners now tinker with their homes as once they did with their automobiles. The relative merits of various kinds of oil burners, fertilizers, and amortization terms dominate social conversation to an al-

[8] Grebler, Blank, and Winnick, *op. cit.*, Chapter VII.
[9] U. S. Bureau of Labor Statistics, "Characteristics of New Housing—First Quarter, 1954."

most painful degree. Will not a whole generation of young families initiated into the rites of home ownership by way of an apprenticeship in a $9,000 or $10,000 home become in due time ready customers for the $15,000 or $20,000 house?

Of course, the larger homes of today no longer duplicate the mansions of an earlier America. The structures built nowadays even by the wealthiest classes would have failed to impress the prosperous castle builders of the 1890's. Except in a few scattered instances millionaires no longer build grand estates; they merely trade existing ones with each other. The expensive town houses of the Golden Nineties are not being replaced by equivalents even in the suburbs. William Vanderbilt's house, conservatively estimated at $3,000,000 when built in 1893, could be matched in today's prices only by a $15,000,000 house, an unthinkable event. In the 1890's the building of $100,000 houses, to cost today at least $500,000, was not uncommon; there are long streets in every large city lined with such homes. One wonders how many homes containing more than 10 rooms have been built in the last 10 years,[10] much less the number of houses costing $500,000 or more.

Very large houses are probably a thing of the past. Income taxes, the steep rise in the cost of domestic and maintenance services and the disappearance of ostentatious glitter have made them obsolete. A shift towards large houses in the new construction market nowadays means more 7- and 8-room houses plus a very thin sprinkling of pocketsize "mansions," and fewer 3- and 4-room houses. Among the prosperous classes, a second house to be used as a vacation retreat is probably considered to be sufficient compensation for a relatively modest year-round house. Further improvements in average housing space standards are therefore likely to be accompanied by a continued "leveling" in the distribution of housing space. America has become a country not only predominantly composed of home owners, but one of single-family houses more homogeneous with respect to size. The term "home owner" will still mask the enormous difference between the owner-occupants of a 1-room shack and a 60-room mansion, but neither type will be as prominent as in the past.

---

[10] Only about 1 out of 25 dwelling units built in 1954 contained 4 or more bedrooms, i.e., 6 or more rooms. U. S. Bureau of Labor Statistics, *op. cit.*

CHAPTER 8

THE CHANGING HOUSEHOLD

The long-term decline in average household size has been accompanied by sharp increases in the proportion of very small households and by even more dramatic decreases in the proportion of very large households. Although the comparability of data covering so long an historical span leaves something to be desired, the trends from 1790 to 1950 that are presented in table 30 nevertheless serve to illustrate the magnitude of change. The relative importance of the 1- and 2-person household has more than tripled since the early days of the Republic, their combined share in the total number of households rising from 11.5 to 37.4 percent by 1950. The large household of 8 or more persons has declined from about a quarter of the total to an insignificant 3 percent by 1950. The tendency toward smaller households is plainly evident by 1900 and may possibly continue into the future, though at a retarded rate.

TABLE **30.**—PERCENT DISTRIBUTION OF HOUSEHOLDS, BY SIZE, FOR THE UNITED STATES: 1950, 1900, AND 1790

Census year	1 person	2 persons	3 persons	4 persons	5 persons	6 persons	7 persons	8 persons	9 persons	10 or more
1950............	9.3	28.1	22.8	18.4	10.4	5.3	2.7	1.4	0.8	0.9
1900............	5.1	15.0	19.6	16.9	14.2	10.9	7.7	5.2	3.2	3.1
1790............	3.7	7.8	11.7	13.8	13.9	13.2	11.2	9.0	6.5	9.0

Source: U. S. Bureau of the Census, *A Century of Population Growth*, p. 98, and *1950 Census of Housing*, Vol. I, *General Characteristics*, Part 1, U. S. Summary, table 10.

While such striking modifications in the size distribution of households do not appear to have been accompanied by equally significant improvements in per capita space standards, household size is nevertheless so important a determinant of density levels that it is necessary to probe into some of the long-run factors governing its change. This excursion into demography also affords an opportunity to bring in some scanty materials on the relation of household composition to utilization and to review the changes in household composition which occurred between 1940 and 1950.

Factors behind the decline in household size

The drop in the birth rate has been the overwhelmingly decisive factor affecting household size.[1] Not only has a falling birth rate meant fewer children per household but also fewer adults, since the aging of the population which accompanies a falling birth rate exerts, as will be shown, powerful leverage in raising the proportion of households to population (decreasing average household size). In 1890 the average household consisted of 4.96 persons of whom 2.69 were adults and 2.27 were children under 20 years of age. In 1950 the average household consisted of 3.37 persons of whom 2.20 were adults and 1.17 were children. Compared to a 32-percent drop in the over-all average, adults declined by 18 percent and children by 49 percent. Between 1890 and 1950 the share of children in the population declined from 46 to 35 percent as adults increased from 54 to 65 percent.

A decline in the number of children per household is an obvious sequel to a lowered birth rate. But the decline in the average number of adults requires more explanation since adults, unlike children, are free to vary the rate at which they set up independent establishments, i.e., "undouble" or "fragmentize," regardless of any change in their number. The question is how much of the decline in adults per household can be attributed to an autonomous change in consumer behavior, that is, an increasing preference for independent households, and how much can be accounted for by mere change in the age composition of the population.

At this point, despite a reluctance to add new terminology to a subject already overloaded with technical terms, the concept of the "headship rate" is introduced. The headship rate is the number of heads of households at any moment divided by the population. In this aggregate sense the headship rate is of little analytic interest since it is the exact equivalent of the ratio of households to population, or the reciprocal of average household size. But the over-all headship rate can be further segregated into age-specific headship rates,[2] taken as the proportion of persons in any age group who are heads of households. Since the act of establishing an independent household is intimately related to the life cycle of the individual, age-specific headship rates trace out a characteristic pattern with reference to age that rises continuously from zero for the youngest age groups to well over 50 percent for older age groups and then declines with extreme old age (table 31 and figure 9). Furthermore, since the decision of adults to set up their own households varies with income, health, marital status, the cost of housing, individual preferences, and so forth, age-specific headship rates are subject to shifts over time.

---

[1] Cf. Grebler, Blank, and Winnick, *op. cit.*, Chapter V.

[2] Although arrived at independently, no originality can be claimed for this measure. Terborgh, Glick, and perhaps others, have made use of age-specific headship rates (variously labeled), chiefly in making household projections.

TABLE **31.**—AGE DISTRIBUTION AND AGE-SPECIFIC HEADSHIP RATES, FOR THE UNITED STATES: 1950 AND 1890

Age distribution and headship rate	Under 25 years	25 to 29 years	30 to 34 years	35 to 39 years	40 to 44 years	45 to 49 years	50 to 54 years	55 to 59 years	60 and over
1950:									
Age distribution..........	41.5	8.1	7.6	7.5	6.8	6.0	5.5	4.8	12.2
Headship rate[1]..........	3.2	33.3	40.2	43.7	46.4	48.7	50.4	52.3	53.0
1890:									
Age distribution..........	56.0	8.9	7.3	6.2	5.1	4.4	3.7	2.7	6.2
Headship rate[1]..........	1.8	27.3	38.5	45.1	47.9	51.6	53.4	56.0	51.8

[1] Percent in each age group who are heads of households.

Source: Ned Shilling, "Net Household Formation—A Demographic Analysis," unpublished master's essay, Columbia University, 1955.

The average number of adults per household (the headship rate of all adults) is affected (*a*) by change in weights, i.e., the relative importance of age groups having high headship rates compared to age groups with low rates, and (*b*) by changes in rates, i.e., shifts in the tendency of any given age group to become heads of households (figure 9). Restating the question raised earlier on the roles played by changing age composition and "spreading out" as factors in reducing the average number of adults per household, what have been the relative influences of changing weights and changing rates?

FIGURE **9.**—AGE-SPECIFIC HEADSHIP RATES, FOR THE UNITED STATES: 1950 AND 1890

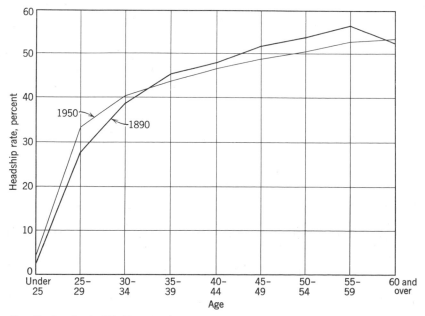

Note: Based on data in table 31.

The answer is quite conclusive: changing age structure, rather than change in consumer behavior, has been the strategic force. If the 1950 population had the same age distribution as prevailed in 1890 and only age-specific headship rates had changed, we would have found a 1950 population of 150.7 million living in 32.1 million households (inclusive of quasi-households), or an average household size of 4.69 as compared to 4.96 in 1890. If, however, age-specific headship rates had remained perfectly constant, the altered age distribution would have led to 41.5 million households in 1950, only 1 million less than the actual 1950 total, resulting in an average household size of 3.63. In other words, behavioral changes on the part of consumers could have accounted for a decline in household size of merely 5 percent while their aging would have caused a decline of 27 percent, or about five-sixths of the over-all drop in household size.[3] The widely held view [4] that spreading out has been a major factor in the decline in household size is, in the light of the facts, untenable. As we shall see, though forces favorable to increased headship rates were present, other trends, particularly an increased proportion of married persons, served as a powerful offset.

In table 31 and figure 9 the movements in both age weights and headship ratios are given in detail. Current interest in the problem of an aging population has been so great and statistical presentation so common that no elaborate discussion of changes in age structure is required here. Suffice it to say that since 1890 the share of men and women over 60 in the population has doubled, from 6 to 12 percent. The share of successively younger age groups down to 30 to 34 has also risen, but by diminishing percentages. The share of the population under 25 years old declined from 56 to about 42 percent.

The increasing age of the population, which played so important a role in reducing household size, was, to repeat, primarily a result of a lowered birth rate. A second important causal factor was the impressive decline in age-specific death rates (table 32). Standardized for age, the national death rate (based on data from death registration States) dropped during the last half century by more than 50 percent, from 17.8 to 8.4 per 1,000.

---

[3] As in all standardization problems, interaction takes place between the variables (headship rates and age weights) so that over-all change can be greater (or less) than the sum of the parts. In this case, for reasons that need not be discussed here, the sum of the two influences almost exactly equals the over-all decline of 32 percent.

[4] Thus the Bureau of the Census comments, ". . . the number of smaller households has been augmented by the changes in the patterns of family living. . . . Usually the household of the past contained not only the head, wife, and children, but often older relatives of the family and sometimes servants. This pattern has changed, with proportionately fewer households including relatives and servants. The long-term trend is one of "spreading out" with each adult group having its own household. Of particular importance is the increasing number of older people. *The growing tendency* of these people to maintain separate households has been an important factor in contributing to an increasingly larger number of small households." *1950 Census of Housing*, Vol. I, *General Characteristics*, p. XXVIII. (Author's italics.)

The decline was expressed in varying degrees in all adult age groups as well as in the child population and had a direct as well as an indirect effect on headship rates.

A glance at figure 9 discloses why changes in age-specific headship rates have had but minor effects on average household size: these rates have moved in opposite directions for various age groups. Headship rates increased for the younger age groups, i.e., up to 35, *decreased* for the middle age span, and increased somewhat for the elderly. It was this decline in the tendency to form independent households among people aged 35 to 59 which reduced the over-all influence of changes in headship rates.[5]

TABLE 32.—DEATH RATE PER 1,000 POPULATION, BY AGE, FOR DEATH-REGISTRATION STATES: 1950 AND 1900

Age	1950	1900	Percent decline, 1900 to 1950	Age	1950	1900	Percent decline, 1900 to 1950
Under 1 year......	33.0	162.4	79.7	45 to 54 years.....	8.5	15.0	43.3
1 to 4 years.......	1.4	19.8	92.9	55 to 64 years.....	19.1	27.2	29.8
5 to 14 years.....	0.6	3.9	84.6	65 to 74 years.....	40.7	56.4	27.8
15 to 24 years....	1.3	5.9	78.0	75 to 84 years.....	93.3	123.3	24.3
25 to 34 years....	1.8	8.2	78.1	85 and over.......	202.0	260.9	22.6
35 to 44 years....	3.6	10.2	64.7				

Source: U. S. Bureau of the Census, *Statistical Abstract of the United States, 1953*, p. 71.

Why was there such contrasting behavior among the various age groups? Curiously, the increase in headship rates among the young and the decline in the middle age groups can be ascribed to the same cause—an increase in the proportion of married people.[6] For the young an increased tendency towards marriage means relatively more independent households since the unmarried young live primarily with their parents. On the other hand, a large proportion of the middle-aged who are unmarried (single,

---

[5] But had headship rates for the middle-aged remained constant or even increased to the extent found for the young and old, the changing age distribution would still have remained the dominant factor in the decline in number of adults per household.

[6] If all persons in a given age group containing an equal number of males and females were married (and living with their spouses in separate dwelling units) the headship rate would be exactly 50 percent for both sexes combined. The effect of an increasing proportion of married persons in any age group is a movement toward this 50 percent level, marriage exerting an upward push in age groups having headship rates lower than 50 percent (young persons) and a downward push in age groups with headship rates above this level. The stated conditions are modified in real life by the fact that (a) the sex ratio in a given age group is not unity, (b) some married couples double up, and (c) there are varying proportions of "unmarried" people in any group whose tendency to establish a private household depends on whether they are single, widowed, divorced, etc. Nevertheless, the tendency described above remains a useful way of stating one effect of marriage on headship rates.

Between 1890 and 1950 the proportion of married people to total population aged 14 and over, standardized for age, increased from about 58 to 65 percent. Bureau of the Census, *Statistical Abstract of the U. S., 1953*, Washington, D. C., 1953, p. 49.

widowed, divorced, or separated) maintain independent establishments.[7] If this group shows an increased tendency toward marriage, the result is frequently a merger of two separate households and a reduction in the headship rate. This is true particularly when the additional marriages are associated with declining death rates, which create fewer widows and widowers, since in two out of three cases the widowed (aged 45 to 54) maintain independent establishments.

The slightly increased proportion of young married people is the result of both the younger ages at which marriage takes place and the increased proclivity toward marriage. For the older group, the increased proportion of married people is largely the result of more marriages remaining intact because of the fall in death rates. Also, though a fact hard to document, remarriage rates may have increased.

The increased headship rate for the elderly (60 plus) is a phenomenon that has received much comment. It is generally assumed that Social Security and greater economic resources have given the old a larger degree of independence. Undoubtedly there is some truth in this. But it must be noted that the increase over the entire 60-year period has been slight, the headship rate rising from 51.8 to 53.0 percent. Further, practically all of this rise antedated Social Security legislation. Between 1940 and 1950, despite high prosperity and greater participation of the old in the labor force, the headship rate for the over-65 group remained virtually unchanged. This observation casts some doubt on the role of general economic factors in causing older people to maintain independent households. It is possible that specific housing market conditions, i.e., the relative availability of inexpensive housing, are more strategic than the general state of the economy. Many of the elderly live on fixed incomes and do not fully share in the changes in business conditions. However, long-run improvement in economic conditions has probably been a strategic factor in raising the proportion of married people to the total population, particularly in the case of the young age group.

It is possible that the long-run changes in the proportion of married people may have obscured a long-term tendency for the headship rate of unmarried, i.e., widowed, single, divorced, separated, adults to rise. The data do not permit an unequivocal answer to this question. That young single working girls and widows frequently maintain their own apartments is clearly visible in any large city. Data for 1940 and 1950 confirm the fact that there is an increased rate of household formation among the unmarried young, but they show no net movement among unmarried adults over 35 years old. In fact, the movement in age-specific headship rates of

---

[7] Thus, in 1950, of the unmarried houshold population aged 20 to 24, only 5.3 percent had independent establishments. Among the unmarried aged 45 to 54 the headship rate was about 41 percent. *1950 Census of Population*, Vol. IV, *Special Reports*, Part 2, Chapter D, Marital Status, table 1.

unmarried adults follows fairly closely the pattern for all adults.   Over
the same decade there have been appreciable declines in the headship rates
of older unmarried men and a slight decline for the corresponding group
of women (appendix table D–1).   Since a majority of these people are
widows or widowers, there is again doubt cast on the belief that up to 1950
the widowed more and more tended to maintain independent households as a
result of better economic conditions.[8]   At any rate, the quantitative influence of unmarried adults on the over-all headship rate would be small
because they constitute a minor fraction of the adult population.

It is quite possible that headship rates for all age groups will increase in
the future.   The 1950 housing market was far from normal, and the
doubling-up rate, though equal to that of 1940, was possibly high in view
of the business prosperity of that year.   Indeed, the drop in the doubling-
up rate since 1950 indicates that some further rise in adult headship rates
has already occurred.   Since the aged will grow in relative importance,
any further tendency for the headship rate of this group to increase would
have great leverage in increasing the relative number of small households
and therefore in depressing the PPR ratio.

The impact of an aging population on housing demand in terms of location, size, and type of unit has received considerable attention in recent
years.   Although an increased demand for certain types of housing is
equally real whether it is the result of *more* older people or a higher headship rate, it would clarify analysis if a distinction between the two were
maintained, which is not always the case.

The incorporation of age-specific headship rates into housing market
analysis has much to recommend it.   From the foregoing analysis it is
clear that total household formation is dependent upon change in the
weight of an age class and a change in its headship rate, the former having been the dominant factor at least historically.   Since the future size
and age distribution of an adult population can be projected about 20
years with a reasonable degree of accuracy,[9] the total number of households can be ascertained by applying age-specific headship rates to each of
the projected age groups.[10]   These rates apparently have not been subject
to wide and violent changes.   Indeed, over the 1940–1950 decade (and to
a large extent over the past 60 years) the only important net movements

---

[8] Between 1940 and 1947 the headship rate of widows declined from 57 to 56 percent (U. S. Bureau
of the Census, *Current Population Reports*, Series P–20, Nos. 10 and 16).   Between 1930 and 1950
there was a net rise in the rate, but other data suggest that most of this rise took place in the depression period of 1930 to 1940.   More recently, however, the headship rate of widows again increased,
reaching 62 percent in 1953 (*Current Population Reports*, Series P–20, Nos. 50 and 53).

[9] For *local* housing market analysis the problem of estimating migration would, of course, still
remain.   Whatever the size of the area, the preferred method of population forecasting would be the
cohort-survival technique, since it alone can yield a reliable future age distribution.

[10] Cf. the discussion by Glick, Larmon, and Landau in "Projections of the Number of Households
and Families, 1955 and 1960," U. S. Bureau of the Census, *Current Population Reports*, P–20, No. 42.

occurred in the younger age groups. That is to say, for the age group of 35 and over, which contains about two-thirds of all household heads, the 1950 total could have been estimated accurately in 1940 by projecting the 1940 headship rates.

Headship rates differ not only by age but also by marital status, sex, location, race, etc. Some of these differences are discussed later in this chapter when household status is more fully analyzed.

The 1-person household

The growth in the proportion of 1-person households which has been so striking in the past (table 30) represents an almost revolutionary change in American utilization patterns. For one thing, it has been seen that 1-person households are relatively lavish users of shelter space and therefore exercise a demand for housing quite disproportionate to their numbers. Second, the 1-person household may possibly be the most volatile sector of housing demand, shifting from headship to other household status more readily than other groups. That is, the "doubling" and "undoubling" of adult individuals may be characterized by wider cyclical swings than is the case for married couples or other types of families.

One-person households may also serve as a reservoir of housing demand. They appear on the market to fill in vacancies in older, deteriorated portions of the housing supply and thus limit any tendency for housing to filter out i.e., to be demolished or boarded up for lack of tenants willing to pay a rent sufficient to meet operating costs. The very condition of prosperity which causes many families to upgrade both their housing and neighborhoods also may tend to accelerate 1-person household formation, and housing which otherwise might be abandoned finds occupants.

TABLE **33.**—CHARACTERISTICS OF NONFARM 1-PERSON HOUSEHOLDS, BY TENURE: 1950

Item	Total	Owner	Renter
Percent of all households..................................	10.0	7.5	12.9
Urban..	10.0	6.7	13.3
Rural nonfarm.......................................	10.1	9.7	10.7
Percent owner-occupants..................................	40.0	...	...
Median value, 1-family house...................... dollars..	...	4,962	...
Median contract rent............................... dollars..	...	...	31.39
Average number of rooms.................................	3.4	4.4	2.5
Percent female...	64.1	66.5	62.5
Percent 65 and over, both sexes...........................	38.7	49.6	31.6
Male...	34.1	43.6	28.5
Female...	41.4	52.7	33.5

Source: *1950 Census of Housing*, Vol. I, *General Characteristics*, Part 1, U. S. Summary, table 10; Vol. II, *Nonfarm Housing Characteristics*, Part 1, Chapter 1, United States, tables A–1, A–2, A–5, and A–8.

Testing such hypotheses is beyond the resources of this study. But even a casual survey of the characteristics of the 1-person household (table 33) reveals the special nature of this portion of the market and makes the above conjectural statements more than mere possibilities. In 1949, the 1-person renter household had a low income, of about $1,200 compared with $2,800 for all renter households. The 1-person owner was even poorer, with an income of less than $1,000 compared to $3,360 for all owners. With both a lower income and lower space requirements, many 1-person households are probably always on the borderline between surrendering or maintaining a separate establishment.

There is little question that 1-person households occupy the cheaper portions of the housing inventory. One-person renters had a median contract rent of $31.39 compared to $35.50 for all renters. The median value of single-family houses occupied by 1-person households was $4,962 compared to $7,388 for all owners. One-person households occupy substandard housing more frequently than others,[11] especially in the owner-occupied sector. With very much lower incomes and only moderately lower rents, the rent-income ratio of 1-person households (Chapter 5) was quite high with little margin for cushioning any economic reverses.

One-person households are, of course, far from being a homogeneous group. Included are the young executive or rich divorcée in an up-to-date apartment as well as the poor aged widow in a city slum or rural town, but, most typically, the 1-person household is an elderly woman living in an urban area. Among 1-person households, women outnumber men two to one and the heaviest concentration of these women is found in the 65-and-over age group. One-person households are predominantly (60 percent) renters, and an overwhelming majority of them are located in urban areas. One-person households are not a uniquely urban phenomenon, however. In fact, they are (relatively) as prevalent in rural nonfarm as in urban areas and in the past have been more so.

The desire for privacy on the part of Americans is never more clearly illustrated than by the increasing importance of 1-person households. Live alone and like it is more than a hortatory slogan. With low income and an average of nearly 3½ rooms (nearly 4½ for owners) there is a real question why lodgers or partners are not sought more often than they have been. Yet of the total number of primary individuals (persons heading a dwelling unit containing no other relatives), about 80 percent are 1-person households. Furthermore, the sharing of dwelling space on the part of primary individuals that does take place is more likely to be among the young. Only one out of six primary individuals 65 or over shared his home. Under 45 years of age the proportion is one out of four.

The relative importance of 1-person households is likely to grow in the future. By 1975 it is entirely probable that there will be several million more 1-person households, few of whom will be accommodated by new private construction. It is more reasonable to expect that these individuals

---

[11] *1950 Census of Housing*, Vol. II, *Nonfarm Housing Characteristics*, Part 1, Chapter 1, United States, table A–4.

will seek out or retain cheap housing wherever it is available. While the drive of the aged toward independent living arrangements has justifiably met with widespread social approval, one of its consequences may nevertheless be a further clogging of an already imperfectly operating filtering process as a regulator of the quality of the housing stock.

Changing household composition

Household size and household composition are, of course, interrelated. A 3-person household (husband, wife, one minor child) differs from a 4-person household (husband, wife, two minor children) not only because it is smaller (and therefore usually needs less housing space) but also because there may be differences in interpersonal relationships; the family has a different structure. It goes without saying that the long-run trend toward smaller households has necessarily altered the composition of our households.

The variations in the PPR ratio by household size discussed in Chapter 4 were in part affected by differences in household composition. In moving up from the 2-person to 3-, 4-, or higher order household size, what are the consequences for housing space requirements if the additions represent infants, children, adults, secondary families, or subfamilies? Households of any given size can have a wide range of compositional possibilities reflecting the age, sex, and type of relationship of its members. Such compositional differences will naturally lead to variations in the amount and type of space demanded. According to the APHA norms referred to in Chapter 2, a 6-person household may require as few as 5 and as many as 8 rooms depending on its particular constitution. These differences in composition account for much of the dispersion around the averages found in the cross-distribution of household size by number of rooms (appendix table A–2).

The 1950 Census data do not allow much exploration of this question. From other sources, particularly the 1947 sample census, a few observations can be gleaned on the quantitative relationship between housing space and household composition. There are serious limitations in these data: fairly large sampling errors, the inability to keep age and income of head constant, and the fact that 1947 housing reports are based on an abnormal market situation. Such data are to be considered more valuable as examples of the types of classification needed than as a source of precise estimates.

In 1947 the median number of rooms occupied by a 2-person (husband-wife) nonfarm renter household was 3.71. A husband-wife family with a child under 18 occupied 3.93 rooms, or only 6 percent more (table 34). If this child were between 6 and 17 years of age, the median was 4.43, or 25 percent higher. This result suggests that the presence of a child under 6 years old exerts only very small pressure on space. In fact, a husband-wife household containing one child under 6 had less space than a husband-wife household without children—probably a freakish result of the failure of those statistics to keep age of household head constant. A great many childless husband-wife households are well past the prime of life and have a different space utilization pattern. The downward adjustment in housing space use after children marry is often incomplete.

TABLE **34.**—MEDIAN NUMBER OF ROOMS FOR NONFARM OCCUPIED DWELLING UNITS, BY TYPE OF HOUSEHOLD AND TENURE: APRIL 1947

Age of related children, and tenure	Husband and wife, no children [1]	Husband and wife, 1 child [1]	Husband and wife, 2 or more children [1]
Owner:			
Under 18 years	5.35	5.29	5.49
Under 6 years	...	4.92	5.16
6 to 17 years	...	5.54	5.80
Renter:			
Under 18 years	3.71	3.93	4.34
Under 6 years	...	3.53	4.11
6 to 17 years	...	4.43	4.72

Tenure	Husband-and-wife primary family with—			
	No secondary families [2]	1 or more secondary families or individuals [2]	No sub-families [3]	1 or more subfamilies [3]
Owner	5.38	7+	5.38	6.10
Renter	4.00	5.23	4.00	5.10

[1] Without sub- or secondary families.
[2] Without subfamilies.
[3] Without secondary families or individuals.

Source: U. S. Bureau of the Census, *Current Population Reports*, P–20, No. 16, table 15.

A husband-wife family with two or more children had more space than a husband-wife one-child household. The increment to space was especially great when the children were 6 to 17 years of age. As a matter of fact, a husband-wife family with but one child aged 6 to 17 held more space than a husband-wife family with two or more children under 6, 4.43 rooms compared to 4.11,[12] suggesting that the aging of children may create a greater demand for space than the mere addition of infants. This finding is in accord with the belief that the demand for 3- and 4-bedroom houses may increase as the current baby crop grows older. In interpreting the data it should be kept in mind that the parents of a child aged 6 to 17 are likely to be older and to have more income than the parents of two infants so that too much reliance cannot be placed on the numerical values given in these examples.

[12] Families with one child 6 to 17 years old may, of course, have other, more mature children in the household or may be retaining space for older children who are away at college.

The space demand of school-age children is also registered among home owners who, of course, have more rooms than renters of corresponding household size and composition. Homeowners with one child between 6 and 17 have more space than homeowners with two or more children under 6.

When household size is augmented by the addition of other family units, unrelated or related to the head of the household (secondary or subfamilies), relatively large additional amounts of space are found. Unlike the case of children, where a simple cause and effect could be assumed, i.e., the addition of children caused parents to seek more space, doubling up may be either the *result* of the availability of extra space or the *reason for* larger dwelling units. The addition of a secondary family to a husband-wife primary family (renter) is associated with an extra 1.23 rooms, or a 31-percent increase in space. Households containing a subfamily have an extra 1.10 rooms, or 27.5 percent more space. In spite of the fact that secondary families are typically smaller than subfamilies they appear to use more space, probably because the greater need for privacy among unrelated adults requires more physical separation of household activities. Secondary families, doubtless, pay rent more often than subfamilies and therefore may demand more for their money.

The greater space requirements of adults can also be observed in data from the 1935–1936 budget studies. With income held constant, the average number of rooms occupied by two types of households nearly equivalent in size but not in composition differ markedly. The type III families [13] shown in table 35 were comprised of two adults and two children under 16, and type IV families consisted of either three adults, four adults, or three adults plus a child under 16. Despite the fact that a type IV family could not be larger and was frequently smaller than type III, it nearly always occupied more rooms.

TABLE **35.**—AVERAGE NUMBER OF ROOMS IN OCCUPIED DWELLING UNITS, BY TYPE OF FAMILY, BY INCOME, FOR FIVE EAST CENTRAL CITIES: 1935 TO 1936

Income	Type III family	Type IV family	Income	Type III family	Type IV family
$250 to $499	5.0	6.6	$1,750 to $1,999	5.6	5.9
$500 to $749	5.2	5.7	$2,000 to $2,249	6.1	5.7
$750 to $999	5.3	5.4	$2,250 to $2,499	5.8	6.2
$1,000 to $1,249	5.2	5.5	$2,500 to $2,999	6.3	6.4
$1,250 to $1,499	5.7	5.8	$3,000 and over	7.0	6.5
$1,500 to $1,749	5.5	6.1			

Source: U. S. Bureau of Labor Statistics, *Family Expenditures in Selected Cities*, 1935–36, Vol. I, Housing Bulletin No. 648, pp. 175, 176. Type III families contain 2 adults plus 2 children under 16; type IV families contain, alternatively, 3 adults, 4 adults, or 3 adults plus 1 child under 16.

[13] No serious loss of accuracy would result if these families had been designated as households in the original source.

The differential space requirements of young children and adults observed in the last two tables reflect the fact that it is "easier" to crowd children than adults. Indeed, our overcrowded dwelling units are made up of a disproportionate number of children. As we have seen in Chapter 4, high PPR ratios are mainly associated with large households. Large household size is due to the presence of large numbers of children rather than of large numbers of adults. Measures of overcrowding in the United States, which are higher in terms of persons than of households, are still higher for the child population. In the sample study of 1935–1936, the proportion of all ages living at densities higher than 1.00 was shown to be 26 percent (table 36). Fully 43 percent of all children under 15 years of age, but only 13 percent of all adults 45 years and older, were in this density group.

TABLE 36.—PERCENT OF PERSONS IN VARIOUS DENSITY GROUPS, BY AGE, FOR SELECTED URBAN PLACES: 1935 AND 1936

Persons-per-room ratio	All ages	Under 15 years	15 to 24 years	25 to 44 years	45 and over
More than 1.00	25.9	43.0	28.8	20.8	12.7
More than 1.50	9.2	17.4	10.1	6.4	3.5
2.00 or more	5.2	9.7	5.3	3.9	2.1

Source: U. S. Public Health Service, *Urban Housing and Crowding*, 1941, p. 24.

The life cycle in household composition

Enough has been shown thus far to demonstrate that, by a relatively small improvement in census data tabulation, an important advance could be made in housing market analysis. Estimates of the *number* of dwelling units likely to be sought could be supplemented by detail on size of dwelling unit. A life cycle pattern of the changing space requirements of common types of families, as Glick has done for other housing characteristics,[14] could be traced from fairly simple cross-tabulations reflecting space differentials among households of different composition at a given moment of time. The data in table 34 suggest, for example, that a newly married couple may seek about 3.5 rooms if they are renters and 5 rooms if they are owners. At the same time, the couple vacates 2 or more rooms in their parents' homes. If their parents reduce their space holdings, the net demand for space arising from a new household is smaller than the gross demand. Indeed, if the new couple had been formed from primary individuals, each having an average of about 2.5 rooms, over-all space requirements would be reduced. Similarly, the adjustments of housing space to new births, aging of children, death of a spouse, in- and out-migration of adults, etc., could be measured, yielding data that permit a finer analysis

[14] Paul Glick, "The Family Cycle," *American Sociological Review*, April 1947, pp. 164–174.

of aggregate housing demand. Even better would be information on the complete distributions from which the averages are derived.

Some aspects of the life cycle process in household composition can even now be derived from census data, though unfortunately without reference to space requirements. In both 1940 and 1950 all persons residing in dwelling units were tabulated by age and assigned to household status classes, i.e., head, wife of head, child of head, grandchild of head, parent of head, other relatives, and two nonrelative groups, lodgers and residential employees. These data partially summarize the life cycle of the individual, since nearly all people remain in the household population from birth to death but change their household status as they age.

An individual begins life in a household headed by his father (or to some extent in his grandparents' home) and remains in the status of a child until his early twenties, the most typical age of marriage. At this point, household status shifts to either head or wife of head; in many cases the new married couple doubles up with an existing household and appears in a variety of household status classes: child, other relative, lodger. During the next two decades children appear and grow up to repeat the cycle of the parents. As their own children leave, the couple remains as a husband-wife, 2-person household. With declining age-specific death rates, the interval of this phase of the life cycle has lengthened. The death of one spouse (generally the husband) causes, in a substantial number of cases, the household to go out of existence; in the majority of cases, however, there is merely a shift in status of the survivor from wife of head to head of household. Finally, increasing age forces an end to headship either by death or entry into a dependency status in other households or a shift from the household population to the nonhousehold population (i.e., to quasi-households).

The life cycle of household status is reflected in the varying proportions of the eight status classes into which each age group is divided. Thus, at age 20 to 24 about 18 percent of the household population were heads of households in 1950, an equal proportion were wives of heads, and 36 percent still had the status of children in their parents' households. In the age group 50 to 54 about 90 percent were either heads of households or wives of heads while only 1 percent were still considered "children" in the house of a parent (figure 10).

Thus, the age-specific headship rate, which will always remain strategic since it is a determinant of the number of households, is but one of a longer list of status rates covering all members of the household. Just as in the case of the headship rate, a characteristic pattern by age is marked out by other household status classes. These patterns, governed in large part by rigid social and biologic factors, are quite stable over time and even reasonably predictable. But since they are influenced by economic and cultural forces, there is no expectation that household status rates will remain completely static. Changing economic conditions leave their imprint, which can be clearly seen in a comparison of 1940 and 1950 data (figure 10). There are also discernible differences in the household status pattern of whites and nonwhites, as well as differences between urban and rural-nonfarm areas and among the various standard metropolitan areas.

FIGURE 10.—PERCENT OF EACH AGE GROUP OF THE NONFARM POPULATION IN SPECIFIED HOUSEHOLD STATUS CLASSES: 1950 and 1940

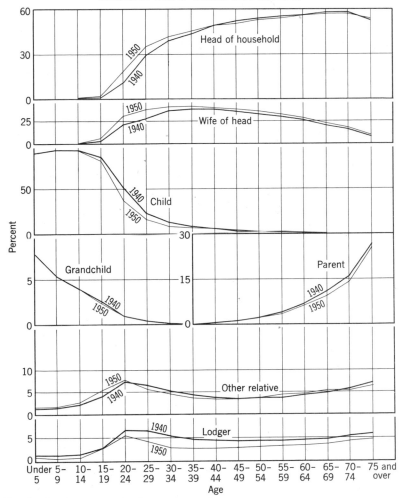

Note: Based on data in appendix table D–3.

Headship status by age, sex, marital status, and location

The three most important household status classes are heads, wives, and children, who constitute the biologic family. In 1950 they accounted for

30, 23, and 36 percent, respectively, of the nonfarm household population, leaving only 11 percent of the total in all other status classes combined. The basic age-specific headship structure has already been described and all that is necessary is the addition of some important details. It should be noted that whatever the date, 1890, 1940, or 1950, the essential contour of the headship rate pattern remains the same: a sharp rise at age of marriage, a slower rise through the middle years as more unmarried but mature people form households, and a small drop with old age as economic and physical resources decline.

A brief word concerning the nature of the household status data and their limitations is in order. In the first place, most of the data refer only to people residing in households. Persons living in quasi-households, including institutions, are omitted. Second, persons are classified only by their relationship to the head *with whom they reside* regardless of other consanguinary and marital ties. Thus, the child category will contain a mature married woman with children of her own as long as she resides in her parents' home and exclude an infant living with grandparents or other relatives. The number of persons classified as children will differ, therefore, from other tabulations of children derived from age distributions. Likewise, the number of husband-wife households falls short of the total number of married women living in households by excluding all married couples not living together with the husband as head, i.e., couples living as subfamilies or secondary families and all couples living apart from each other.[15]

Headship rates of course differ greatly by sex, with the male headship curve lying well above the curve for females at all ages (figure 11). In 1950, the peak headship rate occurred for men between 55 and 59 years of age and then dropped off rapidly. Decreasing employment opportunities and illness with advancing age increasingly limit the possibilities of maintaining separate establishments. In the sixth decade of life, more than 9 out of 10 men in the household population are listed as heads; after 75 the proportion is only 7 out of 10. The headship pattern for women is one which rises steadily with age because of increases in the proportion who become widowed; widows have a stronger propensity toward maintaining their own dwelling units than women of any other marital status.

---

[15] The 1940 and 1950 data differ in one important respect: the former are based on a complete count and the latter on a 20-percent sample. This difference may render less reliable historical comparison of the smaller cells. In addition, there are two minor changes in definition: (*a*) In 1940, the cut-off point for rooming houses was 10 lodgers and in 1950, 5. This change leads to a slight decrease in the total household population and to a decrease in the number of lodgers living in households. (*b*) In 1940, children of resident employees were classified as lodgers and in 1950, as resident employees. This change increases employees, decreases the number of lodgers, and explains the employee status of astonishingly young children in 1950.

FIGURE 11.—HEADSHIP RATES FOR THE NONFARM POPULATION, BY MARITAL STATUS AND SEX, 1950 AND 1940, AND BY SEX AND RESIDENCE, 1950

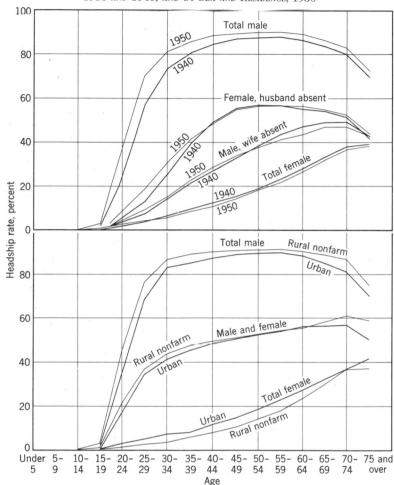

Source: Appendix tables D–1 and D–2.

Among "unmarried" (single, widowed, divorced, or separated) males, headship rates tend to remain low in comparison with married men. At age 50 to 54, for example, only 40 out of 100 unmarried men head establishments compared to 97 married men. There is undoubtedly a reluctance on the part of such men to take on the responsibility of operating an establishment. This is clearly seen in the fact that unmarried women, age for age, have higher headship rates than unmarried men. At age 25 to 29 there are twice as many unmarried women heading households as men, and, at age 50 to 54, 57 percent have achieved this household status compared to 38 percent of the males. The aspiration of most women for both

husband and home apparently makes the second goal more attractive whenever the first eludes them.

Between 1940 and 1950 the headship pattern for both sexes combined
changed slightly, rising among the younger age groups and falling in the
middle span as a result, primarily, of the greater frequency of marriage.
Since married men have such a pronounced tendency toward heading a
household, the effect of more marriages was to raise the headship rate for
men of all ages. For the same reason, the headship rate for women of 25
and over decreased. Only in the younger female age groups was a rise experienced, a rise entirely accounted for by the very sharp increase in headship
among youthful "unmarried" women. The tendency of young women not
yet married to maintain their own apartments is increasingly becoming an
American folkway made possible by jobs and greater social acceptance,
(Even so, only one out of every five "unmarried" women aged 25 to 29 ex-
ercised such independence in 1950.) No doubt this tendency was further
reinforced by the fact that many young women who were married but separated from husbands who were in the Armed Forces (hence included
among the "unmarried") sought private living arrangements. For "unmarried" women of 40 and over, headship rates declined over the decade.
Again, the observation repeatedly found in postwar housing market analyses that more and more widows cling to households of their own is not
to be seen in these data. Young "unmarried" men also increased their
headship rates but not as dramatically as was the case for women. Headship rates among older unmarried men tended to drop over the decade.

Urban-rural nonfarm differentials in headship rates (figure 11) result
from differences in customs and opportunities. Among persons living in
rural areas, the headship rate is higher for the younger age groups and
somewhat lower in middle age, a difference which parallels historical
changes. The reason is the same: a higher proportion of married people.
In the oldest ages, urban headship rates are below the rural, probably because there are more opportunities for entering quasi-households such as
boarding houses and institutions. A second consequence of a higher proportion of married people is also seen: higher headship rates among men
and lower headship rates for women. There are urban and rural differentials even within given marital status categories (not charted, but see appendix table D–2). In rural areas relatively more married men living with
their wives (married couples) have their own households than in urban
areas. Undoubtedly the shortage of housing in rural areas was less severe
than in urban areas and doubling up therefore less necessary.

Other types of household status

The propensity of women to appear in the role of wives of head varies
with age in a manner similar to the headship rate. The most important
difference is that the peak proportion is found at a relatively early age, i.e.,

in the 30 to 39 age group. From the age of 40 on, the proportion of women who are wives of heads declines. As death, divorce, and separation take their toll, the status of many women shifts from wife of head to head of household or (particularly in the more advanced ages) to some other household status or even leads to a withdrawal from private to quasi-households. Between 1940 and 1950 the proportion of wives increased at all ages, particularly for young women. The consequence of this shift was to reduce the number of women living with parents and the number of women heading their own households, which, it was seen, was the principal factor for the decline in the headship rates of the middle aged (figure 10).

Children, i.e., individuals who, regardless of age or marital status, live in a household headed by a parent, form the largest component of the household population and probably always have. Surprisingly, between 1940 and 1950, despite the rise in the birth rate, the proportion of persons classified as children of the household head declined (figure 10). What happened was a movement of young adults out of their parents' homes to set up their own, which more than offset the addition of infants and young children. The result of more young and fewer adult children was, of course, a marked lowering in the average age of children in households. In 1940, 18 percent were under 5 and 12 percent, 20 to 24 years of age; in 1950, the percentages at corresponding ages were 28 and 8 (appendix table D-3).

The proportion of children living with parents declines (with one exception) continuously as they grow older, achieve economic independence, and marry. The exception occurs in the first decade of life when, owing to the tendency of many young married couples to double up, an appreciable number of children dwell with their grandparents. As the subfamily becomes an independent household, the proportion of children increases to a peak at age 10 to 14. Thenceforth children normally become either heads or wives of heads. The complementary nature of this process is seen in the "wishbone" design formed by juxtaposing the curve for children against the curves for heads and wives (figure 10).

In 1950, about 11 percent of all persons 14 years and over living in the household of a parent were married (appendix table D-4). In 7 out of 10 cases their husbands or wives were also present; such couples form the largest component of all doubled-up married couples.

Grandchildren and parents trace out simple patterns, the former status declining and the latter rising continuously with age (figure 10). It is indicative of the wide variety of household patterns to find some people not far from 40 years of age still clinging to their grandparents' homes while at 30 to 34 some parents not only boast sons or daughters old enough, or at least confident enough, to head households of their own but have already doubled up with them. Probably the results in many such instances are due to the way in which headship is reported. As has been said, household status is dependent upon the particular person designated as the head, who then becomes the reference against whom all other members are classified.[16]

The tendency for very old people to double up with children appears surprisingly low and has even decreased since 1940. Only 256 out of 1,000 persons 75 years and older lived with children; nearly two-thirds lived in their own households as heads or wives. Independent living arrangements on the part of the aged seem to be part of an older tradition. Of central importance may be the geographical mobility of the population, which insures the separation of many parents and children. Doubling up among the old would doubtlessly be more widespread, economic factors aside, if children lived more often in the same locality as their parents, as is the case in more static societies.

More than three-quarters of all parents who doubled up with sons or daughters were widowed, widows outnumbering the widowers about 5 to 1. Fifteen percent of all doubled-up parents were married couples and constituted a significant fraction of all doubled-up married couples. About 6 percent of all parents were divorced or otherwise separated from a spouse.

In 1950, about 4 percent of the household population lived in households headed by a relative other than any of the categories specified above. A large proportion, almost 20 percent, of "other relatives" are sons- or daughters-in-law and are consequently found quite frequently in the 20-to-24-year age group. As subfamilies grow older and undouble, the importance of this household status class diminishes sharply and does not assume much importance again until old age. Over the decade the importance of this group declined somewhat except in the 15-to-19 age group. Early marriage often leads not to the exit of a child but to the acquisition of an in-law.

Persons in the lodger category do not necessarily live in lodging-houses as such but may merely share a dwelling unit headed by an individual not related to them. In other census classifications, lodgers in households appear as secondary families and secondary individuals. The age pattern in lodging rates closely resembles that of "other relatives." This resemblance may result from the fact that "other relatives" and household "lodgers" come from the same sector of the population who may elect either

---

[16]Consider a household containing a young married couple, their child, and the husband's mother. If the husband reports himself as head, the household consists of a male head, wife, child, and parent. If the mother is reported as head, the household consists of a female head, a child (son), grandchild, and an "other relative" (i.e., the daughter-in-law). Apart from the solemn provision that no woman can ever be considered a head if her husband lives with her, the Bureau of the Census has no rules for the determination of headship. The head is merely designated by the respondents, as practical a method, perhaps, as any other. It would be difficult to prescribe objective standards for headship. None of the concepts, e.g., chief breadwinner, owner or renter of the dwelling unit, oldest member, decision-maker, is completely satisfactory. In the overwhelming majority of instances, the person reported as head has most or all of these roles.

living arrangement depending upon their particular opportunities, i.e., the availability of relatives in the community. Often people may prefer to live with close friends rather than distant relatives. Not much can be said of the change in household lodging rates over the decade since the data have been affected by change in definition. Twenty-eight percent of the lodgers in 1950 were married persons of whom one-half formed couples and were therefore classifiable as secondary families.

Resident employees, the bulk of whom are servants, comprise a negligibly small fraction of the household population. In 1950 only 3 out of every 1,000 household population were thus classified (appendix table D–3). The current "servant problem" is plainly seen in the data; the number of live-in servants fell by more than half over the decade. Practically the entire group of resident employees are made up of women, particularly in the younger age groups. The shortage of domestics, however, has led to the more frequent employment of elderly female servants.

Doubled-up couples

The most commonly used index of doubling up is the proportion of married couples who do not have their own dwelling unit. Obviously, the concept of doubling could be extended to include family groups other than married couples and even further broadened to the point of including every adult not the head (or wife of head) of a household. Similarly, the measurement could be narrowed to refer only to married couples sharing someone else's dwelling unit and exclude all married couples living in quasi-households (hotels, lodginghouses, institutions, etc.) who are not literally doubled up.[17]

Adhering to the Bureau of the Census concept of doubling, i.e., married couples without own households, the incidence of doubling is analyzed by age in figure 12. It is clear that doubling up is subject to a fairly stable life cycle pattern. It is a common adjustment of the newly married; over one-fifth of the couples in the 15-to-24 age group (husband) fail to establish their own households. In middle age the incidence of doubling falls to extremely low levels with the lowest proportion, i.e., 3 percent, at age 55 to 59. Thenceforth, with advancing age, more and more couples surrender their independent status until, after 75, between 8 and 9 percent of married couples no longer have households of their own.

From 1940 to 1950 the incidence of doubling declined throughout the younger age groups (figure 12). Except for some increase in the doubling

---

[17] The difference resulting from these two definitions of doubling of married couples is quantitatively small. In 1950 there was less than one percentage point spread between the two proportions (in the nonfarm sector), which were 6.64 percent inclusive and 5.80 percent exclusive of married couples not living in households. See *1950 Census of Population*, Vol. II, *Characteristics of the Population*, Part 1, U. S. Summary, table 107, and Vol. IV, *Special Reports*, Part 2, Chapter D, Marital Status, tables 1 and 3.

FIGURE **12.**—PERCENT OF NONFARM MARRIED COUPLES WITHOUT OWN HOUSEHOLD,
BY AGE OF HUSBAND: 1950 AND 1940

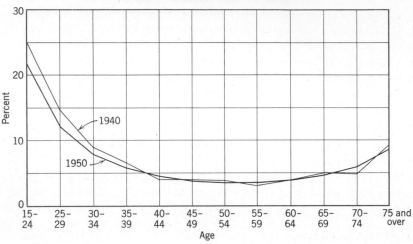

Source: Appendix table D–6.

rate at 70 to 74, hardly any changes were registered for married couples
over 40. The decreased doubling rate for younger married couples is
surprising in view of the fact that younger and younger people were getting
married, many while still in college. Good job opportunities for both
partners, veterans' military allowances and a high rate of geographic
mobility must have provided great incentives to the establishment of independent households.

In view of the decline in the doubling *rate* in the younger age group, it
can scarcely be said, as often it has been, that young married couples suffered exceptional hardship in the late postwar housing market. The large
increase in the *number* of young married couples attracted attention to their
plight, more so than in other years, notwithstanding the fact that their relative position had improved. Owing to the great increase in marriages,
very young doubled married couples in 1950 represented a larger proportion of all doubled-up couples than in the past (figure 13). The share of
older married couples (i.e., 55 and over) also increased, but solely because
of the changing age structure of the population. No change, it was seen,
occurred in the incidence of doubling among older couples.

FIGURE **13.**—PERCENT DISTRIBUTION OF NONFARM MARRIED COUPLES WITHOUT OWN
HOUSEHOLD, BY AGE OF HUSBAND: 1950 AND 1940

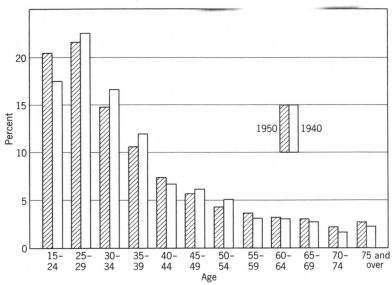

Source: Appendix table D–6.

A P P E N D I X   A

THE PERSONS-PER-ROOM RATIO:
DERIVATION OF CLASS INTERVALS
AND WEIGHTED AVERAGES

The persons-per-room ratio has so seldom been a subject for quantitative analysis that it is worthwhile to discuss some statistical problems associated with its use. First, there arises the question of selecting appropriate class intervals for the presentation of PPR ratio distributions. These class intervals must be fine enough for intensive analysis yet not so numerous as to be unmanageable. Second, since the PPR ratio is a proportion formed from two discrete, integral variables (size of dwelling unit and size of household) having only a limited number of values, the distribution of PPR ratios is discontinuous. Consequently, small differences in the choice of class limits may affect the interpretation of grouped data. Third, an analysis of density patterns cannot effectively be made without resort to an average PPR ratio, a measure used extensively throughout this volume. In its absence, every observation about the level of utilization and its change requires the support of cumbersome (and often misleading) household distributions. The derivation of accurate averages, however, depends upon a proper choice of weights, a point on which there has been more than a little confusion.

The published persons-per-room data in Volume I of the 1950 Housing Census are grouped into four class intervals: 0.75 persons per room or less; 0.76 to 1.00; 1.01 to 1.50; 1.51 or more.[1] In Volume II the class intervals are reduced to three. Neither median nor average PPR ratios are presented; all census reports on these data are given in the form of household distributions.

These published class intervals are clearly too broad for many analytic tasks. In 1950, over 60 percent of all occupied nonfarm households and nearly 70 percent of owner-occupied households were included in the lowest density group. Obviously, combining the majority of households into a single class sharply reduces the investigator's ability to explore very

---

[1] *1950 Census of Housing*, Vol. I, *General Characteristics*, Chapter 1, U. S. Summary, table 11; Vol. II, *Nonfarm Housing Characteristics*, Chapter 1, United States, tables 7, 9, and 10. Finer class intervals are, however, presented in 1940 Census publications.

deeply into utilization patterns.   Since the median value for both the aggregate and individual area distributions is located in the first open end class, an accurate measure of central tendency cannot even be computed from these data.

Both of these deficiencies were corrected by making maximum use of table 5 in Volume II of the Housing Census.   This table presents a complete cross-tabulation, or matrix, of the number of rooms in a dwelling unit and the number of occupants, each distributed into 10 classes.   When values are assigned to the open-end classes (10 or more persons and 10 or more rooms), a step discussed later in this appendix, it becomes possible to develop PPR ratio distributions for each tenure class to almost any degree of fineness.   The 10 x 10 matrix forms 100 cells each yielding a PPR ratio.   For example, all 4-person households living in a 2-room unit are living at PPR ratios of 2.00, in 3-room units at ratios of 1.25, in 4-room units at ratios of 1.00, and so forth.   Because of duplication, i.e., a 1-person household in 2 rooms gives the same PPR ratio as a 2-person household in 4-rooms and a 4-person household in 8 rooms, the 100 cells produce only 63 different PPR ratios.

The 10 x 10 tables yield rich quantities of data which have been extensively, but not completely, exploited in the text of this study.   Not only can a PPR ratio be assigned to each household size class, but by reading down the columns PPR ratios can be derived for each size of dwelling unit. Thus we can learn not only the spatial choices of households differing in size but also its inverse: what sizes of households do dwelling units of various size attract?   It is noted that tables A–1 and A–2 contain no empty cells, implying that there is a wide diversity of occupancy patterns.   One-person households, for instance, are found occupying every size of dwelling unit from the smallest to the largest; and no matter what the size of a dwelling unit, its occupants will range in size from households consisting of a single individual to those comprising 10 or more persons.   While spatial arrangements are highly diversified, the tables also disclose systematic patterns which provide the basis for two major generalizations found in the text: (a) the PPR ratio increases with household size, and (b) the PPR ratio decreases with size of dwelling unit.

These PPR ratio distributions for owners and renters are graphically illustrated in figures A–1 and A–2.   Neither distribution is continuous since PPR ratios are derived from discrete values; there is a zero frequency, for example, for PPR ratios ranging between 0.44 and 0.47, 0.63 and 0.67, 2.00 and 2.25.

A second consequence of crossing the household size distribution with the dwelling size distribution is that it becomes arithmetically impossible for households of some given size to attain certain specified values of the PPR ratio.   The most obvious example is that 1-person households can never form ratios higher than 1.00.   Likewise, a 6-person renter household can never be assigned a PPR ratio less than 0.50 since the maximum number of rooms assumed for renters is 12. The dashes in table 14 indicate which density groups are not mathematically available for each household size class.

TABLE **A–1.**—NUMBER OF ROOMS FOR NONFARM OCCUPIED DWELLING UNITS, BY HOUSEHOLD SIZE AND TENURE: 1950

Household size and tenure	Total	Number of rooms									
		1	2	3	4	5	6	7	8	9	10 or more
Owner-occupied dwelling units..	100.00	1.08	2.44	6.56	18.84	26.47	24.36	10.40	5.59	2.10	2.20
1 person............	7.21	0.42	0.65	1.09	1.49	1.52	1.07	0.46	0.29	0.10	0.12
2 persons...........	28.09	0.31	0.81	2.47	6.00	8.14	5.80	2.39	1.24	0.46	0.47
3 persons...........	22.95	0.14	0.41	1.32	4.69	6.69	5.61	2.19	1.10	0.39	0.41
4 persons...........	19.96	0.09	0.28	0.83	3.66	5.44	5.59	2.19	1.10	0.39	0.39
5 persons...........	11.36	0.05	0.14	0.41	1.64	2.70	3.41	1.53	0.84	0.32	0.32
6 persons...........	5.43	0.03	0.07	0.19	0.70	1.11	1.61	0.84	0.49	0.19	0.20
7 persons...........	2.54	0.02	0.04	0.11	0.32	0.46	0.69	0.42	0.25	0.11	0.12
8 persons...........	1.22	0.01	0.02	0.06	0.16	0.21	0.30	0.20	0.13	0.06	0.07
9 persons...........	0.63	...	0.01	0.04	0.09	0.11	0.14	0.09	0.07	0.04	0.04
10 persons or more...	0.65	0.01	0.01	0.04	0.09	0.09	0.14	0.09	0.08	0.04	0.06
Renter-occupied dwelling units..	100.00	4.90	13.46	25.38	25.77	16.88	8.97	2.63	1.17	0.42	0.39
1 person............	12.50	2.79	3.83	3.14	1.57	0.71	0.29	0.09	0.04	0.02	0.02
2 persons...........	30.57	1.36	5.39	10.17	7.13	4.04	1.70	0.44	0.20	0.07	0.07
3 persons...........	23.38	0.40	2.31	6.39	6.95	4.34	2.09	0.54	0.22	0.07	0.07
4 persons...........	17.07	0.18	1.05	3.28	5.60	3.82	2.12	0.60	0.25	0.09	0.08
5 persons...........	8.49	0.08	0.45	1.25	2.49	2.10	1.37	0.43	0.19	0.07	0.06
6 persons...........	3.96	0.04	0.21	0.55	1.03	0.97	0.70	0.26	0.12	0.04	0.04
7 persons...........	1.92	0.02	0.10	0.29	0.49	0.46	0.34	0.12	0.07	0.02	0.02
8 persons...........	0.99	0.01	0.06	0.15	0.25	0.22	0.17	0.07	0.04	0.01	0.01
9 persons...........	0.55	0.01	0.03	0.09	0.13	0.11	0.09	0.04	0.02	0.02	0.01
10 persons or more...	0.53	0.01	0.03	0.07	0.13	0.11	0.10	0.04	0.02	0.01	0.01
Percent of total rooms...........	100.00	1.27	6.98	19.74	26.75	21.91	13.94	4.79	2.44	0.96	1.21

Source: *1950 Census of Housing*, Vol. II, *Nonfarm Housing Characteristics*, Part 1, Chapter 1, United States, table A–5.

FIGURE **A–1.**—PERCENT DISTRIBUTION OF HOUSEHOLDS IN OWNER-OCCUPIED NONFARM DWELLING UNITS, BY PERSONS-PER-ROOM RATIO: 1950

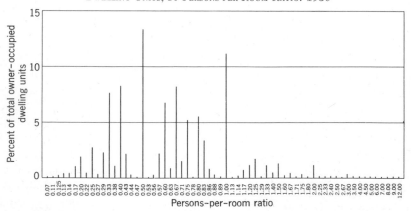

Source: Table A–2.

TABLE A-2.—PERCENT DISTRIBUTION OF NONFARM HOUSEHOLDS AND PERSONS BY TENURE, BY DETAILED PERSONS-PER-ROOM RATIO: 1950

Persons-per-room ratio	Total		Owner		Renter	
	Households	Persons	Households	Persons	Households	Persons
Total....................	100.00	100.00	100.00	100.00	100.00	100.00
0.067........................	0.07	0.02	0.12	0.04	...	...
0.083........................	0.01	...	...	...	0.02	0.01
0.111........................	0.06	0.02	0.10	0.03	0.02	0.01
0.125........................	0.17	0.05	0.29	0.08	0.05	0.01
0.133........................	0.25	0.15	0.47	0.28	...	...
0.143........................	0.29	0.09	0.46	0.14	0.09	0.03
0.167........................	0.73	0.23	1.07	0.31	0.36	0.14
0.200........................	1.36	0.55	1.93	0.81	0.71	0.23
0.222........................	0.27	0.17	0.46	0.27	0.07	0.04
0.250........................	2.31	0.95	2.73	1.16	1.84	0.70
0.267........................	0.21	0.25	0.39	0.45	...	...
0.286........................	1.47	0.90	2.39	1.39	0.44	0.28
0.333........................	6.37	3.51	7.60	4.52	4.99	2.27
0.375........................	0.69	0.63	1.10	0.97	0.22	0.22
0.400........................	6.32	3.99	8.34	5.11	4.04	2.60
0.417........................	0.03	0.04	...	...	0.06	0.10
0.429........................	1.41	1.30	2.19	1.92	0.54	0.52
0.444........................	0.25	0.30	0.39	0.45	0.09	0.12
0.467........................	0.06	0.14	0.12	0.25	...	...
0.500........................	13.35	9.14	13.36	9.90	13.34	8.22
0.533........................	0.03	0.08	0.07	0.15	...	...
0.556........................	0.20	0.30	0.32	0.46	0.07	0.11
0.571........................	1.44	1.76	2.19	2.56	0.60	0.77
0.583........................	0.01	0.02	...	...	0.02	0.05
0.600........................	5.60	5.17	6.73	5.97	4.34	4.18
0.625........................	0.53	0.82	0.84	1.22	0.19	0.31
0.667........................	10.18	8.79	8.25	8.32	12.35	9.38
0.714........................	1.01	1.55	1.53	2.24	0.43	0.69
0.750........................	6.07	5.86	5.17	4.96	7.08	6.96
0.778........................	0.07	0.14	0.11	0.22	0.02	0.05
0.800........................	4.70	5.81	5.49	6.55	3.82	4.91
0.833........................	2.45	3.73	3.41	4.98	1.37	2.19
0.857........................	0.57	1.04	0.84	1.48	0.26	0.50
0.875........................	0.17	0.35	0.25	0.52	0.07	0.15
0.889........................	0.04	0.09	0.06	0.14	0.01	0.03
1.000........................	16.78	18.02	11.11	14.07	23.16	22.90
1.125........................	0.04	0.12	0.07	0.18	0.02	0.05
1.143........................	0.14	0.34	0.20	0.46	0.07	0.18
1.167........................	0.52	1.12	0.69	1.40	0.34	0.76
1.200........................	1.05	1.92	1.11	1.95	0.97	1.87
1.250........................	2.04	3.11	1.64	2.40	2.49	4.00
1.286........................	0.07	0.19	0.09	0.25	0.04	0.12
1.333........................	2.24	3.09	1.16	1.80	3.46	4.70
1.400........................	0.46	0.98	0.46	0.93	0.46	1.04
1.500........................	2.33	3.27	1.33	2.22	3.45	4.57
1.600........................	0.21	0.52	0.21	0.49	0.22	0.57
1.667........................	0.80	1.22	0.41	0.60	1.25	2.00
1.714........................	0.07	0.25	0.09	0.32	0.04	0.17
1.750........................	0.40	0.85	0.32	0.64	0.49	1.11
1.800........................	0.11	0.30	0.11	0.28	0.11	0.33
2.000........................	2.12	2.86	1.07	1.69	3.30	4.30
2.250........................	0.11	0.31	0.09	0.25	0.13	0.39
2.333........................	0.19	0.42	0.11	0.23	0.29	0.64
2.400........................	0.10	0.38	0.09	0.33	0.11	0.44
2.500........................	0.29	0.44	0.14	0.20	0.45	0.73
2.667........................	0.11	0.26	0.06	0.15	0.15	0.40
3.000........................	0.57	1.06	0.34	0.67	0.83	1.52
3.500........................	0.07	0.15	0.04	0.08	0.10	0.23
4.000........................	0.23	0.46	0.15	0.29	0.31	0.66
4.500........................	0.02	0.06	0.01	0.03	0.03	0.10
5.000........................	0.06	0.10	0.05	0.07	0.08	0.13
6.000........................	0.05	0.13	0.04	0.09	0.07	0.18
7.000........................	0.02	0.03	0.02	0.03	0.02	0.04
8.000........................	0.01	0.02	0.01	0.02	0.01	0.03
9.000........................	0.01	0.01	...	0.01	0.01	0.02
12.000........................	0.01	0.02	0.01	0.02	0.01	0.03

Note: Households reporting number of rooms: Total, 35,384,010; owner, 18,730,850; and renter, 16,653,160. Persons in households reporting number of rooms: Total, 115,938,170; owner, 64,101,880; and renter, 51,836,290.

Source: *1950 Census of Housing*, Vol. II, *Nonfarm Housing Characteristics*, Part 1, Chapter 1, United States, table A-5, p. 7.

FIGURE **A–2.**—PERCENT DISTRIBUTION OF HOUSEHOLDS IN RENTER-OCCUPIED NONFARM
DWELLING UNITS, BY PERSONS-PER-ROOM RATIO: 1950

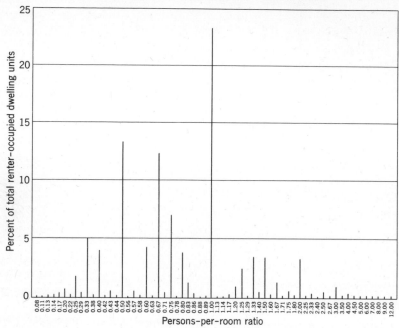

Source: Table A–2.

Furthermore, the distributions of PPR ratios are far from normal; the concentrations at certain values, such as 0.33, 0.50, 1.00, are much greater than at the PPR ratio values immediately adjacent to them.

Obviously, 63 individual PPR ratios are much too numerous for purposes of discussion. The data were therefore condensed into 8 groups: 0.17 or less, 0.18–0.33, 0.34–0.50, 0.51–0.75, 0.76–1.00, 1.01–1.50, 1.51–2.00, 2.01 or more. These class limits permit full comparison with published 1940 and 1950 Census density data, but at the same time afford considerably more detail. Had not the need to make comparison with published data been so overriding, good statistical practice would have dictated a somewhat different grouping pattern. Too many of the selected class limits correspond to concentration points in the original distribution. Thus, nearly 23 percent of renter households are found to have a PPR ratio of exactly 1.00. A significant though lesser degree of concentration is found at 0.50, 0.67, 0.75, etc. (figure A–2). It is no longer a matter of indifference, as is often the case in dealing with continuous distributions, whether the PPR ratio of 1.00 falls at the beginning or end of a class group. An alteration in the selected class limits as small as 0.01 would affect the classification of 40 to 50 percent of the household population (table A–3). It would therefore have been better to select as class limits PPR ratios having zero or very low frequencies. The need to adapt to present and past census data, however, necessitated the use of more customary class limits, even at the expense of statistical finesse. Nevertheless, it would be advisable for students of housing space standards to make their language more exact; a maximum space standard for American households of 1.00 is appreciably different from a standard of 0.99.

TABLE **A–3.**—EFFECT OF SLIGHT CHANGE IN CLASS LIMITS ON DISTRIBUTION OF NONFARM HOUSEHOLD POPULATION, BY PERSONS-PER-ROOM RATIO: 1950

Persons-per-room ratio	Percent	Persons-per-room ratio	Percent
0–0.16	0.34	0–0.17	0.57
0.17–0.32	3.31	0.18–0.33	6.33
0.33–0.49	9.65	0.34–0.50	15.54
0.50–0.74	27.63	0.51–0.75	24.35
0.75–0.99	17.04	0.76–1.00	29.20
1.00–1.49	28.89	1.01–1.50	14.14
1.50–1.99	6.42	1.51–2.00	6.01
2.00 or more	6.71	2.01 or more	3.85
1.00 or more	42.02	1.01 or more	24.00
1.50 or more	13.13	1.51 or more	9.86

Source: Table A–2.

The derivation of weighted average PPR ratios

The 10 x 10 tables also allow the derivation of average PPR ratios for all households, for households of any given size, and for dwelling units of any given size. Moreover, these averages can be readily weighted by an appropriate set of weights, namely, numbers of people rather than numbers of households. Because nearly all published material on PPR ratios are presented in terms of numbers of households, it is not always realized that the PPR ratio refers to the space standards of individuals, not families or households. While PPR ratio distributions by households are useful for such purposes as establishing density patterns, they cannot, because of variations in household size, serve as a basis for aggregate or average PPR ratios nor for changes in these over time. For example, the correct average PPR ratio for a community consisting of three households (a 1-person household living in 2 rooms, PPR ratio = 0.50, a 3-person household living in 4 rooms, PPR ratio = 0.75; and an 8-person household living in 8 rooms, PPR ratio = 1.00) is not 0.75 but 0.86. The community average is computed by dividing the total household population (12) by the total number of occupied rooms (14). It would be incorrect to reason that the average PPR ratio is equal to the sum of the individual PPR ratios (2.25) divided by the number of households (3). The latter average is erroneous because the weights employed were households rather than population.

Failure to make the distinction between population and household weights leads to another type of error, one already alluded to in the text. Because larger households have higher PPR ratios, any distribution of PPR ratios by number of households understates the amount of overcrowding and overstates the prevalence of favorable density situations, both looked at from the point of view of *the individuals involved.* To say that only 3 percent of all households live at densities higher than 1.50 is to overlook the fact that this group may contain 6 or more percent of the population, since a disproportionate number of large households are involved. Likewise, if 15 percent of all households lived at densities of 0.33 or less, but all of these were 1-person households, such a favorable space standard would be enjoyed by less than 5 percent of the population.

The utility of the 10 x 10 table is further enhanced by providing a convenient source of both total population and total room counts by tenure. Obviously, the total population living in 3-room units equals the number of 1-person households living in such units plus twice the number of 2-person households plus 3 times the number of 3-person households, and so on. Likewise, the total number of rooms in 3-room occupied units is 3 times the number of households (occupied dwelling units) four times the number of households in 4-room units, etc.

Two questions required settlement before proceeding with the above estimates: (*a*) the treatment of nonreporting households, i.e., households who did not report room counts and (*b*) an estimate of average household size and average number of rooms for the open-end classes, households of 10 or more persons and occupied dwelling units with 10 or more rooms. The problem of nonreporting cases was resolved by distributing them in accordance with the density patterns of the reporting cases. That is, the percentage distributions derived from reporting households was applied to all households including the nonreporting.

The assignment of average values to the open-end classes was handled partly by estimation and partly by assumption. The average size of households containing 10 or more people was estimated by subtracting from total household population the number of persons contained in households of 1 to 9 persons and subtracting from the total number of households the number of households accounted for by the same nine household size classes. The two residuals yield a quotient of 12.3 persons per household of 10 or more persons; the decimal place was dropped and 12 persons adopted as the average for both owners and renters, there being no firm basis for drawing a distinction between the two tenure classes.

The average number of rooms in occupied dwelling units containing 10 or more rooms was arbitrarily assumed to be 12 for renters and, because of the very large size of many single-family homes, 15 for owners. Since the open-end class is relatively small, even a poor guess cannot lead to very wide margins of error. In table A–4, average PPR ratios for owner households were recomputed on the assumption that the true averages were as low as 12 or as high as 20 rooms. The differences in the results are quite negligible for the aggregate PPR ratios (0.01); the largest relative error involved amounts to 6.5 percent in the estimate of the PPR ratio of the largest sized households.

TABLE A-4.—PERSONS-PER-ROOM RATIO BY HOUSEHOLD SIZE—EFFECT OF VARIOUS ASSUMED AVERAGES FOR OPEN-END CLASS OF ROOMS SIZE DISTRIBUTION, FOR NONFARM OWNER-OCCUPIED DWELLING UNITS: 1950

Household size	Persons-per-room ratio if true average equals--			Percent error[1] in assuming 15-room average if true average equals--	
	12 rooms	15 rooms	20 rooms	12 rooms	20 rooms
Total....................	0.63	0.62	0.61	-1.2	+2.0
1 person........................	0.22	0.22	0.21	-1.1	+1.8
2 persons.......................	0.39	0.38	0.38	-1.0	+1.6
3 persons.......................	0.56	0.55	0.54	-1.0	+1.7
4 persons.......................	0.72	0.71	0.70	-1.0	+1.7
5 persons.......................	0.86	0.85	0.83	-1.4	+2.4
6 persons.......................	1.00	0.98	0.95	-1.8	+3.1
7 persons.......................	1.14	1.12	1.07	-2.3	+3.9
8 persons.......................	1.30	1.27	1.22	-2.6	+4.3
9 persons.......................	1.46	1.42	1.35	-3.0	+5.0
10 persons or more..............	1.89	1.82	1.71	-3.9	+6.5

[1] Percentage errors are computed from unrounded data.

Source: *1950 Census of Housing*, Vol. II, *Nonfarm Housing Characteristics*, Part 1, Chapter 1, United States, table A-5.

How valid is this technique, i.e., the use of a cross-classification by size of household and size of dwelling unit as a source for PPR ratios? One check, at least as far as the aggregate results are concerned, is to regroup the derived PPR ratios into the same class intervals found in published census tables and examine the differences. In table A-5 such a comparison shows that divergences between the estimated and published density groupings tend to be gratifyingly small (and statistically insignificant).

TABLE A-5.—ESTIMATED AND PUBLISHED DISTRIBUTIONS OF NONFARM HOUSEHOLDS, BY PERSONS PER ROOM

Persons-per-room ratio	Total		Owner		Renter	
	Estimated	Published	Estimated	Published	Estimated	Published
0.75 or less.............	60.8	60.6	68.6	68.5	52.0	51.5
0.76 to 1.00.............	24.8	24.7	21.3	21.3	28.7	28.6
1.01 to 1.50.............	8.9	9.1	6.8	6.9	11.3	11.7
1.51 or more.............	5.6	5.6	3.4	3.3	8.0	8.3

Source: *1950 Census of Housing*, Vol. I, *General Characteristics*, Part 1, U. S. Summary, table 11, p. 8; table A-2.

Computation of PPR ratios by income, rent, and value

The cross-tabulations of dwelling units presented in the census reports *(1950 Census of Housing,* Vol. II, *Nonfarm Housing Characteristics)* have proven highly useful in the determination of persons-per-room ratios by various household or dwelling unit characteristics.

Volume II of the 1950 Housing Census includes, in table A-5, a cross-tabulation of dwelling units by number of rooms and by income of the household.[2]   From this table the average number of rooms per dwelling unit is computed for each income class.   From table A–7 in the same volume the average number of persons per household in each income class (i.e., the same households shown in the income distribution in table A–5) is computed.[3]   The persons-per-room ratio for an income class is then the ratio of average number of persons to average number of rooms.   Persons not reporting income do not, of course, enter into this ratio, while persons in households which reported income but did not report number of rooms do.   The implicit assumption is simply that the density ratios of persons in the relatively few households that did not report rooms were not appreciably different from those of other persons.

The computation of PPR ratios by rent and value [4] classes was carried out in precisely the manner indicated above for income groups.   From tables A–1 and A–2 of Volume II, the average number of persons per household by value of home and by contract monthly rent, respectively, was derived.   The average number of rooms per dwelling unit by these attributes was computed from table A–5.   In no case were the averages assumed for the open-end classes considered to be crucial in accounting for variations in density ratios.

Standardization for changes in household size and tenure

In Chapter 3 reference is made to the standardization of density changes from 1940 to 1950 to determine the separate and combined effects of the changing household size distribution and the changing tenure ratio.   What difference would it make if in 1950 households were distributed by size and tenure as they were in 1940 but maintained their 1950 per capita space standards?   The answers were supplied in the text, but some statement of method is necessary.

In standardizing for the change in household size the distribution of households by size must be transformed to a distribution of population by household size.   The reason for this transformation is the need to weight persons-per-room ratios by population rather than by households.   In order to determine the over-all density of a standardized distribution of persons in households of varying size, the number of persons in each household size class was divided by the 1950 PPR ratio derived for that household size, yielding the number of occupied rooms.   The computations performed for each size class were summed to give the total number of rooms occu-

---

[2] Reported income is limited to income of the primary family or primary individual in the household.

[3] Since the open-end class for the distribution by number of persons is "7 or more," an average was estimated from the more detailed distribution in table A–5.

[4] Value of home refers only to owner-occupied dwelling units "in one unit structures" and located on "one-unit properties."   Thus PPR ratios by value do not necessarily apply to all owner-occupied dwelling units.

pied, which in combination with the total number of persons, yields the over-all PPR ratio.

Similarly, in standardizing for the changing tenure ratio, the conventional tenure ratio in terms of households was transformed to a tenure ratio in terms of population. The difference between these two measures, however, is not very great.

A slight association exists between the shift in tenure that took place and the change in the household size distribution. Very small and very large households changed to owner-occupancy to a lesser extent than did those of more average size. The effect of tenure change on density, therefore, is not completely free of the effect of changing household size. This interaction accounts for the fact that the combined effect of tenure and household size change is less than the sum of the two components.

A P P E N D I X   B

RENT INCREASED OVER THE DECADE
—BUT HOW MUCH?

The Bureau of Labor Statistics rent index as a measure of the changing cost of housing space was rejected for two reasons: (*a*) its limited coverage and (*b*) its inadequacy (with respect to the questions raised in Chapter 5) as a reflector of the changing cost of housing space to the average consumer. The first deficiency needs no further explanation, but it is worthwhile to discuss the statistical evidence for the second. Maisel has already pointed out the wide gap between rent changes measured by the Bureau of Labor Statistics and those obtained from Bureau of the Census data.[1] To use New York City as an example, BLS data indicate a 6 percent rent increase from April 1940 to roughly April 1950. The increase in average contract rent for the entire New York City rental inventory was 19 percent or over 3 times as much. Maisel also listed some of the factors which explain the divergences between the two measures of rent change. These factors largely involve changes in the composition of the inventory as new units come in at high rents and relatively low rent units disappear from the rental inventory because of demolition and tenure shift. The BLS index is designed to measure price change for an identical sample and tries to exclude the effect on average rent levels caused by changing composition.

Many people have gained the impression that new construction is the crucial element in any reconciliation of the Bureau of the Census and BLS measures of rent change and that, by and large, the BLS index comes reasonably close to measuring the rent changes of dwelling units built before 1940, that is, both the changing cost of shelter to tenants living in structures existing before rent control and the gross income of landlords after allowance for the filling of vacancies is described reasonably well by the BLS index.

The contrary is true. Analysis of census rent data (table B–1) has produced one interesting observation: the decade rise in median rents of the inventory already standing in 1940 was nearly as much as for the entire inventory. Hence the sizable increases in average or median rent over

[1] Sherman J. Maisel, "Have We Underestimated the Increase in Shelter Rent?" *Journal of Political Economy*, April 1949.

the decade were not primarily accounted for by new construction.   The increase in median rent in New York City of structures built before 1940 was 14.6 percent compared to the 15.6 percent increase in the median for all units.   The experience for other cities (table B–1) varies, but one generalization holds: the increase in the rents of the pre-rent control inventory lies very much closer to the over-all increase than to the change indicated by BLS.   In fact, in a number of cities, the rent of the older inventory rose more than the rent of the entire inventory.

TABLE **B–1.**—MEDIAN RENT, 1950 AND 1940, AND BY YEAR BUILT, 1950, FOR 31 CITIES

City	Median rent (dollars)				Col. 2 as percent of col. 1	Percent increase		
	1950			1940, total		Rent of all units, 1940 to 1950 (cols. 1 and 4)	Rent of 1940 inventory (cols. 3 and 4)	BLS rent index, 1940 to 1950
	Total	Units built 1945 or later	Units built 1939 or earlier					
	(1)	(2)	(3)	(4)	(5)	(6)	(7)	(8)
Baltimore, Md............	40.30	71.96	38.54	23.60	178.6	70.8	63.3	15.5
Birmingham, Ala.........	22.47	51.91	18.99	12.41	231.0	81.1	53.0	(¹)
Boston, Mass.............	35.35	47.57	35.12	28.41	134.6	24.4	23.6	18.4
Buffalo, N. Y.............	32.09	54.25	31.87	25.20	169.1	27.3	26.5	18.4
Chicago, Ill..............	44.04	60.64	44.26	31.51	137.7	39.8	40.5	31.1
Cincinnati, Ohio........	29.77	77.77	28.22	19.24	261.2	54.7	46.7	13.5
Cleveland, Ohio.........	34.92	48.53	34.97	25.35	139.0	37.8	37.9	19.5
Denver, Colo............	38.52	81.24	36.93	23.67	210.9	62.7	56.0	18.1
Detroit, Mich............	43.19	81.08	43.65	32.77	187.7	31.8	33.2	20.3
Houston, Texas..........	44.82	54.12	44.87	22.35	120.7	100.5	100.8	33.9
Indianapolis, Ind.......	38.84	80.43	37.97	21.28	207.1	82.5	78.4	22.6
Jacksonville, Fla.......	34.39	62.72	34.33	14.95	182.4	130.0	129.6	38.4
Kansas City, Mo.........	39.06	69.31	39.04	22.70	177.4	72.1	40.0	23.5
Los Angeles, Calif......	41.30	75.45	39.39	27.83	182.7	48.4	41.5	20.0
Memphis, Tenn...........	29.84	60.77	25.84	13.08	203.7	128.1	97.6	25.9
Milwaukee, Wis..........	43.37	52.82	43.35	29.66	121.8	46.2	46.2	31.7
Minneapolis, Minn......	38.55	48.99	38.83	27.70	127.1	39.2	40.2	24.6
Mobile, Ala.............	27.80	35.56	22.82	12.06	127.9	130.5	89.2	20.0
New Orleans, La.........	24.22	41.30	23.87	15.38	170.5	57.5	55.2	12.3
New York, N. Y..........	42.50	78.07	42.08	36.71	183.7	15.8	14.6	6.1
Norfolk, Va.............	35.83	75.99	30.83	18.06	212.1	98.4	70.7	15.8
Philadelphia, Pa........	36.18	78.78	35.90	25.64	217.7	41.1	40.0	18.1
Pittsburgh, Pa..........	35.74	91.21	35.30	24.62	255.2	45.2	43.4	15.9
Portland, Oreg..........	37.74	79.16	37.01	20.14	209.8	87.4	83.8	22.3
Richmond, Va............	28.84	71.61	27.75	18.01	248.3	60.1	54.1	11.9
St Louis, Mo............	28.50	(²)	28.58	20.13	...	41.6	42.0	20.0
San Francisco, Calif....	40.23	82.83	40.41	30.13	205.9	33.5	34.1	13.2
Savannah, Ga............	20.83	58.51	16.73	11.17	280.9	86.5	49.8	15.7
Scranton, Pa............	28.64	³43.27	29.04	22.26	151.1	28.7	30.5	14.4
Seattle, Wash...........	39.28	77.06	39.79	22.25	196.2	76.5	78.8	18.4
Washington, D. C........	53.72	70.93	51.94	41.42	132.0	29.7	25.4	6.6
Average.................	...	...	...	...	...	61.0	53.8	20.1

¹ Not available.
² Class containing median value is "$100 or more."
³ Median based on only 70 units.

Source: *1950 Census of Housing*, Vol. I, *General Characteristics*, table 31, and Vol. II, *Nonfarm Housing Characteristics*, table B–2; *1940 Census of Housing*, Vol. II, *General Characteristics*, Part 1, table 86.   BLS rent index computed from monthly dates closest to April 1950 and 1940; the monthly data (old series) were provided by the N. Y. Regional Office of the Bureau of Labor Statistics.

A similar picture can be developed for the total nonfarm rental inventory. In 1940, median rent was $21.41 and in 1950, $35.50.   Over the decade some 2½ million new rental units (equal to 15 percent of the 1940 rental inventory) were built at rent levels considerably above the current averages. But it is clear that new construction did not play a statistically important role in the rise in rent over the decade; had there been *no new construction of rental units*, the median rent in 1950 would have been very nearly the same, i.e., $34.26 compared to $35.50, even without allowance for the greater demand for existing houses that would have ensued.

For the 30 or so cities surveyed, the average (unweighted) increase in the BLS index was 20 percent compared to a 54-percent (unweighted average) increase in rents for the 1940 rental stock. The relationship between the two rent changes varied greatly from city to city, however, and only a loose relationship was observable.[2] It may be concluded that the BLS index does not serve as a reliable first approximation to the over-all rent change of even the older rental inventory. Cities in which the BLS index changed by nearly equal amounts varied greatly in over-all rent change, and some cities with roughly equal over-all rent change varied widely in the movement of its BLS index.

How can the differences in the two rent measures, the BLS index and the census medians, be explained? Granted that both measures successfully accomplished the tasks they were designed to fulfill, the divergence is reconcilable by the following factors:

1. The BLS samples only those units occupied by moderate income families. The percentage rent change in the nonsampled population may have been greater than for the sampled population.

2. The BLS index does not reflect the increase in rents arising from increased services. It is known that 1950 contract rents included payment for services and facilities, such as furniture, light, water, and refrigeration, to a greater degree than in earlier years.[3]

3. Many changes occurred in the composition of the rental inventory (apart from units built since 1940): (*a*) Demolition (or other loss) of units will raise or lower the average of the surviving units depending on whether the rent level of the nonsurvivors is below or above the existing average. It is probable that demolitions were concentrated among the cheaper units and tended to have an upward pull on the average. (*b*) Conversions will probably raise the average since they are motivated by a desire to increase the total rent payment for a given amount of space. Conversions will not, however, invariably raise average rent even if the rent of the newly converted units is higher than the prevailing average. For example, given an inventory of, say, 10 units with an average rent of $40, the splitting of one $80 unit into two $55 units will cause the average rent in the community

---

[2] A Spearman coefficient of correlation of 0.40 was derived when both rent changes were ranked against each other.

[3] Louis Winnick, "Long-Run Changes in the Valuation of Real Estate by Gross Rents," *The Appraisal Journal*, October 1952, pp. 490–491. Gross rent as used in this study is equivalent to census contract rent.

to fall although both the individual landlord's income and the community's aggregate rent payments rise.   To elevate the average, the net difference between the rent of the old unit and the total rent of the new units, divided by the increase in units must exceed the prevailing average.   Thus, if the $80 dwelling unit is subdivided into two units, the combined rent of the latter must total more than $120 if the prevailing $40 average rent is to rise.   Likewise, with a prevailing average of $40, the splitting of a $15 unit into two $30 units will cause the community's average rent to rise despite the fact that the rents of the newly added units are below the prevailing average.[4]

How do conversions affect median rents?   It all depends upon which half of the distribution the old unit came from and to which half the new units go.   With a prevailing median of $35, the breakup of a $50 unit into two $30 units will cause the median to fall; if into two $40 units, the median will rise; if into one $40 unit and one $30 unit, the median will also drop slightly.

Studies of conversions are quite scarce and the few existing ones do not give information on the change in total rent for a given amount of dwelling space.   While one cannot be certain, the likelihood is great that conversions have been an important factor in the rise in average rents over the decade.   After all, a large number of all conversions resulted from the fact that owners could lease the added units at economic rents which were very much above ceiling rents.   It is highly improbable that very many owners would have bothered with conversions if they could not have obtained a rental above the existing median ($21 in 1940 and $35 in 1950). There are cases in New York City where owners have obtained 50 to 80 percent more rent for a converted basement than for substantially better and larger units in the rest of the structure.   (c) Tenure shifts.   It is difficult to state conclusively whether the shift to home ownership of rental dwelling units tended to raise over-all average rent, although the evidence points in that direction.   The houses most affected by tenure shifts were single-family detached.   In 1940, the median rent of rented single-family detached units was considerably below the median rent of all rental units. Even, therefore, if all rented single-family houses had shifted tenure, the effect would be an increase in the median rent of the entire rental inven-

---

[4] Increase in aggregate rent $= 2\ (\$30) - \$15 = \$45$
   Increase in units $= 1$
   Aggregate rent $= \$445$
   Aggregate units $= 11$
   Average rent $= \$40.45$

If a unit is added without affecting any existing units, average rents will rise or fall depending upon whether the added unit rents for more or less than the prevailing average.   The rule holds for both positive and negative conversion as long as both numerator and denominator have the same sign, i.e., the conversion of a dwelling unit to, say, nonresidential use will cause average rents to rise if the rent of the given unit was below the prevailing average and vice versa.

tory.   Actually, between 1940 and 1950 the median rent of single-family houses remaining in the rental inventory rose by half as much again as the over-all median, establishing a presumption that it was the relatively cheap single-family houses which moved to the home ownership market and thus tended to produce an even greater upward pull on average rent.   Or, put differently, it was worthwhile for landlords to place on the rental market only those 1-family houses which could command a relatively high rent.

TABLE **B–2.**—MEDIAN CONTRACT RENT, 1940, AND BY YEAR BUILT, FOR NONFARM RENTER-OCCUPIED DWELLING UNITS, 1950

(In dollars)

Year built	1950	1940
Total..................................	35.50	21.41
After 1940...............................	42.75	...
1940 to 1944...........................	37.62	...
1945 to 1950...........................	51.40	...
Before 1940.............................	34.26	...

Source: *1950 Census of Housing*, Vol. I, *General Characteristics*, Part 1, U. S. Summary, table 14, and Vol. II, *Nonfarm Housing Characteristics*, Part 1, Chapter 1, United States, table A–2; *1940 Census of Housing*, Vol. II, *General Characteristics*, Part 1, U. S. Summary, table 14.

APPENDIX C

SUMMARY OF RESULTS OF THE
MULTIPLE CORRELATION PROBLEM IN CHAPTER 5

The variables selected for study are:

X_1-Percentage change in PPR ratio (renters), 1940 to 1950
X_2-Percentage change in contract rent per room (renters), 1940 to 1950
X_3-Percentage change in household size (renters), 1940 to 1950
X_4-Percentage change in median income of the experienced labor force, 1940 to 1950

The data (given in table C–1) relate to 89 cities with a population of 100,000 or more in 1950.
   The equation of multiple regression:

$$X_1 = 4.79\% + 0.073\ X_2 + 0.395\ X_3 - 0.045\ X_4$$

On the assumption of normal sampling distributions, the net regression coefficients are each statistically significant at the 0.01 level. That is, if the true values of the coefficients are zero, random sampling variability could lead to the computed coefficient less than 1 time out of 100.
   The coefficient of multiple correlation equals 0.479 and is significant at the 0.01 confidence level.
   The coefficients of partial (or net) correlation are:

$r_{12.34} = +0.446$	$r_{23.14} = -0.379$
$r_{13.24} = +0.312$	$r_{24.13} = +0.585$
$r_{14.23} = -0.335$	$r_{34.12} = +0.272$

The primary subscripts, i.e., those to the left of the decimal point, indicate the two variables, the correlation of which is measured and the secondary subscripts, to the right, indicate variables whose effect has been taken into account. Thus, $r_{12.34}$ shows that a correlation coefficient of 0.446 is obtained between changes in PPR ratios (X_1) and changes in rent (X_2), after all the influence of changes in household size (X_3) and income (X_4) upon either X_1 or X_2 has been eliminated. Similar interpretations can be applied to the other coefficients of partial correlation.
   All coefficients of partial correlation are significant at the 0.05 level.

TABLE C-1.—Selected Data, by Tenure, for 105 Cities of 100,000 Inhabitants or More: 1950 and 1940

Year and city	Occupied dwelling units		Population in private households		Persons per household		Rooms per dwelling unit		Persons per room			Median value of single-family units	Average contract rent per unit	Average contract rent per room	Median income of experienced labor force
	Owner	Renter	Owner	Renter	Owner	Renter	Owner	Renter	Total	Owner	Renter	Owner	Renter	Renter	Owner and renter
Akron, Ohio:															
1950............	51,921	29,177	182,432	85,537	3.51	2.93	5.99	3.92	0.63	0.59	0.75	$8,511	$40.01	$10.21	$2,698
1940............	32,489	34,012	121,729	118,767	3.75	3.49	6.11	4.78	0.67	0.61	0.73	3,629	23.78	4.97	964
Albany, N. Y.:															
1950............	15,243	26,383	51,338	76,008	3.37	2.88	6.40	4.44	0.59	0.53	0.65	11,790	41.02	9.24	2,422
1940............	11,787	26,189	42,072	83,821	3.57	3.20	6.72	4.93	0.60	0.53	0.65	6,690	31.72	6.43	908
Allentown, Pa.:															
1950............	17,597	12,830	62,800	38,247	3.57	2.98	6.70	4.39	0.58	0.53	0.68	8,384	39.33	8.96	2,249
1940............	10,054	15,266	37,053	56,732	3.69	3.72	7.20	5.54	0.60	0.51	0.67	(¹)	25.78	4.65	(¹)
Atlanta, Ga.:															
1950............	36,985	55,682	132,133	173,878	3.57	3.12	5.56	3.20	0.80	0.64	0.98	8,204	32.10	10.03	1,892
1940............	20,769	61,231	78,115	215,604	3.76	3.52	5.74	3.36	0.90	0.66	1.05	3,492	19.13	5.69	578
Austin, Texas:															
1950............	18,385	17,100	62,175	52,589	3.38	3.08	5.04	3.59	0.74	0.67	0.86	8,171	44.62	12.43	1,895
1940............	9,385	13,134	33,630	47,393	3.58	3.61	5.20	3.74	0.85	0.69	0.96	(¹)	22.68	6.06	(¹)
Baltimore, Md.:															
1950............	138,817	129,905	502,427	417,846	3.62	3.22	6.16	3.94	0.17	0.59	0.82	7,144	43.15	10.95	(¹)
1940............	92,960	134,622	354,361	477,590	3.81	3.55	6.25	4.54	0.70	0.61	0.78	3,062	25.82	5.69	(¹)
Berkeley, Calif.:															
1950............	17,400	19,127	54,780	47,815	3.15	2.50	5.98	3.50	0.60	0.53	0.70	12,290	49.70	14.20	2,691
1940............	12,978	15,232	41,515	42,551	3.20	2.79	5.98	4.15	0.59	0.53	0.67	(¹)	34.48	8.23	(¹)
Birmingham, Ala.:															
1950............	43,409	49,254	155,051	160,602	3.57	3.26	5.45	3.27	0.79	0.66	1.00	6,552	27.50	8.41	2,084
1940............	21,324	50,474	82,430	181,013	3.87	3.59	5.76	3.50	0.88	0.67	1.02	2,811	15.78	4.51	621
Boston, Mass.:															
1950............	54,266	163,837	212,488	520,266	3.92	3.18	6.64	4.24	0.69	0.59	0.75	9,460	38.39	9.05	2,283
1940............	41,326	156,157	179,088	563,036	4.33	3.61	7.06	4.52	0.74	0.61	0.80	4,979	30.26	6.69	856
Bridgeport, Conn.:															
1950............	15,640	30,360	55,372	97,656	3.54	3.22	5.81	4.18	0.70	0.61	0.77	11,633	33.62	8.04	2,378
1940............	10,711	28,625	42,325	102,113	3.95	3.57	6.02	4.45	0.75	0.66	0.80	5,295	25.34	5.69	861
Buffalo, N. Y.:															
1950............	71,721	92,964	259,591	293,798	3.62	3.16	6.42	4.76	0.61	0.57	0.66	8,816	35.81	7.52	2,617
1940............	48,871	103,066	188,236	371,964	3.85	3.61	6.42	5.17	0.66	0.60	0.70	4,467	27.26	5.27	826
Cambridge, Mass.:															
1950............	7,190	25,605	27,793	79,772	3.87	3.12	6.95	4.26	0.68	0.56	0.73	9,980	42.75	10.04	2,268
1940............	5,485	23,232	23,949	84,073	4.37	3.62	7.56	4.63	0.72	0.58	0.78	5,191	32.93	7.11	908
Camden, N. J.:															
1950............	21,471	13,006	79,466	43,112	3.70	3.31	6.12	4.30	0.65	0.60	0.77	5,433	36.94	8.59	2,344
1940............	11,354	19,124	43,692	72,698	3.85	3.80	6.41	5.29	0.67	0.60	0.72	2,626	22.17	4.19	785

¹ Not available.

TABLE C–1.—SELECTED DATA, BY TENURE, FOR 105 CITIES OF 100,000 INHABITANTS OR MORE: 1950 AND 1940—Cont.

| Year and city | Occupied dwelling units | | Population in private households | | Persons per household | | Rooms per dwelling unit | | Persons per room | | | Median value of single-family units | Average contract rent per unit | Average contract rent per room | Median income of experienced labor force |
	Owner	Renter	Owner	Renter	Owner	Renter	Owner	Renter	Total	Owner	Renter	Owner	Renter	Renter	Owner and renter
Canton, Ohio:															
1950.................	20,887	13,961	72,832	41,281	3.49	2.96	5.80	3.96	0.65	0.60	0.75	$7,954	$38.19	$9.64	$2,436
1940.................	14,141	15,325	53,100	53,987	3.76	3.52	6.06	4.71	0.68	0.62	0.75	3,863	2,480	5.27	924
Charlotte, N. C.:															
1950.................	16,266	20,633	57,987	69,285	3.56	3.36	6.00	3.77	0.73	0.59	0.89	9,086	36.03	9.56	2,014
1940.................	6,854	18,112	27,495	69,127	4.01	3.82	6.32	3.87	0.85	0.63	0.99	4,533	20.78	5.37	618
Chattanooga, Tenn.:															
1950.................	15,365	22,651	52,664	73,866	3.43	3.26	5.41	3.45	0.78	0.63	0.95	5,367	27.63	8.01	1,833
1940.................	9,204	24,267	34,705	90,566	3.77	3.73	5.49	3.70	0.89	0.69	1.01	2,824	16.49	4.46	654
Chicago, Ill.:															
1950.................	329,993	757,265	1,187,031	2,251,880	3.60	2.97	5.52	3.74	0.74	0.65	0.80	12,232	47.02	12.58	2,724
1940.................	230,975	718,769	902,786	2,397,849	3.91	3.34	5.54	4.07	0.79	0.71	0.82	4,975	33.53	8.24	890
Cincinnati, Ohio:															
1950.................	60,287	98,650	201,465	276,808	3.34	2.81	5.60	3.20	0.73	0.60	0.88	12,254	34.20	10.69	2,343
1940.................	45,127	90,682	158,644	279,376	3.52	3.08	5.65	3.30	0.79	0.62	0.93	6,158	23.30	7.05	850
Cleveland, Ohio:															
1950.................	113,453	152,520	408,932	498,000	3.60	3.27	5.81	4.12	0.70	0.62	0.79	10,024	37.74	9.16	2,614
1940.................	80,340	161,727	313,011	544,748	3.89	3.37	5.90	4.42	0.72	0.66	0.76	4,243	26.24	5.94	826
Columbus, Ohio:															
1950.................	51,995	58,053	175,745	171,822	3.38	2.96	5.79	4.13	0.64	0.58	0.72	8,591	39.86	9.65	2,409
1940.................	30,950	52,647	107,730	182,451	3.48	3.47	6.21	4.83	0.65	0.56	0.72	4,304	25.13	5.20	875
Corpus Christi, Texas:															
1950.................	14,189	16,272	54,090	52,292	3.81	3.21	4.85	3.22	0.88	0.79	1.00	7,447	41.85	13.00	2,201
1940.................	5,624	9,984	21,785	34,256	3.87	3.43	4.41	3.05	1.01	0.88	1.12	(1)	22.43	7.35	(1)
Dallas, Texas:															
1950.................	71,701	63,539	234,398	183,702	3.27	2.89	5.22	3.43	0.71	0.63	0.84	8,099	49.31	14.38	2,315
1940.................	29,354	54,737	102,361	185,183	3.49	3.38	5.35	3.60	0.81	0.65	0.94	3,235	22.50	6.25	635
Dayton, Ohio:															
1950.................	37,854	33,665	132,224	99,421	3.49	2.95	5.63	3.72	0.68	0.62	0.79	9,252	43.27	11.63	2,794
1940.................	24,053	35,887	84,265	121,007	3.50	3.39	5.84	4.44	0.69	0.60	0.76	4,016	26.03	5.86	1,015
Denver, Colo.:															
1950.................	67,356	62,950	226,247	159,981	3.36	2.54	5.46	3.23	0.68	0.62	0.79	9,657	43.42	13.44	2,409
1940.................	37,186	59,591	124,288	177,527	3.34	2.98	5.54	3.61	0.72	0.60	0.83	3,510	25.53	7.07	787
Des Moines, Iowa:															
1950.................	36,935	19,361	123,212	46,809	3.34	2.42	5.34	3.22	0.65	0.62	0.75	7,480	42.47	13.19	2,464
1940.................	23,011	23,618	80,690	74,179	3.51	3.14	5.52	3.99	0.70	0.64	0.79	2,764	26.61	6.67	906
Detroit, Mich.:															
1950.................	276,313	236,101	1,022,380	729,236	3.70	3.09	5.82	4.12	0.68	0.64	0.75	9,357	45.00	10.92	2,963
1940.................	166,933	258,614	670,178	917,504	4.01	3.55	5.91	4.48	0.74	0.68	0.79	4,201	32.89	7.34	1,037

¹ Not available.

TABLE C-1.—SELECTED DATA, BY TENURE, FOR 105 CITIES OF 100,000 INHABITANTS OR MORE: 1950 AND 1940—Cont.

Year and city	Occupied dwelling units		Population in private households		Persons per household		Rooms per dwelling unit		Persons per room			Median value of single-family units	Average contract rent per unit	Average contract rent per room	Median income of experienced labor force
	Owner	Renter	Owner	Renter	Owner	Renter	Owner	Renter	Total	Owner	Renter	Owner	Renter	Renter	Owner and renter
Duluth, Minn.:															
1950	19,340	11,972	66,363	32,189	3.43	2.69	5.50	3.64	0.66	0.62	0.74	$7,227	$34.68	$9.53	$2,530
1940	13,422	14,397	48,926	46,789	3.65	3.25	5.67	4.18	0.70	0.64	0.78	3,710	23.31	5.58	851
Elizabeth, N. J.:															
1950	12,261	19,550	45,701	63,894	3.73	3.27	6.20	4.20	0.69	0.60	0.78	11,421	40.90	9.74	2,550
1940	8,993	18,987	36,884	71,190	4.10	3.75	6.46	4.69	0.73	0.64	0.80	5,989	30.62	6.53	1,010
El Paso, Texas:															
1950	14,810	19,419	58,196	65,194	3.93	3.36	5.09	2.89	0.94	0.77	1.16	8,803	36.52	12.64	2,111
1940	7,585	17,246	29,334	63,878	3.87	3.70	5.12	3.06	1.02	0.75	1.21	(1)	14.21	4.64	(1)
Erie, Pa.:															
1950	19,524	17,743	70,721	54,910	3.62	3.09	6.26	4.40	0.63	0.59	0.70	8,333	36.31	8.25	2,609
1940	11,897	18,524	45,923	68,698	3.86	3.65	6.68	5.32	0.64	0.58	0.70	3,596	22.99	4.40	820
Evansville, Ind.:															
1950	21,549	17,854	70,960	53,788	3.29	3.01	4.75	3.38	0.77	0.69	0.89	6,557	36.72	10.86	2,397
1940	10,144	17,619	35,074	60,711	3.46	3.45	5.06	3.69	0.82	0.68	0.93	(1)	21.31	5.78	(1)
Fall River, Mass.:															
1950	8,620	24,038	31,399	77,775	3.64	3.24	6.24	4.48	0.68	0.58	0.72	7,942	23.15	5.17	1,933
1940	6,234	23,565	24,762	88,502	3.97	3.76	6.52	4.68	0.75	0.61	0.80	3,625	17.37	3.71	635
Flint, Mich.:															
1950	32,876	15,501	114,060	45,959	3.47	2.96	5.52	4.02	0.66	0.63	0.74	6,970	47.38	11.79	3,214
1940	21,348	19,219	80,516	68,886	3.77	3.58	5.65	4.58	0.72	0.67	0.78	3,235	25.74	5.62	1,232
Fort Wayne, Ind.:															
1950	26,258	14,742	86,497	40,989	3.29	2.78	5.57	3.85	0.63	0.59	0.72	8,452	45.12	11.72	2,706
1940	17,484	15,514	61,636	52,496	3.53	3.38	5.94	4.72	0.64	0.59	0.72	4,010	25.99	5.51	946
Fort Worth, Texas:															
1950	50,777	34,761	165,045	99,823	3.25	2.87	4.83	3.15	0.75	0.67	0.91	6,605	44.24	14.04	2,263
1940	21,964	29,656	74,168	97,529	3.38	3.29	5.01	3.52	0.80	0.67	0.93	2,212	18.65	5.30	592
Gary, Ind.:															
1950	19,696	17,627	72,891	56,307	3.70	3.19	4.95	3.66	0.80	0.75	0.87	8,911	40.33	11.02	2,900
1940	10,615	19,390	43,409	66,049	4.09	3.41	5.08	3.72	0.87	0.80	0.92	3,997	28.03	7.53	1,201
Grand Rapids, Mich.:															
1950	33,138	20,972	112,491	57,920	3.39	2.76	6.20	4.24	0.58	0.55	0.65	8,498	36.33	8.57	2,663
1940	23,100	24,423	81,834	79,159	3.54	3.24	6.44	4.90	0.60	0.55	0.65	3,432	21.57	4.40	850
Hartford, Conn.:															
1950	11,627	39,777	42,269	122,474	3.64	3.08	6.25	3.98	0.71	0.58	0.77	12,809	39.83	10.01	2,358
1940	7,696	36,557	31,243	128,772	4.06	3.52	6.84	4.35	0.76	0.59	0.81	7,054	31.78	7.31	1,003
Houston, Texas:															
1950	90,653	90,199	307,891	268,797	3.40	2.98	5.38	3.57	0.71	0.63	0.84	7,846	47.63	13.34	2,444
1940	36,354	71,176	130,894	241,948	3.60	3.40	5.41	3.72	0.81	0.67	0.91	3,486	24.24	6.52	732

1 Not available.

TABLE C-1.—SELECTED DATA, BY TENURE, FOR 105 CITIES OF 100,000 INHABITANTS OR MORE: 1950 AND 1940—Cont.

Year and city	Occupied dwelling units		Population in private households		Persons per household		Rooms per dwelling unit		Persons per room			Median value of single-family units	Average contract rent per unit	Average contract rent per room	Median income of experienced labor force
	Owner	Renter	Owner	Renter	Owner	Renter	Owner	Renter	Total	Owner	Renter	Owner	Renter	Renter	Owner and Renter
Indianapolis, Ind.:															
1950	69,559	62,187	235,871	177,284	3.39	2.85	5.37	3.68	0.69	0.63	0.78	$7,436	$41.00	$11.14	$2,551
1940	40,796	71,435	139,290	236,989	3.41	3.32	5.75	4.31	0.69	0.59	0.77	3,644	23.88	5.54	871
Jacksonville, Fla.:															
1950	28,115	29,792	96,275	96,643	3.42	3.24	5.57	3.80	0.71	0.61	0.85	6,943	37.11	9.77	1,886
1940	14,012	31,365	50,666	116,360	3.62	3.71	5.83	4.12	0.79	0.62	0.90	3,501	17.75	4.31	581
Jersey City, N. J.:															
1950	20,390	64,566	77,659	210,889	3.81	3.27	5.88	4.12	0.75	0.65	0.79	7,119	37.38	9.07	2,577
1940	14,593	65,091	59,521	238,120	4.08	3.66	6.14	4.34	0.80	0.66	0.84	4,673	30.76	7.09	972
Kansas City, Kans.:															
1950	25,456	13,509	88,232	39,108	3.47	2.89	5.12	3.34	0.73	0.68	0.87	5,086	34.08	10.20	2,452
1940	16,920	17,148	60,069	59,558	3.55	3.47	5.27	4.15	0.75	0.67	0.84	1,936	16.33	3.93	(¹)
Kansas City, Mo.:															
1950	72,642	75,516	242,714	188,992	3.34	2.50	5.74	3.19	0.66	0.58	0.78	7,287	42.03	13.18	2,415
1940	37,761	84,342	129,497	251,830	3.43	2.99	6.00	3.87	0.69	0.57	0.77	3,202	24.75	6.40	747
Knoxville, Tenn.:															
1950	18,341	16,484	66,379	52,152	3.62	3.16	5.22	3.38	0.80	0.69	0.94	5,292	32.33	9.57	1,919
1940	9,977	18,624	38,347	70,934	3.84	3.81	5.39	3.83	0.87	0.71	0.99	2,361	17.89	4.67	622
Little Rock, Ark.:															
1950	15,970	15,017	51,428	42,872	3.22	2.85	5.40	3.44	0.68	0.60	0.83	7,413	39.45	11.47	2,002
1940	8,707	15,965	30,402	51,738	3.49	3.24	5.63	3.62	0.77	0.62	0.90	(¹)	18.91	5.22	(¹)
Long Beach, Calif.:															
1950	40,924	50,239	120,373	120,126	2.94	2.39	4.99	3.35	0.65	0.59	0.71	9,202	46.16	13.78	2,766
1940	18,520	39,865	54,406	106,189	2.94	2.66	4.97	3.48	0.70	0.59	0.77	3,711	27.94	8.03	878
Los Angeles, Calif.:															
1950	305,393	361,294	982,340	891,305	3.22	2.47	5.41	3.30	0.66	0.59	0.75	10,821	46.70	14.15	2,601
1940	166,094	326,993	529,973	912,988	3.19	2.79	5.51	3.61	0.69	0.58	0.77	3,958	29.45	8.18	845
Louisville, Ky.:															
1950	51,971	56,854	182,561	172,325	3.51	3.03	5.06	3.23	0.79	0.69	0.94	7,010	36.37	11.26	2,279
1940	32,226	57,729	117,497	194,256	3.65	3.36	5.25	3.50	0.84	0.70	0.96	3,320	19.68	5.62	707
Memphis, Tenn.:															
1950	54,146	59,206	195,516	183,898	3.61	3.11	5.23	3.07	0.82	0.69	1.01	7,967	33.78	11.00	1,953
1940	24,793	56,288	92,289	189,087	3.72	3.36	5.28	3.17	0.91	0.70	1.06	3,141	17.42	5.50	563
Miami, Fla.:															
1950	37,896	40,489	119,083	111,970	3.14	2.77	5.34	3.60	0.66	0.59	0.77	10,440	59.93	16.65	2,061
1940	18,321	30,162	63,735	101,689	3.48	3.37	5.37	3.87	0.77	0.65	0.87	3,819	26.46	6.84	654
Milwaukee, Wis.:															
1950	79,945	105,789	282,012	321,253	3.53	3.04	5.47	4.20	0.68	0.64	0.72	11,082	45.90	10.93	2,732
1940	52,917	111,418	195,069	378,581	3.69	3.40	5.79	4.50	0.71	0.64	0.76	4,974	30.32	6.74	934

¹ Not available.

TABLE C-1.—SELECTED DATA, BY TENURE, FOR 105 CITIES OF 100,000 INHABITANTS OR MORE: 1950 AND 1940—Cont.

Year and city	Occupied dwelling units		Population in private households		Persons per household		Rooms per dwelling unit		Persons per room			Median value of single-family units	Average contract rent per unit	Average contract rent per room	Median income of experienced labor force
	Owner	Renter	Owner	Renter	Owner	Renter	Owner	Renter	Total	Owner	Renter	Owner	Renter	Renter	Owner and renter
Minneapolis, Minn.:															
1950	83,737	75,608	290,440	196,427	3.47	2.60	5.69	3.42	0.66	0.61	0.76	$10,126	$41.30	$12.08	$2,445
1940	58,764	84,070	215,874	258,316	3.67	3.07	5.84	3.96	0.70	0.63	0.78	4,158	29.07	7.34	910
Mobile, Ala.:															
1950	17,620	18,831	63,827	60,360	3.62	3.21	5.11	3.30	0.82	0.71	0.97	6,158	31.07	9.42	1,969
1940	6,443	14,069	24,914	51,394	3.87	3.65	5.46	3.50	0.90	0.71	1.04	(1)	14.99	4.28	(1)
Montgomery, Ala.:															
1950	12,232	18,241	43,260	59,285	3.54	3.25	5.47	3.47	0.79	0.65	0.94	7,509	33.00	9.51	1,686
1940	5,872	16,060	21,747	54,919	3.70	3.42	5.65	3.30	0.89	0.66	1.04	(1)	13.98	4.24	(1)
Nashville, Tenn.:															
1950	21,013	28,794	74,799	88,412	3.56	3.07	5.43	3.29	0.78	0.66	0.93	5,613	28.26	8.59	1,694
1940	14,185	31,619	52,809	110,671	3.72	3.50	5.43	3.46	0.88	0.69	1.01	2,595	17.28	4.99	564
Newark, N. J.:															
1950	28,705	93,826	108,525	307,988	3.78	3.28	6.12	4.10	0.74	0.62	0.80	10,821	38.25	9.33	2,347
1940	20,209	91,985	82,945	337,815	4.10	3.67	6.33	4.39	0.79	0.65	0.84	5,776	29.84	6.79	813
New Bedford, Mass.:															
1950	11,168	21,998	37,966	68,574	3.40	3.12	6.27	4.63	0.62	0.54	0.67	7,696	24.89	5.38	1,876
1940	7,899	22,741	27,739	80,706	3.51	3.55	6.49	4.89	0.67	0.54	0.73	3,340	17.81	3.64	626
New Haven, Conn.:															
1950	14,865	32,026	52,688	99,793	3.54	3.12	6.08	4.23	0.68	0.58	0.74	12,187	33.64	7.95	2,328
1940	11,126	31,354	44,301	112,294	3.98	3.58	6.34	4.54	0.74	0.63	0.79	6,023	26.86	5.92	803
New Orleans, La.:															
1950	56,091	109,962	200,218	348,585	3.57	3.17	5.20	3.50	0.81	0.69	0.90	9,699	30.55	8.73	1,939
1940	31,552	101,488	123,637	358,369	3.92	3.53	5.49	3.64	0.89	0.71	0.97	3,854	17.80	4.89	563
New York, N. Y.:															
1950	450,185	1,907,734	1,695,185	5,878,375	3.77	3.08	5.90	3.75	0.77	0.64	0.82	11,920	49.03	13.07	2,513
1940	323,143	1,724,776	1,304,840	5,923,099	4.04	3.43	6.18	3.98	0.82	0.65	0.86	5,925	41.26	10.37	887
Norfolk, Va.:															
1950	19,303	34,731	66,989	109,086	3.47	3.14	5.96	3.80	0.71	0.58	0.83	7,764	39.57	10.41	1,862
1940	10,625	26,778	40,391	94,489	3.80	3.53	6.23	4.27	0.75	0.61	0.83	3,483	21.83	5.11	663
Oakland, Calif.:															
1950	63,303	65,582	198,848	165,913	3.14	2.53	5.47	3.30	0.65	0.57	0.77	10,487	59.65	18.08	2,796
1940	42,593	56,732	134,267	157,430	3.15	2.77	5.52	3.78	0.65	0.57	0.73	4,178	27.37	7.24	1,063
Oklahoma City, Okla.:															
1950	43,997	34,866	141,036	94,404	3.21	2.71	5.09	3.30	0.69	0.63	0.82	7,684	41.06	12.44	2,341
1940	22,027	37,467	75,412	120,135	3.42	3.21	5.11	3.46	0.81	0.67	0.93	3,256	21.30	6.16	672
Omaha, Nebr.:															
1950	43,654	29,053	153,231	80,923	3.51	2.79	5.49	3.56	0.68	0.64	0.78	7,766	46.59	13.09	2,443
1940	28,672	33,463	104,829	110,261	3.66	3.30	5.61	4.06	0.73	0.65	0.81	3,124	25.93	6.39	809

1 Not available.

TABLE C-1.—SELECTED DATA, BY TENURE, FOR 105 CITIES OF 100,000 INHABITANTS OR MORE: 1950 AND 1940—Cont.

Year and city	Occupied dwelling units		Population in private households		Persons per household		Rooms per dwelling unit		Persons per room			Median value of single-family units	Average contract rent per unit	Average contract rent per room	Median income of experienced labor force
	Owner	Renter	Owner	Renter	Owner	Renter	Owner	Renter	Total	Owner	Renter	Owner	Renter	Renter	Owner and renter
Pasadena, Calif.:															
1950	20,414	15,791	61,351	37,659	3.01	2.38	6.06	3.71	0.54	0.50	0.64	$11,870	$53.87	$14.52	$2,400
1940	12,208	15,153	37,158	42,035	3.04	2.77	6.31	4.32	0.56	0.48	0.64	(1)	29.54	6.84	(1)
Paterson, N. J.:															
1950	14,351	27,877	49,315	85,635	3.44	3.07	5.76	4.30	0.61	0.60	0.71	9,738	34.02	7.91	2,341
1940	10,059	28,626	37,130	100,536	3.69	3.51	5.89	4.64	0.72	0.62	0.76	4,432	24.06	5.29	673
Peoria, Ill.:															
1950	18,298	15,541	61,402	43,518	3.36	2.80	5.39	3.48	0.69	0.62	0.80	8,617	44.00	12.64	2,571
1940	13,851	16,608	47,245	52,815	3.41	3.18	5.49	3.88	0.71	0.62	0.82	4,658	29.23	7.53	971
Philadelphia, Pa.:															
1950	328,035	256,663	1,203,587	776,750	3.67	3.03	6.52	3.92	0.63	0.56	0.77	7,009	40.19	10.25	2,407
1940	197,017	309,963	758,212	1,119,633	3.85	3.61	6.73	4.87	0.63	0.57	0.74	3,265	27.59	5.67	770
Phoenix, Ariz.:															
1950	17,480	16,765	55,762	44,701	3.19	2.67	4.97	3.28	0.71	0.64	0.81	7,939	46.41	14.15	2,354
1940	6,777	12,510	23,556	39,428	3.48	3.15	5.09	3.37	0.82	0.68	0.94	(1)	22.12	6.56	(1)
Pittsburgh, Pa.:															
1950	80,951	109,941	304,131	342,935	3.76	3.12	5.80	3.65	0.74	0.65	0.85	8,277	41.08	11.25	2,440
1940	56,381	118,782	229,216	426,860	4.07	3.59	5.90	3.91	0.82	0.69	0.92	4,895	29.21	7.47	819
Portland, Oreg.:															
1950	74,674	52,031	228,950	125,016	3.07	2.40	5.74	3.31	0.59	0.53	0.73	8,025	41.26	12.47	2,631
1940	49,303	52,760	151,614	139,777	3.08	2.65	5.77	3.81	0.57	0.53	0.70	3,219	21.77	5.71	858
Providence, R. I.:															
1950	22,902	49,357	82,016	153,474	3.58	3.11	6.31	4.37	0.65	0.57	0.71	11,032	30.76	7.04	2,021
1940	18,748	48,753	74,305	172,412	3.96	3.54	6.43	4.62	0.71	0.62	0.77	5,642	23.50	5.09	709
Reading, Pa.:															
1950	18,677	13,627	66,036	39,328	3.54	2.89	6.86	4.26	0.57	0.52	0.68	6,525	34.86	8.18	2,219
1940	13,107	16,691	48,045	60,594	3.67	3.63	6.98	5.15	0.61	0.53	0.70	3,189	24.36	4.73	691
Richmond, Va.:															
1950	30,463	34,586	108,966	107,813	3.58	3.12	6.09	3.90	0.68	0.59	0.80	8,263	34.81	8.93	2,116
1940	14,814	36,103	57,299	130,247	3.87	3.61	6.41	4.15	0.77	0.60	0.87	4,617	22.77	5.49	711
Rochester, N. Y.:															
1950	51,218	48,340	181,100	134,109	3.54	2.77	6.34	3.99	0.61	0.56	0.70	8,952	42.03	10.53	2,538
1940	35,782	54,257	134,937	179,239	3.77	3.30	6.59	4.73	0.64	0.57	0.70	4,453	29.29	6.19	952
Sacramento, Calif.:															
1950	24,755	18,535	78,879	46,456	3.19	2.51	5.38	3.51	0.63	0.59	0.71	10,218	44.87	12.78	2,830
1940	14,340	17,838	46,662	52,231	3.25	2.93	5.39	3.85	0.68	0.60	0.76	4,292	28.68	7.45	1,176
St. Louis, Mo.:															
1950	89,811	168,325	304,378	498,408	3.39	2.96	4.99	3.31	0.80	0.68	0.89	9,211	33.10	10.00	2,367
1940	62,829	172,043	222,933	564,650	3.55	3.28	5.15	3.55	0.84	0.69	0.92	4,093	22.69	6.39	748

1 Not available.

TABLE C–1.—SELECTED DATA, BY TENURE, FOR 105 CITIES OF 100,000 INHABITANTS OR MORE: 1950 AND 1940—Cont.

Year and city	Occupied dwelling units		Population in private households		Persons per household		Rooms per dwelling unit		Persons per room			Median value of single-family units	Average contract rent per unit	Average contract rent per room	Median income of experienced labor force
	Owner	Renter	Owner	Renter	Owner	Renter	Owner	Renter	Total	Owner	Renter	Owner	Renter	Renter	Owner and renter
St. Paul, Minn.:															
1950	51,444	40,715	183,913	111,921	3.58	2.75	5.62	3.53	0.68	0.64	0.78	$9,665	$40.20	$11.39	$2,588
1940	37,940	42,617	142,432	136,597	3.75	3.21	5.79	3.98	0.72	0.65	0.81	4,022	27.49	6.91	922
Salt Lake City, Utah:															
1950	30,939	23,422	111,909	63,682	3.62	2.72	5.25	3.35	0.73	0.69	0.81	9,158	45.87	13.69	2,522
1940	20,594	20,774	78,705	65,896	3.82	3.17	5.31	3.54	0.79	0.72	0.90	3,517	25.74	7.27	940
San Antonio, Texas:															
1950	63,119	48,841	237,500	159,428	3.76	3.26	4.67	3.29	0.87	0.81	0.99	6,530	38.54	11.71	1,957
1940	24,848	40,897	93,171	148,567	3.75	3.63	4.86	3.32	0.94	0.77	1.09	2,502	16.15	4.86	425
San Diego, Calif.:															
1950	48,472	56,318	144,873	158,270	2.99	2.81	5.19	3.62	0.67	0.58	0.78	9,693	44.04	12.17	2,451
1940	26,031	37,931	78,187	108,147	3.00	2.85	5.28	3.83	0.66	0.57	0.74	3,570	26.12	6.82	731
San Francisco, Calif.:															
1950	94,594	163,140	293,648	397,543	3.10	2.44	5.46	3.37	0.65	0.57	0.72	11,927	44.58	13.23	2,700
1940	64,398	141,613	209,106	368,433	3.25	2.60	5.56	3.53	0.67	0.58	0.74	5,175	32.34	9.16	1,062
Savannah, Ga.:															
1950	11,391	23,448	39,114	77,752	3.43	3.32	5.71	3.97	0.74	0.60	0.84	6,816	25.49	6.42	1,747
1940	4,923	21,483	17,658	76,184	3.59	3.55	6.29	4.10	0.79	0.57	0.86	(1)	14.62	3.57	(1)
Scranton, Pa.:															
1950	16,505	19,920	58,376	64,102	3.54	3.22	6.47	4.76	0.61	0.55	0.68	6,208	31.37	6.59	2,154
1940	13,667	21,964	55,221	82,967	4.04	3.78	6.55	4.92	0.70	0.62	0.77	3,259	23.56	4.79	631
Seattle, Wash.:															
1950	87,402	67,180	275,799	153,215	3.16	2.28	5.55	3.13	0.62	0.57	0.73	9,231	43.11	13.77	2,770
1940	56,080	70,274	178,652	172,518	3.19	2.45	5.53	3.28	0.65	0.58	0.75	3,391	24.00	7.32	914
Shreveport, La.:															
1950	18,292	18,967	61,770	58,939	3.38	3.11	5.47	3.39	0.73	0.62	0.92	8,460	31.96	9.43	1,957
1940	9,749	17,160	35,726	59,514	3.66	3.47	5.48	3.58	0.83	0.67	0.97	(1)	19.58	5.47	(1)
Somerville, Mass.:															
1950	9,644	18,321	38,616	61,688	4.00	3.37	6.50	4.61	0.68	0.62	0.73	7,496	36.04	7.82	2,377
1940	6,894	19,370	28,340	73,040	4.11	3.77	6.77	4.94	0.71	0.61	0.76	4,102	28.29	5.73	969
South Bend, Ind.:															
1950	24,127	10,299	82,390	30,096	3.41	2.92	5.57	4.01	0.64	0.61	0.73	8,331	44.67	11.14	3,295
1940	14,811	13,083	54,979	44,900	3.71	3.43	5.90	4.74	0.67	0.63	0.72	3,440	24.39	5.15	913
Spokane, Wash.:															
1950	33,551	19,443	106,040	47,234	3.16	2.43	5.26	3.21	0.64	0.60	0.76	7,327	40.45	12.60	2,749
1940	21,339	17,579	68,148	47,117	3.19	2.68	5.30	3.49	0.67	0.60	0.77	2,579	21.05	6.03	792

[1] Not available.

TABLE C-1.—SELECTED DATA, BY TENURE, FOR 105 CITIES OF 100,000 INHABITANTS OR MORE: 1950 AND 1940—Cont.

| Year and city | Occupied dwelling units | | Population in private households | | Persons per household | | Rooms per dwelling unit | | Persons per room | | | Median value of single-family units | Average contract rent per unit | Average contract rent per room | Median income of experienced labor force |
	Owner	Renter	Owner	Renter	Owner	Renter	Owner	Renter	Total	Owner	Renter	Owner	Renter	Renter	Owner and renter
Springfield, Mass.:															
1950	19,776	26,932	71,254	82,816	3.60	3.08	6.26	4.51	0.63	0.58	0.68	$9,324	$36.72	$8.14	$2,434
1940	11,719	28,584	44,799	100,490	3.82	3.52	6.68	4.94	0.66	0.57	0.71	4,671	28.30	5.73	941
Syracuse, N. Y.:															
1950	30,065	33,139	108,511	96,120	3.61	2.90	6.68	4.32	0.60	0.54	0.67	10,510	41.38	9.58	2,350
1940	19,314	37,695	71,953	128,202	3.73	3.40	6.85	5.09	0.62	0.54	0.67	5,619	27.98	5.50	857
Tacoma, Wash.:															
1950	30,863	17,091	96,029	42,574	3.11	2.49	5.28	3.28	0.63	0.59	0.76	7,002	35.77	10.91	2,745
1940	20,865	15,221	65,394	40,270	3.13	2.65	5.32	3.74	0.63	0.59	0.71	2,498	19.82	5.30	911
Tampa, Fla.:															
1950	20,126	18,020	66,115	53,014	3.29	2.94	5.50	3.75	0.67	0.60	0.78	5,733	33.49	8.93	1,635
1940	10,969	18,945	39,422	65,835	3.59	3.48	5.77	4.26	0.73	0.62	0.82	2,380	15.16	3.56	484
Toledo, Ohio:															
1950	54,483	35,909	182,759	105,492	3.35	2.94	6.06	4.37	0.59	0.55	0.67	8,030	40.46	9.26	2,820
1940	36,651	42,690	130,360	142,434	3.56	3.34	6.15	4.87	0.63	0.58	0.69	3,651	25.94	5.33	831
Trenton, N. J.:															
1950	19,171	13,116	75,854	42,740	3.96	3.26	6.61	4.26	0.65	0.60	0.76	6,635	41.35	9.71	2,407
1940	11,863	17,731	48,718	69,834	4.11	3.94	6.56	5.79	0.66	0.63	0.68	3,031	26.88	4.64	748
Tulsa, Okla.:															
1950	33,979	24,701	109,861	65,788	3.23	2.66	5.22	3.34	0.68	0.62	0.80	8,138	40.32	12.07	2,495
1940	16,853	24,491	58,997	77,545	3.50	3.17	5.30	3.69	0.76	0.66	0.86	3,314	23.95	6.49	695
Utica, N. Y.:															
1950	13,039	16,817	45,737	50,059	3.51	2.98	6.37	4.71	0.59	0.55	0.63	9,624	32.93	6.99	2,239
1940	8,931	17,984	33,412	62,785	3.74	3.49	6.75	5.12	0.63	0.55	0.68	4,267	23.15	4.52	704
Washington, D. C.:															
1950	72,362	151,780	273,233	439,302	3.78	2.89	6.66	3.55	0.70	0.57	0.82	14,498	57.42	16.17	2,763
1940	51,944	121,501	207,094	420,156	3.99	3.46	6.76	3.83	0.77	0.59	0.90	7,926	44.30	11.57	1,085
Waterbury, Conn.:															
1950	12,127	17,513	44,163	57,424	3.64	3.28	5.74	4.37	0.70	0.63	0.75	11,253	30.90	7.07	2,501
1940	7,942	17,445	32,297	65,337	4.07	3.75	5.99	4.71	0.75	0.68	0.80	(1)	25.50	5.41	(1)
Wichita, Kans.:															
1950	31,297	22,981	99,985	59,534	3.19	2.59	5.05	3.26	0.68	0.63	0.79	7,829	45.01	13.81	2,505
1940	14,550	20,225	48,526	62,900	3.34	3.11	5.45	3.79	0.71	0.61	0.82	2,730	21.68	5.72	893
Wilmington, Del.:															
1950	16,143	15,444	59,511	47,526	3.69	3.08	6.66	4.26	0.62	0.55	0.72	9,274	42.21	9.91	2,385
1940	11,531	17,762	45,988	64,108	3.99	3.61	6.92	4.85	0.66	0.58	0.74	4,978	28.94	5.97	890

1 Not available.

TABLE C–1.—SELECTED DATA, BY TENURE, FOR 105 CITIES OF 100,000 INHABITANTS OR MORE: 1950 AND 1940—Cont.

Year and city	Occupied dwelling units		Population in private households		Persons per household		Rooms per dwelling unit		Persons per room			Median value of single-family units	Average contract rent per unit	Average contract rent per room	Median income of experienced labor force
	Owner	Renter	Owner	Renter	Owner	Renter	Owner	Renter	Total	Owner	Renter	Owner	Renter	Renter	Owner and renter
Worcester, Mass.:															
1950..........	21,193	33,788	76,055	111,711	3.59	3.31	6.20	4.83	0.64	0.58	0.68	$9,941	$34.35	$7.11	$2,367
1940..........	14,728	34,084	57,942	127,352	3.93	3.74	6.49	5.07	0.70	0.61	0.74	5,068	26.44	5.21	955
Yonkers, N. Y.:															
1950..........	15,225	29,684	57,036	92,471	3.75	3.12	6.56	4.02	0.68	0.57	0.77	15,973	49.21	12.24	2,817
1940..........	9,474	29,042	37,685	102,907	3.98	3.54	6.75	4.40	0.73	0.59	0.81	8,691	39.08	8.88	1,034
Youngstown, Ohio:															
1950..........	27,840	17,680	106,146	57,639	3.81	3.26	5.82	4.16	0.69	0.65	0.78	7,659	36.03	8.66	2,640
1940..........	20,069	21,128	85,174	80,797	4.24	3.82	5.86	4.64	0.77	0.72	0.82	4,092	25.53	5.50	929

Source: Cols. 1 and 2, "Occupied dwelling units (households)": *1950 Census of Housing*, Vol. I, *General Characteristics*, Parts. 2–6, table 19; *1940 Census of Housing*, Vol. II, *General Characteristics*, Parts 2–5, table 8.

Cols. 3 and 4, "Population in private households": Estimated from source for cols. 1 and 2.

Cols. 5 and 6, "Persons per household": Col. 3 ÷ col. 1, and col. 4 ÷ col. 2.

Cols. 7 and 8, "Rooms per dwelling unit": 1950, estimated from *1950 Census of Housing*, Vol. I, *General Characteristics*, Parts 2–6, table 19; 1940, estimated from *1940 Census of Housing*, Vol. II, *General Characteristics*, Parts 2–5, table 8.

Cols. 9 to 11, "Persons per room": Quotient of population in private households (cols. 3 and 4) and total number of rooms in occupied dwelling units (same source as cols. 5 and 6).

Col. 12, "Median value of single-family, owner-occupied dwelling units": *1950 Census of Housing*, Vol. I, *General Characteristics*, Parts 2–6, table 21; *1940 Census of Housing*, Vol. III, *Characteristics by Monthly Rent of Value*, Parts 2 and 3, table 2.

Col. 13, "Average contract rent, renter-occupied dwelling units": *1950 Census of Housing*, Vol. V, *Block Statistics*, table 1; *1940 Census of Housing*, Vol. II, *General Characteristics*, Part 1, U. S. Summary, table 87.

Col. 14, "Average contract rent per room": Col. 13 ÷ col. 8.

Col. 15, "Median income of experienced labor force": *1950 Census of Population*, Vol. II, *Characteristics of the Population*, Part 1, U. S. Summary, table 94; *1940 Census of Population*, Vol. III, *The Labor Force*, Parts 2–5, table 15.

APPENDIX D

Tables to Chapter 8

TABLE **D-1.**—HEADSHIP RATES, BY AGE, MARITAL STATUS, AND SEX, FOR THE NONFARM
POPULATION: 1950 AND 1940

| | Male | | | | | | Female | | | |
| | Total[1] | | Married, wife present | | Other | | Total[1] | | Other than married, husband present | |
Age	1950	1940	1950	1940	1950	1940	1950	1940	1950	1940
10 to 14 years......	0.1	...	...	...	...	...	...	...	...	...
15 to 19 years......	2.3	0.9	78.8	75.1	1.8	1.4	0.6	0.3	2.8	1.8
20 to 24 years......	37.9	22.3					2.7	2.0		
25 to 29 years......	70.1	57.1	88.4	85.9	9.8	7.7	4.2	3.9	18.8	12.9
30 to 34 years......	81.7	73.9	92.6	91.2	15.7	14.2	5.9	6.3	30.7	25.5
35 to 39 years......	85.9	80.7	94.6	93.5	22.1	21.3	8.4	9.6	40.8	39.6
40 to 44 years......	88.2	84.7	95.8	96.1	28.3	27.4	11.3	12.6	48.5	49.1
45 to 49 years......	89.4	87.1	96.4	96.2	34.0	33.4	14.8	15.7	54.6	55.3
50 to 54 years......	90.1	87.7	96.8	96.4	37.8	38.7	18.3	19.4	56.6	57.2
55 to 59 years......	90.3	87.8	96.9	97.0	41.7	43.9	21.8	23.3	57.0	56.9
60 to 64 years......	88.8	86.5	96.4	96.2	44.0	46.8	26.3	27.9	55.1	56.1
65 to 69 years......	86.2	83.9	95.7	95.3	46.7	48.9	32.2	33.7	54.7	54.6
70 to 74 years......	82.7	80.0	94.5	95.3	47.3	49.0	37.0	38.3	51.9	52.4
75 years and over...	72.4	69.8	91.8	91.2	41.3	42.8	38.8	39.4	42.0	43.3

[1] Percentages based on household population.

Source: *1950 Census of Population*, Vol. II, *Characteristics of the Population*, Part 1, U. S. Summary,
tables 105 and 107, pp. 189 and 192; *1940 Census of Population*, Vol. IV, *Characteristics by Age*, Part 1,
U. S. Summary, tables 6, 9, and 10, pp. 17, 25, and 26, and *Types of Families*, table 8, p. 103.

TABLE **D-2.**—HEADSHIP RATES, BY AGE, MARITAL STATUS, AND SEX, FOR THE URBAN AND
RURAL-NONFARM POPULATION: 1950

| Area and age | Both sexes[1] | Male | | | Female | |
		Total[1]	Married, wife present[2]	Other[2]	Total[1]	Other than married, husband present[2]
URBAN						
10 to 14 years..............	0.1	0.1	...	...	...	...
15 to 19 years..............	1.4	2.1	77.4	1.9	0.7	3.1
20 to 24 years..............	17.9	35.8			3.1	
25 to 29 years..............	34.6	68.1	87.3	10.2	4.7	19.3
30 to 34 years..............	41.6	80.3	91.8	16.3	6.6	31.2
35 to 39 years..............	45.2	85.0	94.0	22.5	9.1	41.4
40 to 44 years..............	48.3	87.5	95.4	28.2	12.2	49.4
45 to 49 years..............	50.8	88.9	96.1	33.7	15.7	55.6
50 to 54 years..............	53.0	89.6	96.6	37.3	19.2	57.4
55 to 59 years..............	55.0	89.9	96.7	41.1	22.7	57.4
60 to 64 years..............	56.3	88.2	96.2	42.8	27.2	55.1
65 to 69 years..............	56.5	85.3	95.3	44.6	32.7	54.0
70 to 74 years..............	56.5	81.2	93.8	44.6	37.2	50.6
75 years and over..........	51.2	70.2	90.6	39.1	37.9	40.5
RURAL NONFARM						
10 to 14 years..............	0.1	0.1	...	...	...	...
15 to 19 years..............	1.5	2.8	82.6	1.4	0.3	1.7
20 to 24 years..............	21.4	45.2			1.5	
25 to 29 years..............	37.7	76.9	92.0	8.0	2.4	16.1
30 to 34 years..............	43.7	86.2	95.1	13.8	3.6	27.4
35 to 39 years..............	47.0	89.2	96.5	20.8	5.7	37.9
40 to 44 years..............	49.4	90.5	97.2	28.5	7.8	43.8
45 to 49 years..............	51.3	91.4	97.5	34.8	11.0	49.4
50 to 54 years..............	52.8	91.8	97.6	39.6	14.4	52.5
55 to 59 years..............	54.4	91.8	97.7	44.0	18.2	54.8
60 to 64 years..............	55.9	90.6	97.3	47.7	22.9	54.9
65 to 69 years..............	58.4	88.6	96.9	52.8	30.5	57.7
70 to 74 years..............	60.9	86.4	96.4	54.2	36.6	56.7
75 years and over..........	59.0	77.3	94.5	46.5	41.5	46.8

[1] Household population only.   [2] Percentages based on total population.

Source: See table 30.

TABLE **D-3.**—PERCENT DISTRIBUTION OF PERSONS IN HOUSEHOLDS BY RELATIONSHIP TO HEAD, BY AGE AND SEX, URBAN AND RURAL NONFARM (WITH NONWHITE FOR URBAN): 1950 AND 1940

Area, year, age, and sex	Head	Wife	Child	Grand-child	Parent	Other rela-tive	Lodger	Resident em-ployee
TOTAL								
Both Sexes								
1950, all ages.......	30.0	23.4	35.7	1.9	1.9	4.1	2.8	0.3
Under 5 years............	...	...	89.8	7.7	...	1.6	0.8	...
5 to 9 years............	...	...	92.2	5.4	...	1.6	0.7	...
10 to 14 years...........	0.1	...	92.4	4.0	...	2.6	0.8	0.1
15 to 19 years...........	1.4	6.2	81.3	2.6	...	5.5	2.7	0.3
20 to 24 years...........	18.7	30.2	36.5	0.9	...	7.8	5.7	0.3
25 to 29 years...........	35.3	38.7	15.7	0.3	...	5.8	4.0	0.2
30 to 34 years...........	42.1	40.9	9.3	...	0.1	4.5	2.9	0.2
35 to 39 years...........	45.6	40.8	6.6	...	0.1	3.9	2.7	0.3
40 to 44 years...........	48.5	39.6	4.9	...	0.3	3.7	2.7	0.3
45 to 49 years...........	50.9	38.0	3.2	...	0.9	3.6	2.9	0.4
50 to 54 years...........	53.0	35.6	2.0	...	2.0	3.7	3.1	0.5
55 to 59 years...........	54.9	32.7	1.1	...	3.7	3.8	3.2	0.6
60 to 64 years...........	56.2	28.1	0.6	...	6.5	4.3	3.6	0.7
65 to 69 years...........	57.0	23.3	0.3	...	9.9	4.9	4.0	0.6
70 to 74 years...........	57.6	17.4	...	...	14.5	5.7	4.2	0.5
75 years and over........	53.3	8.9	...	...	25.6	7.0	4.9	0.3
1940, all ages.......	28.3	21.1	38.0	1.7	1.8	4.3	4.1	0.7
Under 5 years............	...	...	89.6	7.7	...	1.5	1.2	...
5 to 9 years............	...	...	91.9	5.3	...	1.6	1.2	...
10 to 14 years...........	...	...	92.5	3.9	...	2.3	1.3	...
15 to 19 years...........	0.6	3.6	84.9	2.4	...	4.9	2.6	1.0
20 to 24 years...........	11.5	21.3	50.2	0.9	...	7.6	6.9	1.5
25 to 29 years...........	29.3	33.3	23.2	0.3	...	6.5	6.6	0.9
30 to 34 years...........	39.1	36.9	12.9	0.1	...	5.1	5.2	0.7
35 to 39 years...........	44.4	37.6	8.0	...	0.1	4.3	4.8	0.7
40 to 44 years...........	48.3	37.1	5.2	...	0.3	3.9	4.5	0.7
45 to 49 years...........	51.5	35.7	3.3	...	0.9	3.6	4.3	0.8
50 to 54 years...........	53.9	32.8	2.1	...	2.1	3.9	4.4	0.9
55 to 59 years...........	55.6	29.9	1.2	...	3.9	4.2	4.3	1.0
60 to 64 years...........	56.3	26.0	0.6	...	6.9	4.6	4.5	1.0
65 to 69 years...........	57.3	20.9	...	...	10.9	5.2	4.9	0.8
70 to 74 years...........	57.7	15.3	...	...	15.8	5.4	5.3	0.5
75 years and over........	52.9	7.8	...	...	26.6	6.4	6.0	0.3
Male								
1950, all ages.......	52.0	...	37.7	2.0	1.0	4.1	3.2	0.1
Under 5 years............	...	...	89.9	7.7	...	1.6	0.8	...
5 to 9 years............	...	...	92.4	5.4	...	1.5	0.7	...
10 to 14 years...........	0.1	...	92.4	4.0	...	2.7	0.8	0.1
15 to 19 years...........	2.3	...	87.7	2.8	...	4.8	2.4	0.1
20 to 24 years...........	37.9	...	45.5	1.1	...	8.7	6.7	0.1
25 to 29 years...........	70.1	...	17.6	0.3	...	7.1	4.8	0.1
30 to 34 years...........	81.7	...	9.2	...	...	5.5	3.4	0.1
35 to 39 years...........	85.9	...	6.2	...	...	4.5	3.2	0.1
40 to 44 years...........	88.2	...	4.3	...	0.1	4.0	3.3	0.1
45 to 49 years...........	89.4	...	2.8	...	0.3	3.6	3.7	0.1
50 to 54 years...........	90.1	...	1.6	...	0.8	3.5	4.0	0.1
55 to 59 years...........	90.3	...	0.8	...	1.5	3.2	4.1	0.1
60 to 64 years...........	88.8	...	0.4	...	2.9	3.3	4.5	0.1
65 to 69 years...........	86.2	...	0.2	...	5.1	3.5	4.9	0.1
70 to 74 years...........	82.7	...	...	...	8.5	3.9	4.8	0.1
75 years and over........	72.4	...	...	...	17.5	4.7	5.3	0.1

TABLE **D-3.**—PERCENT DISTRIBUTION OF PERSONS IN HOUSEHOLDS BY RELATIONSHIP TO HEAD, BY AGE AND SEX, URBAN AND RURAL NONFARM (WITH NONWHITE FOR URBAN): 1950 AND 1940—Cont.

Area, year, age, and sex	Head	Wife	Child	Grand-child	Parent	Other rela-tive	Lodger	Resident em-ployee
TOTAL--Cont.								
Male--Cont.								
1940, all ages.......	48.0	...	40.0	1.7	1.0	4.3	4.8	0.1
Under 5 years.............	...	...	89.8	7.6	...	1.4	1.2	...
5 to 9 years..............	...	...	92.1	5.3	...	1.5	1.1	...
10 to 14 years............	...	...	92.8	3.9	...	2.1	1.2	...
15 to 19 years............	0.9	...	89.9	2.6	...	4.2	2.3	0.1
20 to 24 years............	22.3	...	60.7	1.2	...	8.1	7.5	0.2
25 to 29 years............	57.1	...	26.8	0.3	...	7.8	7.7	0.2
30 to 34 years............	73.9	...	13.4	0.1	...	6.2	6.2	0.2
35 to 39 years............	80.7	...	7.8	...	...	5.1	6.1	0.2
40 to 44 years............	84.7	...	4.7	...	0.1	4.3	6.0	0.2
45 to 49 years............	87.1	...	2.7	...	0.3	3.7	5.9	0.2
50 to 54 years............	87.7	...	1.6	...	0.9	3.6	6.1	0.2
55 to 59 years............	87.8	...	0.9	...	1.8	3.6	5.8	0.2
60 to 64 years............	86.5	...	0.4	...	3.5	3.6	5.8	0.2
65 to 69 years............	83.9	...	...	...	6.1	3.8	6.1	0.2
70 to 74 years............	80.0	...	...	...	9.9	3.8	6.3	0.1
75 years and over........	69.8	...	...	...	19.0	4.3	6.8	0.1
Female								
1950, all ages.......	9.6	45.2	33.7	1.8	2.8	4.1	2.4	0.4
Under 5 years.............	...	...	89.6	7.8	...	1.7	0.9	...
5 to 9 years.............	...	...	92.0	5.5	...	1.7	0.7	...
10 to 14 years............	...	...	92.4	4.0	...	2.6	0.9	0.1
15 to 19 years............	0.6	11.9	75.4	2.4	...	6.2	3.0	0.4
20 to 24 years............	2.7	55.2	29.0	0.7	...	7.1	4.9	0.4
25 to 29 years............	4.2	73.3	14.0	0.2	...	4.7	3.3	0.3
30 to 34 years............	5.9	78.3	9.5	...	...	3.6	2.4	0.3
35 to 39 years............	8.4	78.5	7.0	...	0.1	3.3	2.2	0.4
40 to 44 years............	11.3	76.7	5.4	...	0.5	3.4	2.2	0.5
45 to 49 years............	14.8	73.6	3.7	...	1.4	3.6	2.2	0.7
50 to 54 years............	18.3	68.9	2.4	...	3.2	4.0	2.3	0.8
55 to 59 years............	21.8	63.2	1.4	...	5.8	4.4	2.4	1.0
60 to 64 years............	26.3	54.0	0.7	...	9.7	5.3	2.8	1.2
65 to 69 years............	32.2	43.0	0.4	...	14.0	6.0	3.3	1.1
70 to 74 years............	37.0	31.8	...	...	19.5	7.2	3.7	0.8
75 years and over........	38.8	15.6	...	...	31.7	8.8	4.6	0.4
1940, all ages.......	9.4	41.4	36.2	1.6	2.5	4.3	3.3	1.2
Under 5 years.............	...	...	89.5	7.8	...	1.5	1.2	...
5 to 9 years.............	...	...	91.7	5.3	...	1.7	1.2	...
10 to 14 years............	...	...	92.1	3.9	...	2.6	1.3	...
15 to 19 years............	0.3	7.0	80.1	2.3	...	5.6	2.9	1.8
20 to 24 years............	2.0	40.1	41.1	0.8	...	7.1	6.4	2.6
25 to 29 years............	3.9	63.4	19.9	0.2	...	5.4	5.5	1.6
30 to 34 years............	6.3	71.5	12.4	0.1	...	4.2	4.2	1.3
35 to 39 years............	9.6	73.6	8.2	...	0.2	3.6	3.5	1.2
40 to 44 years............	12.6	73.5	5.6	...	0.6	3.5	2.9	1.3
45 to 49 years............	15.7	71.5	3.8	...	1.5	3.5	2.6	1.4
50 to 54 years............	19.4	66.5	2.5	...	3.3	4.1	2.7	1.6
55 to 59 years............	23.3	59.8	1.5	...	6.1	4.7	2.8	1.8
60 to 64 years............	27.9	50.5	0.7	...	10.1	5.6	3.3	1.8
65 to 69 years............	33.7	39.4	...	...	15.1	6.5	3.9	1.4
70 to 74 years............	38.3	28.6	...	...	21.0	6.9	4.4	0.9
75 years and over........	39.4	14.0	...	...	32.6	8.1	5.4	0.4

TABLE **D-3.**—PERCENT DISTRIBUTION OF PERSONS IN HOUSEHOLDS BY RELATIONSHIP TO HEAD, BY AGE AND SEX, URBAN AND RURAL NONFARM (WITH NONWHITE FOR URBAN): 1950 AND 1940—Cont.

Area, year, age, and sex	Head	Wife	Child	Grand-child	Parent	Other rela-tive	Lodger	Resident em-ployee
URBAN, TOTAL								
Both Sexes								
1950, all ages.......	30.6	23.4	34.4	1.8	2.0	4.3	3.2	0.3
Under 5 years............	...	...	89.3	8.1	...	1.7	1.0	...
5 to 9 years.............	...	...	91.9	5.6	...	1.7	0.8	...
10 to 14 years..........	0.1	...	92.3	4.0	...	2.7	0.9	...
15 to 19 years..........	1.4	5.4	81.8	2.5	...	5.6	3.0	0.2
20 to 24 years..........	17.9	28.2	38.1	0.9	...	8.1	6.5	0.3
25 to 29 years..........	34.6	37.4	16.7	0.3	...	6.2	4.6	0.2
30 to 34 years..........	41.6	40.0	10.1	...	...	4.8	3.3	0.2
35 to 39 years..........	45.2	40.2	7.0	...	0.1	4.2	3.1	0.3
40 to 44 years..........	48.3	39.1	5.0	...	0.3	3.9	3.1	0.3
45 to 49 years..........	50.8	37.5	3.2	...	0.9	3.8	3.3	0.4
50 to 54 years..........	53.0	35.0	2.0	...	2.1	3.9	3.5	0.5
55 to 59 years..........	55.0	32.0	1.1	...	3.9	4.0	3.5	0.5
60 to 64 years..........	56.3	27.2	0.5	...	6.8	4.5	4.0	0.7
65 to 69 years..........	56.5	22.4	0.3	...	10.5	5.1	4.5	0.6
70 to 74 years..........	56.5	16.5	...	...	15.7	6.0	4.8	0.5
75 years and over.......	51.2	8.4	...	...	27.4	7.4	5.4	0.3
1940, all ages.......	28.5	21.0	37.1	1.5	1.9	4.6	4.6	0.7
Under 5 years............	...	...	88.9	8.1	...	1.6	1.4	...
5 to 9 years.............	...	...	91.5	5.5	...	1.7	1.3	...
10 to 14 years..........	...	...	92.4	3.9	...	2.4	1.3	...
15 to 19 years..........	0.5	2.8	85.7	2.4	...	5.0	2.7	0.9
20 to 24 years..........	10.4	19.2	52.8	0.9	...	7.8	7.4	1.5
25 to 29 years..........	27.8	31.6	25.1	0.3	...	7.0	7.3	1.0
30 to 34 years..........	37.9	35.8	13.9	0.1	...	5.6	5.9	0.8
35 to 39 years..........	43.5	36.9	8.5	...	0.1	4.7	5.5	0.8
40 to 44 years..........	47.7	36.6	5.3	...	0.4	4.2	5.1	0.7
45 to 49 years..........	51.1	35.2	3.3	...	0.9	3.9	4.8	0.8
50 to 54 years..........	53.6	32.3	2.0	...	2.1	4.1	4.9	0.9
55 to 59 years..........	55.3	29.3	1.1	...	4.1	4.4	4.8	1.0
60 to 64 years..........	55.9	25.4	0.5	...	7.2	4.9	5.1	1.0
65 to 69 years..........	56.3	20.2	...	...	11.5	5.5	5.7	0.8
70 to 74 years..........	56.1	14.5	...	...	17.1	5.8	6.0	0.5
75 years and over.......	50.3	7.3	...	...	28.6	6.8	6.8	0.3
Male								
1950, all ages.......	52.7	...	36.4	1.9	1.0	4.3	3.6	0.1
Under 5 years............	...	...	89.4	8.0	...	1.6	0.9	...
5 to 9 years.............	...	...	92.1	5.5	...	1.6	0.8	...
10 to 14 years..........	0.1	...	92.3	4.0	...	2.8	0.8	...
15 to 19 years..........	2.1	...	87.6	2.7	...	4.9	2.6	...
20 to 24 years..........	35.8	...	46.6	1.1	...	8.9	7.6	0.1
25 to 29 years..........	68.1	...	18.4	0.3	...	7.6	5.5	...
30 to 34 years..........	80.3	...	9.8	...	...	5.9	3.9	...
35 to 39 years..........	85.0	...	6.3	...	...	4.9	3.7	0.1
40 to 44 years..........	87.5	...	4.3	...	0.1	4.2	3.8	0.1
45 to 49 years..........	88.9	...	2.7	...	0.3	3.8	4.1	0.1
50 to 54 years..........	89.6	...	1.5	...	0.8	3.6	4.5	0.1
55 to 59 years..........	89.9	...	0.7	...	1.5	3.3	4.5	0.1
60 to 64 years..........	88.2	...	0.3	...	3.0	3.4	5.0	0.1
65 to 69 years..........	85.3	...	0.2	...	5.3	3.6	5.4	0.1
70 to 74 years..........	81.2	...	...	...	9.2	4.1	5.5	0.1
75 years and over.......	70.2	...	...	...	19.0	4.9	5.9	0.1

TABLE **D–3.**—Percent Distribution of Persons in Households by Relationship to Head, by Age and Sex, Urban and Rural Nonfarm (with Nonwhite for Urban): 1950 and 1940—Cont.

Area, year, age, and sex	Head	Wife	Child	Grand-child	Parent	Other rela-tive	Lodger	Resident em-ployee
URBAN, TOTAL--Cont.								
Male--Cont.								
1940, all ages.......	48.1	...	39.1	1.7	1.0	4.6	5.5	0.1
Under 5 years.............	...	...	89.1	8.1	...	1.5	1.4	...
5 to 9 years.............	...	...	91.7	5.5	...	1.6	1.3	...
10 to 14 years...........	...	...	92.7	3.9	...	2.1	1.3	...
15 to 19 years...........	0.8	...	90.1	2.5	...	4.2	2.4	0.1
20 to 24 years...........	19.9	...	62.6	1.1	...	8.2	8.1	0.1
25 to 29 years...........	53.9	...	28.7	0.3	...	8.3	8.6	0.2
30 to 34 years...........	71.6	...	14.3	0.1	...	6.7	7.1	0.2
35 to 39 years...........	79.0	...	8.2	...	...	5.6	7.0	0.2
40 to 44 years...........	83.4	...	4.8	...	0.1	4.6	6.9	0.2
45 to 49 years...........	86.2	...	2.7	...	0.3	3.9	6.6	0.1
50 to 54 years...........	86.9	...	1.6	...	0.9	3.8	6.7	0.1
55 to 59 years...........	87.1	...	0.8	...	1.8	3.7	6.4	0.1
60 to 64 years...........	85.7	...	0.4	...	3.6	3.7	6.5	0.1
65 to 69 years...........	82.7	...	...	...	6.4	3.9	7.0	0.1
70 to 74 years...........	78.2	...	...	...	10.7	3.9	7.2	0.1
75 years and over........	67.1	...	...	...	20.7	4.4	7.7	0.1
Female								
1950, all ages.......	10.3	44.9	32.5	1.7	3.0	4.4	2.8	0.4
Under 5 years.............	...	...	89.1	8.1	...	1.8	1.0	...
5 to 9 years.............	...	...	91.7	5.6	...	1.9	0.8	...
10 to 14 years...........	...	...	92.2	4.0	...	2.7	0.9	...
15 to 19 years...........	0.7	10.3	76.5	2.4	...	6.3	3.3	0.4
20 to 24 years...........	3.1	51.6	31.1	0.7	...	7.4	5.6	0.4
25 to 29 years...........	4.7	70.8	15.2	0.2	...	5.0	3.8	0.3
30 to 34 years...........	6.6	76.1	10.3	...	...	3.9	2.8	0.3
35 to 39 years...........	9.1	76.6	7.5	...	0.2	3.6	2.6	0.4
40 to 44 years...........	12.2	75.0	5.6	...	0.6	3.6	2.5	0.5
45 to 49 years...........	15.7	72.1	3.7	...	1.5	3.8	2.5	0.7
50 to 54 years...........	19.2	67.4	2.4	...	3.4	4.3	2.6	0.8
55 to 59 years...........	22.7	61.6	1.4	...	6.0	4.7	2.7	1.0
60 to 64 years...........	27.2	52.0	0.7	...	10.2	5.6	3.2	1.2
65 to 69 years...........	32.7	40.9	0.3	...	14.8	6.4	3.8	1.1
70 to 74 years...........	37.2	29.4	...	...	20.8	7.6	4.3	0.8
75 years and over........	37.9	14.3	...	...	33.3	9.1	5.0	0.4
1940, all ages.......	10.0	40.9	35.2	1.5	2.7	4.6	3.8	1.3
Under 5 years.............	...	...	88.7	8.2	...	1.6	1.4	...
5 to 9 years.............	...	...	91.3	5.5	...	1.8	1.3	...
10 to 14 years...........	...	...	92.0	3.9	...	2.6	1.4	...
15 to 19 years...........	0.3	5.5	81.5	2.3	...	5.5	3.1	1.8
20 to 24 years...........	2.2	36.0	44.2	0.8	...	7.4	6.8	2.7
25 to 29 years...........	4.4	59.9	21.9	0.2	...	5.8	6.1	1.7
30 to 34 years...........	7.0	68.7	13.6	0.1	...	4.6	4.8	1.3
35 to 39 years...........	10.4	71.3	8.8	...	0.2	4.0	4.0	1.3
40 to 44 years...........	13.4	71.8	5.9	...	0.6	3.8	3.3	1.3
45 to 49 years...........	16.4	70.0	3.9	...	1.5	3.8	3.0	1.4
50 to 54 years...........	20.1	64.8	2.5	...	3.4	4.5	3.1	1.6
55 to 59 years...........	24.1	58.1	1.4	...	6.3	5.1	3.2	1.8
60 to 64 years...........	28.5	48.6	0.7	...	10.6	6.0	3.8	1.8
65 to 69 years...........	33.9	37.3	...	...	15.9	6.9	4.6	1.4
70 to 74 years...........	37.9	26.5	...	...	22.3	7.3	5.1	0.9
75 years and over........	37.7	12.7	...	...	34.5	8.5	6.1	0.4

TABLE **D-3.**—Percent Distribution of Persons in Households by Relationship to Head, by Age and Sex, Urban and Rural Nonfarm (with Nonwhite for Urban): 1950 and 1940—Cont.

Area, year, age, and sex	Head	Wife	Child	Grand-child	Parent	Other rela-tive	Lodger	Resident em-ployee
URBAN, NONWHITE								
Both Sexes								
1950, all ages.......	27.8	17.1	32.3	4.5	1.7	7.9	8.1	0.6
Under 5 years.............	...	...	73.1	17.4	...	6.0	3.4	...
5 to 9 years..............	...	...	78.7	13.1	...	5.7	2.4	...
10 to 14 years............	...	...	80.4	9.4	...	7.4	2.7	0.1
15 to 19 years............	1.3	4.4	70.6	5.7	...	12.2	5.4	0.4
20 to 24 years............	15.2	21.3	32.3	2.0	...	15.7	12.8	0.8
25 to 29 years...........	30.6	29.1	15.0	0.6	...	11.0	12.9	0.7
30 to 34 years............	39.1	32.1	8.5	...	0.1	8.2	11.3	0.8
35 to 39 years............	44.4	32.2	5.1	...	0.3	6.6	10.5	0.9
40 to 44 years............	49.4	29.8	3.5	...	0.9	5.7	9.8	0.9
45 to 49 years............	53.1	27.6	2.0	...	1.9	5.0	9.2	1.0
50 to 54 years............	56.1	24.0	1.4	...	3.5	4.9	9.1	1.0
55 to 59 years............	58.5	21.0	0.7	...	5.5	4.9	8.4	0.9
60 to 64 years............	58.5	17.3	0.4	...	8.6	5.4	8.8	1.0
65 to 69 years............	57.9	13.7	0.3	...	12.4	6.1	8.9	0.7
70 to 74 years............	56.9	9.0	...	...	16.9	7.4	9.2	0.6
75 years and over........	49.9	4.6	...	...	25.5	10.6	9.0	0.4
1940, all ages.......	27.1	15.8	31.6	3.4	1.7	7.1	12.1	1.3
Under 5 years.............	...	...	73.7	15.6	...	5.1	5.6	...
5 to 9 years..............	...	...	79.2	11.0	...	5.3	4.5	...
10 to 14 years............	...	...	80.7	7.9	...	6.7	4.7	...
15 to 19 years............	1.1	3.7	70.7	4.7	...	11.1	7.8	0.9
20 to 24 years............	12.4	18.5	34.6	1.5	...	13.4	17.0	2.5
25 to 29 years............	27.5	25.9	14.8	0.4	...	9.8	19.3	2.3
30 to 34 years............	37.0	27.9	8.3	0.2	...	7.2	17.4	2.0
35 to 39 years............	43.8	28.2	4.7	0.1	0.3	5.4	15.6	1.8
40 to 44 years............	49.6	25.8	2.9	...	1.0	4.6	14.5	1.7
45 to 49 years............	53.5	24.2	1.8	...	2.1	4.1	12.7	1.6
50 to 54 years............	55.7	21.4	1.2	...	3.9	4.2	12.0	1.5
55 to 59 years............	57.6	19.1	0.7	...	6.3	4.0	10.9	1.3
60 to 64 years............	57.6	15.7	0.5	...	9.3	4.4	11.2	1.3
65 to 69 years............	57.3	11.6	...	...	13.8	5.0	11.3	0.9
70 to 74 years............	55.1	7.6	...	...	18.9	5.9	11.8	0.8
75 years and over........	46.9	4.0	...	...	28.6	8.1	11.8	0.6
Male								
1950, all ages.......	43.0	...	33.9	4.8	0.7	7.9	9.4	0.2
Under 5 years.............	...	...	73.4	17.4	...	5.9	3.3	...
5 to 9 years..............	...	...	79.0	13.2	...	5.3	2.4	...
10 to 14 years............	0.1	...	80.6	9.5	...	7.1	2.6	0.1
15 to 19 years............	1.7	...	76.7	6.3	...	10.6	4.6	0.1
20 to 24 years............	27.7	...	37.9	2.3	...	18.0	13.9	0.2
25 to 29 years............	55.1	...	16.0	0.7	...	12.9	15.1	0.2
30 to 34 years............	68.1	...	8.2	...	0.1	9.6	13.7	0.3
35 to 39 years............	73.9	...	4.9	...	0.1	7.5	13.2	0.3
40 to 44 years............	77.6	...	3.2	...	0.2	6.0	12.7	0.4
45 to 49 years............	79.9	...	1.8	...	0.6	5.0	12.3	0.4
50 to 54 years............	80.9	...	1.2	...	0.9	4.5	12.1	0.4
55 to 59 years............	82.0	...	0.6	...	1.6	4.3	11.1	0.4
60 to 64 years............	80.7	...	0.4	...	2.9	4.1	11.4	0.5
65 to 69 years............	78.2	...	0.3	...	5.1	4.4	11.5	0.4
70 to 74 years............	74.9	...	...	...	8.0	5.2	11.5	0.3
75 years and over........	66.0	...	...	...	15.4	7.5	10.7	0.4

TABLE **D-3.**—PERCENT DISTRIBUTION OF PERSONS IN HOUSEHOLDS BY RELATIONSHIP TO HEAD, BY AGE AND SEX, URBAN AND RURAL NONFARM (WITH NONWHITE FOR URBAN): 1950 AND 1940—Cont.

Area, year, age, and sex	Head	Wife	Child	Grand-child	Parent	Other rela-tive	Lodger	Resident em-ployee
URBAN, NONWHITE--Cont.								
Male--Cont.								
1940, all ages.......	40.9	...	33.3	3.6	0.7	7.0	14.0	0.6
Under 5 years............	...	...	74.0	15.7	...	4.9	5.4	...
5 to 9 years............	...	...	79.6	11.0	...	4.9	4.4	...
10 to 14 years...........	...	...	81.5	8.0	...	6.0	4.5	...
15 to 19 years...........	1.3	...	76.7	5.1	...	9.8	6.8	0.2
20 to 24 years...........	22.4	...	42.3	1.9	...	15.0	17.6	0.7
25 to 29 years...........	48.5	...	16.4	0.5	...	11.3	22.3	1.0
30 to 34 years...........	60.8	...	8.5	0.2	...	8.2	21.3	1.1
35 to 39 years...........	67.9	...	4.6	0.1	0.1	6.1	20.2	0.9
40 to 44 years...........	72.5	...	2.7	...	0.2	4.8	18.9	0.8
45 to 49 years...........	76.3	...	1.6	...	0.5	4.1	16.7	0.7
50 to 54 years...........	77.7	...	1.1	...	1.1	3.9	15.6	0.7
55 to 59 years...........	79.4	...	0.6	...	1.9	3.6	13.9	0.6
60 to 64 years...........	78.3	...	0.3	...	3.2	3.5	14.1	0.6
65 to 69 years...........	76.2	...	...	...	5.6	3.7	14.0	0.5
70 to 74 years...........	71.5	...	...	...	9.3	4.3	14.4	0.5
75 years and over........	62.7	...	...	...	16.9	5.4	14.6	0.4
Female								
1950, all ages.......	14.2	32.3	30.8	4.3	2.7	7.9	6.9	0.9
Under 5 years............	...	...	72.9	17.4	...	6.2	3.5	...
5 to 9 years............	...	...	78.4	12.9	...	6.2	2.4	0.1
10 to 14 years...........	...	...	80.1	9.2	...	7.7	2.7	0.1
15 to 19 years...........	1.0	8.1	65.5	5.1	...	13.6	6.1	0.6
20 to 24 years...........	5.9	36.9	28.2	1.7	...	14.0	12.0	1.3
25 to 29 years...........	11.1	52.3	14.2	0.6	...	9.4	11.1	1.2
30 to 34 years...........	15.5	58.1	8.7	...	0.1	7.1	9.3	1.2
35 to 39 years...........	20.1	58.8	5.2	...	0.5	5.8	8.3	1.3
40 to 44 years...........	24.3	56.5	3.7	...	1.5	5.4	7.2	1.4
45 to 49 years...........	28.6	53.0	2.3	...	3.2	5.1	6.4	1.5
50 to 54 years...........	31.7	47.7	1.7	...	5.9	5.2	6.2	1.6
55 to 59 years...........	34.7	42.3	0.9	...	9.4	5.5	5.8	1.5
60 to 64 years...........	36.5	34.5	0.4	...	14.3	6.6	6.2	1.5
65 to 69 years...........	41.3	24.9	0.4	...	18.4	7.4	6.8	1.0
70 to 74 years...........	41.3	16.7	...	...	24.6	9.3	7.2	0.9
75 years and over........	37.4	8.1	...	...	33.3	13.1	7.6	0.4
1940, all ages.......	14.8	29.8	30.1	3.2	2.6	7.1	10.4	2.0
Under 5 years............	...	...	73.3	15.6	...	5.3	5.7	...
5 to 9 years............	...	...	78.8	10.9	...	5.7	4.6	...
10 to 14 years...........	...	...	80.0	7.7	...	7.3	4.9	...
15 to 19 years...........	0.9	6.9	65.5	4.3	...	12.2	8.7	1.5
20 to 24 years...........	5.3	31.8	29.1	1.3	...	12.2	16.6	3.7
25 to 29 years...........	11.5	45.7	13.6	0.4	...	8.6	17.0	3.2
30 to 34 years...........	17.6	50.7	8.2	0.2	...	6.3	14.2	2.8
35 to 39 years...........	23.4	52.1	4.8	0.1	0.6	4.8	11.7	2.6
40 to 44 years...........	27.6	50.5	3.0	...	1.8	4.3	10.2	2.5
45 to 49 years...........	30.8	48.4	1.9	...	3.8	4.0	8.7	2.5
50 to 54 years...........	33.0	43.5	1.4	...	6.9	4.5	8.4	2.4
55 to 59 years...........	35.3	38.8	0.8	...	10.7	4.5	7.8	2.1
60 to 64 years...........	36.9	31.5	0.6	...	15.4	5.3	8.3	2.1
65 to 69 years...........	40.7	21.8	...	...	21.1	6.1	9.0	1.3
70 to 74 years...........	40.7	14.2	...	...	27.3	7.3	9.4	1.0
75 years and over........	35.3	7.0	...	...	37.2	10.1	9.7	0.7

TABLE **D-3.**—Percent Distribution of Persons in Households by Relationship to Head, by Age and Sex, Urban and Rural Nonfarm (with Nonwhite for Urban): 1950 and 1940—Cont.

Area, year, age, and sex	Head	Wife	Child	Grand-child	Parent	Other rela-tive	Lodger	Resident em-ployee
RURAL NONFARM								
Both Sexes								
1950, all ages.......	28.3	23.3	39.7	2.0	1.6	3.3	1.5	0.3
Under 5 years............	...	...	91.1	6.9	...	1.4	0.6	...
5 to 9 years.............	...	...	92.9	5.1	...	1.4	0.6	...
10 to 14 years...........	0.1	...	92.7	4.0	...	2.4	0.7	0.1
15 to 19 years...........	1.5	8.3	79.8	2.8	...	5.3	1.9	0.3
20 to 24 years...........	21.4	36.6	30.8	0.9	...	6.8	3.1	0.3
25 to 29 years...........	37.7	43.3	12.2	0.3	...	4.5	1.8	0.2
30 to 34 years...........	43.7	44.2	7.3	...	...	3.3	1.2	0.2
35 to 39 years...........	47.0	43.0	5.5	...	0.1	2.9	1.3	0.3
40 to 44 years...........	49.4	41.5	4.4	...	0.3	2.7	1.4	0.3
45 to 49 years...........	51.3	39.8	3.2	...	0.7	2.9	1.6	0.5
50 to 54 years...........	52.8	38.0	2.2	...	1.7	3.0	1.8	0.5
55 to 59 years...........	54.4	35.5	1.3	...	3.1	3.1	1.9	0.6
60 to 64 years...........	55.9	31.5	0.7	...	5.3	3.7	2.2	0.7
65 to 69 years...........	58.4	26.1	0.4	...	8.0	4.1	2.4	0.6
70 to 74 years...........	60.9	20.1	...	...	11.1	4.8	2.6	0.5
75 years and over........	59.0	10.2	...	...	20.7	6.1	3.7	0.3
1940, all ages.......	27.7	21.4	40.8	1.8	1.5	3.5	2.6	0.6
Under 5 years............	...	...	91.1	6.8	...	1.3	0.8	...
5 to 9 years.............	...	...	92.7	4.9	...	1.5	0.9	...
10 to 14 years...........	...	...	92.7	3.9	...	2.2	1.1	...
15 to 19 years...........	0.8	5.7	82.8	2.6	...	4.9	2.2	1.0
20 to 24 years...........	14.8	27.7	42.1	1.0	...	7.0	5.5	1.4
25 to 29 years...........	33.6	38.1	17.6	0.3	...	5.2	4.4	0.9
30 to 34 years...........	42.5	40.1	9.9	0.1	...	3.7	3.0	0.7
35 to 39 years...........	47.1	39.8	6.6	0.1	0.1	3.1	2.5	0.7
40 to 44 years...........	50.4	38.7	4.5	...	0.3	2.9	2.4	0.7
45 to 49 years...........	53.0	37.1	3.1	...	0.8	2.7	2.4	0.8
50 to 54 years...........	54.9	34.5	2.2	...	1.9	3.0	2.7	0.9
55 to 59 years...........	56.4	31.7	1.4	...	3.5	3.3	2.7	1.0
60 to 64 years...........	57.9	28.0	0.7	...	5.9	3.7	2.8	1.1
65 to 69 years...........	60.0	22.8	...	...	9.1	4.4	3.0	0.8
70 to 74 years...........	62.0	17.1	...	...	12.5	4.6	3.3	0.6
75 years and over........	59.1	9.0	...	...	21.8	5.6	4.3	0.3
Male								
1950, all ages.......	49.9	...	41.8	2.1	0.9	3.3	1.8	0.1
Under 5 years............	...	...	91.2	6.9	...	1.3	0.5	...
5 to 9 years.............	...	...	93.0	5.0	...	1.3	0.6	...
10 to 14 years...........	0.1	...	92.5	4.0	...	2.5	0.7	0.1
15 to 19 years...........	2.8	...	87.7	3.1	...	4.5	1.7	0.1
20 to 24 years...........	45.2	...	41.7	1.3	...	7.9	3.7	0.2
25 to 29 years...........	76.9	...	14.9	0.3	...	5.4	2.3	0.1
30 to 34 years...........	86.2	...	8.0	...	...	4.1	1.6	0.1
35 to 39 years...........	89.2	...	5.6	...	...	3.4	1.6	0.1
40 to 44 years...........	90.5	...	4.3	...	0.1	3.1	1.8	0.1
45 to 49 years...........	91.4	...	3.0	...	0.3	3.1	2.1	0.2
50 to 54 years...........	91.8	...	1.9	...	0.8	3.0	2.3	0.2
55 to 59 years...........	91.8	...	1.0	...	1.5	2.9	2.6	0.2
60 to 64 years...........	90.6	...	0.5	...	2.7	3.1	2.8	0.2
65 to 69 years...........	88.6	...	0.3	...	4.5	3.4	3.1	0.2
70 to 74 years...........	86.4	...	...	...	6.8	3.5	3.1	0.2
75 years and over........	77.3	...	...	...	14.3	4.3	4.0	0.1

TABLE **D-3.**—PERCENT DISTRIBUTION OF PERSONS IN HOUSEHOLDS BY RELATIONSHIP TO HEAD, BY AGE AND SEX, URBAN AND RURAL NONFARM (WITH NONWHITE FOR URBAN): 1950 AND 1940—Cont.

Area, year, age, and sex	Head	Wife	Child	Grand-child	Parent	Other rela-tive	Lodger	Resident em-ployee
RURAL NONFARM--Cont.								
Male--Cont.								
1940, all ages.......	47.7	...	42.6	1.9	0.9	3.6	3.1	0.2
Under 5 years............	...	...	91.2	6.7	...	1.2	0.8	...
5 to 9 years.............	...	...	92.8	4.9	...	1.4	0.8	...
10 to 14 years...........	...	...	93.0	3.9	...	2.1	1.0	...
15 to 19 years...........	1.3	...	89.3	2.8	...	4.3	2.1	0.1
20 to 24 years...........	29.6	...	54.9	1.3	...	7.9	6.0	0.4
25 to 29 years...........	66.2	...	21.5	0.4	...	6.3	5.3	0.3
30 to 34 years...........	80.6	...	10.8	0.1	...	4.5	3.7	0.3
35 to 39 years...........	85.8	...	6.8	0.1	...	3.8	3.3	0.3
40 to 44 years...........	88.6	...	4.4	...	0.1	3.3	3.3	0.3
45 to 49 years...........	90.2	...	2.8	...	0.3	3.0	3.5	0.2
50 to 54 years...........	90.1	...	1.9	...	0.8	3.0	3.8	0.3
55 to 59 years...........	89.9	...	1.1	...	1.7	3.1	3.8	0.3
60 to 64 years...........	89.0	...	0.5	...	3.2	3.2	3.9	0.3
65 to 69 years...........	87.1	...	...	...	5.3	3.5	3.9	0.2
70 to 74 years...........	84.2	...	...	...	8.1	3.5	4.1	0.2
75 years and over........	75.2	...	...	...	15.7	4.1	4.9	0.1
Female								
1950, all ages.......	7.3	46.0	37.6	2.0	2.2	3.3	1.2	0.4
Under 5 years............	...	...	91.0	7.0	...	1.5	0.6	...
5 to 9 years.............	...	...	92.8	5.1	...	1.5	0.6	0.1
10 to 14 years...........	...	0.1	93.0	3.9	...	2.3	0.7	0.1
15 to 19 years...........	0.3	16.2	72.4	2.5	...	6.0	2.0	0.5
20 to 24 years...........	1.5	67.2	21.7	0.7	...	6.0	2.5	0.4
25 to 29 years...........	2.4	82.2	9.9	0.2	...	3.6	1.3	0.3
30 to 34 years...........	3.6	86.0	6.6	...	...	2.6	0.9	0.3
35 to 39 years...........	5.7	85.2	5.3	...	0.1	2.4	0.9	0.4
40 to 44 years...........	7.8	83.3	4.5	...	0.5	2.4	1.0	0.5
45 to 49 years...........	11.0	79.8	3.5	...	1.2	2.7	1.1	0.7
50 to 54 years...........	14.4	75.3	2.6	...	2.7	2.9	1.2	0.9
55 to 59 years...........	18.2	69.8	1.6	...	4.7	3.4	1.3	1.0
60 to 64 years...........	22.9	61.5	0.9	...	7.7	4.2	1.6	1.2
65 to 69 years...........	30.5	50.2	0.5	...	11.2	4.8	1.8	1.1
70 to 74 years...........	36.6	39.2	...	...	15.2	6.0	2.1	0.8
75 years and over........	41.5	19.9	...	...	26.9	7.8	3.4	0.5
1940, all ages.......	7.7	42.9	38.9	1.8	2.1	3.4	2.1	1.1
Under 5 years............	...	...	91.0	6.8	...	1.3	0.8	...
5 to 9 years.............	...	...	92.6	5.0	...	1.6	0.9	...
10 to 14 years...........	...	...	92.5	3.9	...	2.4	1.1	...
15 to 19 years...........	0.3	11.1	76.5	2.4	...	5.6	2.4	1.8
20 to 24 years...........	1.4	52.6	31.6	0.7	...	6.2	5.1	2.3
25 to 29 years...........	2.6	74.3	13.8	0.2	...	4.1	3.6	1.4
30 to 34 years...........	4.2	80.5	8.9	0.1	...	2.9	2.3	1.1
35 to 39 years...........	6.9	81.2	6.4	...	0.2	2.4	1.8	1.1
40 to 44 years...........	9.9	79.8	4.8	...	0.5	2.4	1.4	1.3
45 to 49 years...........	13.1	76.9	3.5	...	1.3	2.5	1.3	1.4
50 to 54 years...........	16.9	71.6	2.5	...	2.9	3.0	1.4	1.6
55 to 59 years...........	21.0	65.2	1.7	...	5.3	3.6	1.4	1.8
60 to 64 years...........	26.0	56.7	0.9	...	8.7	4.3	1.7	1.8
65 to 69 years...........	33.0	45.5	...	...	12.8	5.2	2.0	1.4
70 to 74 years...........	39.5	34.5	...	...	17.0	5.7	2.4	1.0
75 years and over........	43.8	17.5	...	...	27.6	7.1	3.6	0.5

Source: *1950 Census of Population*, Vol. II, *Characteristics of the Population*, Part 1, U. S. Summary, table 107, p. 192; *1940 Census of Population*, Vol. IV, *Characteristics by Age*, Part 1, U. S. Summary, table 11, p. 28.

TABLE **D-4.**—NONFARM POPULATION 14 YEARS OLD AND OVER IN SELECTED HOUSEHOLD
RELATIONSHIP GROUPS, BY MARITAL STATUS AND SEX: 1950

Relationship and sex	Total	Married, total	Married, spouse present	Widowed
BOTH SEXES				
Child..............................	15,074,870	1,645,440	1,113,570	...
Parent.............................	2,360,940	476,160	343,950	1,806,210
Other relative.....................	3,316,370	780,390	470,490	...
Lodger.............................	3,121,930	885,020	462,710	...
MALE				
Child..............................	7,761,170	602,670	408,810	...
Parent.............................	594,240	201,840	167,880	372,570
Other relative.....................	1,456,490	402,720	264,840	...
Lodger.............................	1,742,410	505,120	235,390	...
FEMALE				
Child..............................	7,313,700	1,042,770	704,760	...
Parent.............................	1,766,700	274,320	176,070	1,433,640
Other relative.....................	1,859,880	377,670	205,650	...
Lodger.............................	1,379,520	379,900	227,320	...

Source: *1950 Census of Population*, Vol. IV, *Special Reports*, Part 2, Chapter D, Marital Status, tables
1 and 3.

TABLE **D-5.**—PERCENT DISTRIBUTION OF PERSONS 14 YEARS OLD AND OVER IN NONFARM HOUSEHOLDS BY FAMILY STATUS, BY MARITAL STATUS AND SEX: 1950

Family status	Both sexes	Male						
		Total	Single	Married			Widowed	Divorced
				Wife present	Wife absent			
					Separated	Other		
Total[1]....................	100.0	100.0	100.0	100.0	100.0	100.0	100.0	100.0
In households.....................	94.5	92.8	83.2	99.2	81.3	51.6	87.9	77.8
In primary families.............	86.3	85.8	70.8	98.3	38.4	23.7	51.7	39.3
Head.........................	33.5	62.7	3.1	93.3	9.2	7.8	24.6	10.0
Wife.........................	29.7	...	...	...	...	...	...	...
Child........................	15.7	16.8	59.0	1.4	16.1	7.3	1.8	17.6
Son- or daughter-in-law.......	1.1	1.4	...	2.1	0.2	0.5	0.2	0.1
Grandchild...................	0.4	0.4	1.6	...	0.3	0.2	...	0.2
Parent.......................	2.5	1.3	...	0.6	2.3	1.7	19.0	2.0
Other relative...............	3.5	3.2	7.1	0.9	10.2	6.2	6.1	9.4
Primary individuals.............	4.6	3.4	4.7	...	21.7	16.0	25.7	21.0
In secondary families...........	0.8	0.8	0.6	0.8	1.0	0.7	0.5	0.8
Secondary individuals...........	2.8	3.1	6.9	...	20.2	10.8	10.1	16.7

Family status	Female						
	Total	Single	Married			Widowed	Divorced
			Husband present	Husband absent			
				Separated	Other		
Total[1]....................	100.0	100.0	100.0	100.0	100.0	100.0	100.0
In households.....................	96.1	89.4	99.2	92.9	76.0	95.0	93.2
In primary families.............	87.0	75.5	98.4	65.8	56.0	62.1	61.3
Head.........................	6.4	3.6	...	32.5	21.4	30.8	29.9
Wife.........................	57.4	...	93.5	...	...	...	...
Child........................	14.7	59.9	2.3	18.3	18.1	2.2	18.6
Son- or daughter-in-law.......	0.8	...	1.3	0.2	1.3	0.1	0.2
Grandchild...................	0.4	1.5	0.1	0.5	0.5	...	0.2
Parent.......................	3.6	...	0.6	5.5	4.9	23.3	4.5
Other relative...............	3.8	10.5	0.7	8.9	9.8	5.7	8.0
Primary individuals.............	5.7	6.5	...	15.2	12.2	26.9	21.7
In secondary families...........	0.8	0.6	0.8	2.1	1.1	0.4	1.3
Secondary individuals...........	2.6	6.7	...	9.7	6.7	5.4	8.9

[1] Includes population in quasi-households, not shown separately.

Source: *1950 Census of Population*, Vol. IV, *Special Reports*, Part 2, Chapter D, Marital Status, tables 1 and 3.

TABLE **D-6.**—NONFARM MARRIED COUPLES WITHOUT OWN HOUSEHOLD, BY AGE OF HUSBAND: 1950 AND 1940

Age of husband	1950	1940	Percent distribution		Proportion of married couples without own household	
			1950	1940	1950	1940
Total....................	1,978,240	1,613,311	100.0	100.0	6.6	7.2
15 to 24 years..............	403,935	283,469	20.4	17.6	21.2	24.9
25 to 29 years..............	426,790	367,827	21.6	22.8	11.6	14.1
30 to 34 years..............	292,440	268,985	14.8	16.7	7.4	8.8
35 to 39 years..............	209,545	193,242	10.6	12.0	5.4	6.5
40 to 44 years..............	147,885	108,456	7.5	6.7	4.2	3.9
45 to 49 years..............	109,800	100,908	5.6	6.3	3.6	3.8
50 to 54 years..............	87,805	81,062	4.4	5.0	3.2	3.6
55 to 59 years..............	71,625	51,148	3.6	3.2	3.1	3.0
60 to 64 years..............	65,905	49,452	3.3	3.1	3.6	3.8
65 to 69 years..............	59,145	43,695	3.0	2.7	4.3	4.7
70 to 74 years..............	46,005	26,986	2.3	1.7	5.5	4.7
75 years and over..........	57,360	38,081	2.9	2.4	8.2	8.8

Source: *1950 Census of Population*, Vol. II, *Characteristics of the Population*, Part 1, U. S. Summary, tables, 104, 105, and 107; *1940 Census of Population*, Vol. IV, *Characteristics by Age*, table 9, and *Types of Families*, table 8.

A P P E N D I X   E

ERRORS IN CENSUS REPORTS

It is hardly to be expected that so extensive an undertaking as a de-
cennial census, requiring the use of thousands of relatively inexperienced
enumerators, can ever be carried out without committing some errors
along the way. The quality of the 1950 Census is undoubtedly as good
as, and perhaps better than, those in the past. The 1950 Census differs
in one respect: for the first time a serious effort was made, by way of a
Post-Enumeration Survey, to learn something about the nature of certain
kinds of errors.

The most pervasive shortcoming revealed by the Post-Enumeration Survey was a tendency on the part of enumerators to undercount both population and dwelling units. A discussion of such errors has been included
in the published Census volumes on population and housing.

Apart from errors of underenumeration, which affect to varying degrees
the interpretation of all census data, there are other and more specific
flaws to be found in nearly all the reports on the characteristics of population, households, and dwelling units. Those which concern this study
most are the errors connected with size of dwelling units and households.
A tabulation of the differences between published census data and the
Post-Enumeration Survey on number of rooms is given in table E–1.
The reader may find this table useful in evaluating the analysis of changes
in size of dwelling unit given in Chapter 7. Apparently, census enumerators not infrequently reported what was in fact a 5-room dwelling unit to
be a 6- or 4-room dwelling unit. Indeed, in a few instances a 1-room unit
was returned as a unit containing 9 or more rooms.

To a lesser extent, similar errors were committed in the classification
of number of persons in household. The Post-Enumeration Survey findings
on this type of error are not shown here. Slips in machine tabulations of
local area data resulted, in a few instances, in some rather large discrepancies
in the size distributions of dwelling units or households as between Volumes
I and II of the Census of Housing. Examples may be found in the published data for Hartford, New Orleans, San Francisco, San Antonio, and
one or two other areas. Whenever such divergences appeared, local PPR
ratios were derived from the more reliable distributions given in Volume II.

Unfortunately, it has not been possible to make any systematic allowances for error in any of the PPR ratios presented in this monograph. It

is clear, however, that the aggregate PPR ratio would scarcely be affected
if the Post-Enumeration Survey results had been substituted for the published data. Comparison of published census and Post-Enumeration
Survey data on average number of rooms per dwelling unit indicates only
a 0.03 percent difference. The difference in the household population
count of enumerated dwelling units was 0.14 percent. It is true that about
2.5 percent of all dwelling units were missed in the census. Depending
on what assumptions are made about the average number of rooms and
average household size of the missed dwelling units, the aggregate PPR
ratio derived from census data may be understated by as much as 0.94 percent. In other words, the 1950 PPR ratio may be 0.6992 compared to a
derived ratio of 0.6927, hardly a significant difference.

TABLE **E-1.**—NUMBER OF ROOMS IN NONFARM OCCUPIED DWELLING UNITS BASED ON 1950
CENSUS AND POST-ENUMERATION SURVEY

(Thousands of dwelling units. Details do not necessarily add to totals)

Number of rooms	1950 Census	Post-Enumeration Survey	Percent distribution		Difference	
			1950 Census	Post-Enumeration Survey	Amount	Percent of 1950 Census count
Total occupied dwelling units......................	37,105	38,026	...	...	-921	-2.5
Reporting number of rooms..	36,549	37,814	100.0	100.0	-1,265	-3.5
1 room..........................	1,015	1,164	2.8	3.1	-149	-14.7
2 rooms.........................	2,719	2,935	7.4	7.8	-216	-7.9
3 rooms.........................	5,548	5,681	15.2	15.0	-133	-2.4
4 rooms.........................	8,000	8,374	21.9	22.1	-374	-4.7
5 rooms.........................	8,055	7,842	22.0	20.7	+213	+2.6
6 rooms.........................	6,298	6,431	17.2	17.0	-133	-2.1
7 rooms.........................	2,597	2,982	7.1	7.9	-385	-14.8
8 rooms.........................	1,303	1,344	3.6	3.6	-41	-3.1
9 rooms or more.................	1,014	1,063	2.8	2.8	-49	-4.8

Source: 1950 data based on *1950 Census of Housing*, Vol. I, *General Characteristics*, Part 1, U. S. Summary, table 9; Post-Enumeration Survey data based on unpublished tabulations.

The errors in some of the PPR ratios of smaller subgroups may, of course,
be more sizable. Any attempt to indicate the errors in the PPR ratios by
income, rent, and household size would involve a full analysis of the Post-
Enumeration Survey, a task for which neither time nor resources were
available. One fact should be remembered, however, in any study of
changes over time in the rate of housing utilization—a problem to which a
considerable portion of this monograph is addressed: the 1940 Housing
Census contained many errors quite similar in character to the one dis-
closed by the Post-Enumeration Survey. The likelihood is therefore great
that the estimates of change in the PPR ratios are more accurate than either
the 1940 or 1950 levels.

INDEX